D0895332

Managing the New Careerists

*The Diverse
Career Success
Orientations
of Today's Workers*

C. Brooklyn Derr

Managing the New Careerists

Jossey-Bass Publishers

San Francisco • London • 1986

MANAGING THE NEW CAREERISTS
The Diverse Career Success Orientations of Today's Workers
  by C. Brooklyn Derr

Copyright © 1986 by: Jossey-Bass Inc., Publishers
                     433 California Street
                     San Francisco, California 94104
                            &
                     Jossey-Bass Limited
                     28 Banner Street
                     London EC1Y 8QE

Copyright under International, Pan American, and
Universal Copyright Conventions. All rights
reserved. No part of this book may be reproduced
in any form—except for brief quotation (not to
exceed 1,000 words) in a review or professional
work—without permission in writing from the publishers.

Library of Congress Cataloging-in-Publication Data

Derr, C. Brooklyn (Clyde Brooklyn)
    Managing the new careerists.

    (Jossey-Bass management series) (Jossey-Bass social
and behavioral science series)
    Bibliography: p. 277
    Includes index.
    1. Supervision of employees—United States.
2. Personnel management—United States. I. Title.
II. Series. III. Series (Jossey-Bass social and
behavioral science series)
HF5549.2.U5D47   1986   658.3'02   85-45901
ISBN 0-87589-677-4

Manufactured in the United States of America

The paper in this book meets the guidelines for
permanence and durability of the Committee on
Production Guidelines for Book Longevity of the
Council on Library Resources.

JACKET DESIGN BY WILLI BAUM

FIRST EDITION

Code 8608

A joint publication in
The Jossey-Bass
Management Series
and
The Jossey-Bass
Social and Behavioral Science Series

To my children—
Bentley, Danielle, Yvette,
and Zachary Derr—
very different future careerists

Preface

A traditional assumption has been that careerists—career-oriented people—have historically been motivated by the money, status, and creative tasks that come with promotions. According to this assumption, they begin their careers on the first step of a ladder that leads to the president's office, or as close to it as they can get. The manager's main task has thus involved pointing people in the direction of the ladder and calling their attention to the tempting rewards on each rung.

Such managerial simplicity, however, has eroded under the complexities of the 1980s. *Managing the New Careerists* identifies five different career success orientations. Only one of them is the traditional ladder-climbing pattern. As I am using the term here, a *career* is a long-term work history characterized by an intended and intentional sense of direction that allows and honors aspects of one's personal life. Americans are becoming more career-centered even while the work force is diversifying as part of the general societal shift toward pluralism—more types of education, more varieties of families, more political special-interest groups, more alternative life styles. A majority of today's workers probably have different goals than those of the organization they work for.

My early study of career dynamics was influenced by my

association with Edgar H. Schein and Michael Driver. Both Schein's writing on career anchors and Driver's work defining career concepts as conceptual maps influenced my thinking and research. In 1976, the U.S. Navy helped me identify 150 high-potential officers as "future admirals" and invited me to study why so many of them would drop out, if past statistics held true. I discovered that one subset of this sample wanted *only* to be admirals. But the navy thought this group, which I call *getting-ahead* careerists, included all 150 officers; actually only 62 percent of this far-from-random sample fell into that category. The rest wanted something else; being an admiral was not their idea of success. They obviously had the talent and the intelligence to convince the navy they could and should be admirals, but they were working for a different set of rewards.

From this sample of 150 officers, I identified three other groups. Some were *getting-secure* people, working for a comfortable niche where they had an understanding with the navy; they offered very hard work and unfaltering loyalty in exchange for a high-level and high-status job that would use their talents and reward their loyalty. About 16 percent of the officers belonged in this group. They were motivated by a sense of job security and life-long organizational identity.

A second minority group, only about 4 percent of the 150, was composed of the *getting-free* careerists. They wanted personal autonomy at all costs, "space," and loose supervision. They were willing to accept a supervisor's definition of deadlines, budgets, and standards; but they wanted to figure out how to attain their objectives by themselves.

About 28 percent were in the navy for excitement, challenge, and the technical content of the work itself. These *getting-high* types had pinpointed the centers of action, of challenging work, and of creativity. Getting there had involved going after enough promotions to qualify them for exciting assignments; but if increased status and pay had not been part of the promotion package, it would not have mattered. The navy hardly seemed to be their natural home.

My further studies of other professional groups, my career portraits of successful people in a variety of fields, and a major study involving multinational executives that I conducted in Europe have confirmed the validity of this concept of diverse career orientations. These additional studies have also produced a fifth type of career orientation: *getting-balanced* careerists. These individuals give equal priority, attention, and time to their careers, to important relationships, and to self-development activities. They are disciplined, intelligent workers; at times they will work around the clock on projects, but they consider such periods exceptional times, out-of-balance times. A getting-ahead careerist considers this pattern normal, of course.

How This Book Will Help Managers

Managing the New Careerists will help managers understand the shape and direction of American business, with some attention to the multinational market. It will give them conceptual information and some practical examples on which to test this information. For almost twenty years, career management has been an important concern, but many of the books available are self-help collections of strategies that assume a getting-ahead orientation. Books about how to manage others, on the other hand, often deal with issues of motivation and political game playing without acknowledging the variety of motives underlying worker behavior.

With such genuine and deep-seated diversity on the part of workers, how should managers respond? I would propose two strategies for managing this diversity of orientation. The first is better motivation through more "valuable" rewards. Managers who have only carrots and sticks in their repertoires of rewards and sanctions are going to be less successful at motivating people who really do not want carrots or who are not afraid of sticks. This book describes the characteristics of the new careerists who hold these five diverse orientations and suggests ways to manage them effectively by minimizing the discrepancy between what they want and what the organization wants.

The second strategy is downplaying organizational conflict and covert politics. The motives, values, and talents of a careerist, as well as the constraints on his or her abilities, constitutes the *internal career.* The business world in which people try to achieve their goals is the *external career*—the demands, requirements, and opportunities of a particular enterprise with its own culture, style, and rewards. A manager who can improve the match between person and job—between internal and external career—will reduce the chance of having to outmaneuver someone who is playing antiorganizational *career politics* or who is maximizing his or her internal career while minimizing the inevitable negative side effects of such actions. Obviously, the less covert the politics and the better the work match, the longer the organization can keep its valuable and skilled employees productive.

A reality that managers of the 1980s must face is the new economy—thriving, but characterized by lower levels of employment along with low inflation, deregulation, a strong dollar, and new technology (McGinley, 1984). Many large companies, even those with record sales, profits, and dividends, are dismissing workers, trimming white-collar staffs, and cutting salaries. Swain and Swain, a New York firm that provides counseling and placement for laid-off careerists, reported that its white-collar business is as active now as during the recession ("Labor Letter Column," 1984). It is more crucial than ever to make the best use of resources—human and financial. Simultaneously, with layoffs continuing and the squeeze on working salaries tightening, more and more careerists are opting for a cautious strategy: to stay put no matter what, at least for awhile. Better career matching also means that employees can be given work they genuinely like to do rather than being "bribed" by increasingly higher salaries to do work that would be very attractive to someone else. Fewer dissatisfactions mean increased productivity. Canny managers need to be attentive to coping patterns that are not beneficial either to the company or the worker and instead find new ways of involving, motivating, and encouraging.

In short, American business is moving toward a more pluralistic work force, one in which private agendas are as important as the external ones imposed by the demands, possibilities, and limitations of the company itself. Managers' own successful careers, therefore, may depend on understanding internal career profiles and on learning to use the differences in career orientation to the company's advantage. Managers will need to design career development systems that accommodate different types of workers and use their strengths more successfully.

Who Should Read This Book

Managing the New Careerists is written primarily to help managers understand and use career diversity. It is an approach that assumes a strong internal and individual career success map. It is designed to help people reach their definitions of career success—which may or may not involve changing jobs. It is designed for managers who are exploring their own internal career orientations and those of their employees. It aims to assist human resource specialists in providing more flexible options in planning career development programs and to aid career counselors in assessing, diagnosing, and testing clients. Researchers will also find this book helpful as an introduction to a typology of careers. Naturally the concepts presented here will also be useful to any individual working on a career plan and forming strategies to achieve personal success.

This volume will be most helpful to thinking managers who are looking for some way to explain the diversity and pluralism of the workplace. At a time when individuals are expressing more pluralism than ever before, the workplace is offering the same old choices, or possibly even fewer. It is crucial for managers to understand the different objectives, strategies, and tactics of workers and their different definitions of a successful career. There are more forms of career success than simply getting ahead, and these other forms are valid, viable, and valuable. Management needs to expand its thinking about what motivates people and move beyond valuing only one or two types of careerists. The human resource and career development specialists can help managers do this, and the material in this book is designed to aid them in this effort.

Overview of the Contents

Part One describes the scene in which American businesses operate today. Chapter One documents the ground swell of pluralism in our society that has already changed—probably permanently—the nature of the workplace, expectations and assumptions about work, and the new career "contract" that managers must negotiate with their workers. Chapter Two describes the new managers and their challenges and constraints in managing diversity and provides the model for assessing a career success map. Chapter Three discusses the external career, describing and defining a context for action that includes the realities of the job market, the legitimate and enforceable demands of businesses, and the life cycle–work cycle correlations that make it possible to generalize about large patterns among American careerists. Chapter Four is a detailed analysis of the strategies and options offered by career politics: how they work, why they are inevitable, and how to manage political actors creatively and productively.

Part Two analyzes the five major definitions of career success that can be identified as major trends for American workers in the 1980s. Supplementing the conventional up-the-ladder pattern of the classic getting-ahead type (Chapter Five) are getting-secure (Chapter Six), getting-free (Chapter Seven), getting-high (Chapter Eight), and getting-balanced (Chapter Nine) careerists. The case studies and examples are composites drawn from my research, career counseling, and reports received from others. Chapter Ten discusses career transitions: how and when major redefinitions of career success occur and how to manage them profitably.

Part Three explains how to apply the principles of managing the new careerists. In Chapter Eleven we explore the instruments an individual careerist can use in assessing his or her career success map: identifying work-related motives, values, talents, and perceived constraints. This chapter also describes how to score and interpret the evaluation instruments. Chapter Twelve discusses how a manager can deal with the practical problems of keeping diverse careerists motivated. Chapter Thirteen provides some basic data on the pluralistic challenges and opportunities facing the multinational manager, particularly in the European sector. Chapter Fourteen is designed to make the concept of multiple career success orientations useful to specialists in organizational development, training, personnel, and career development. Chapter Fifteen assists career counselors in applying the same concepts.

Acknowledgments

The main currents of this project have been fed by many streams of thought and experience. It is a pleasure to acknowledge my teachers, students, and colleagues in this joint adventure.

Special thanks go to Susan Nero at the University of California at Los Angeles and Antioch University of Los Angeles for valuable input during the conceptualization phase, including collaborating with me in testing the concepts during residential courses we cotaught for American University/National Training Laboratory Institute of Applied Behavior Science Program at Airlie House, Virginia. Other colleagues who significantly sharpened the ideas in the book and helped prepare the manuscript are Paul Evans, Andre Laurent, and Linda Brimm of the European Institute of Business Administration, Fontainebleau, France, and Gene Dalton and Paul Thompson of Brigham Young University, Provo, Utah.

Other teacher-colleagues who have shaped my work on careers over the years right up to the present include Edgar H. Schein, Massachusetts Institute of Technology; Michael Driver, University of Southern California; Douglas T. Hall, Boston University; John Gabarro and Jeffrey Sonnenfeld, Harvard University; Lotte Bailyn, Massachusetts Institute of Technology; Robert Morrison, Naval Personnel Research and Development Center; James Clawson, University of Virginia; Francine Hall, University of New Hampshire; David Kolb, Case Western Reserve University; Tom DeLong, Brigham Young University; Richard Williams and Barbara Lawrence, University of California at Los Angeles; Terrence Deal, Vanderbilt University; Ronald Burke, York University; John Seybolt, University of Utah; Marshal Chatwin, Monterey Peninsula College; Manfred Kets de Vries, European Institute of Business Administration; Donald Levine, Brooklyn College; Per Dalin, International Learning Cooperative; and Michael Arthur, Suffolk University.

Clients, managers, and human resource specialists who willingly read the manuscript in various stages and brought their own executive expertise to bear on what might otherwise have been a somewhat academic treatise are Victoria Laney, IBM; Carol Willett, Central Intelligence Agency; David Figgat, American Express; Chris Jacobs, Honeywell; John Bennion, superintendent of schools, Salt Lake City, and James Bergera, superintendent of schools, Provo, Utah; Linda Quass, private human resource consultant; Patrick Gallegos, Evans and Sutherland; Tolly Kizilos, Honeywell; Herbert Scholten, Federal Express; Charles Kramer, World Bank; John Geisler, First Interstate Bank; Jim Smith, 3-M Corporation; John Nielson, Utah Power and Light; Baron Derr, Sheet Metal and Air Conditioning Contractors Association; David Knibbe, Arthur Young; and Gregory Kuhlman, Brooklyn College.

Institutions that provided major research and writing support are the University of Utah, which provided writing time and a research sabbatical, and the Raoul de Vitry d' Avancourt Chair Program in International Human Resource Management at the European Institute of Business Administration (INSEAD), which supported my European research. Colleagues who translated institutional policies with personal good will included INSEAD staff members Didier Berthoud, Avivah Wittenburg, Hans Werner, Lister Vickery, Petra-Jane Barron, Christine Harrison, Sylvia Menou, and Henriette Robilliard. University of Utah colleagues who provided major support include Garth Mangum, director of the Institute for Human Resource Management; Jerome Wiest, chair of the Department of Management; Iver E. Bradley, dean of the College of Business; and faculty colleagues Thayne Robson, Arben Clark, Joseph Bentley, Reed Richardson, and Ann Wendt. Capable research assistants made portions of the job much easier: Linda Anderson, Carl Summers, Claire Turner, Michelle Egan, Shirley Miller, Renee McConnell, Cecelia Gyberg, and Charles Despres.

It is a pleasure to acknowledge my debt to my students—experienced and mature adult learners—in the American University/National Training Laboratory Program who were pursuing masters' degrees in human resource development and who provided valuable feedback: William O'Connell, Saga Corporation; Mary Ann Ruth, Internal Revenue Service; Daniel Robinson, U.S. Air Force; Maresa Guerin, Catholic Youth Ministry; Ivan Monrad, American Telephone and Telegraph; James Dyck and Elizabeth McLagan, World Bank; Susan Stanley and Connie Johnson, Digital Equipment Corporation; Maurice Dubras, Atomic Energy Commission of Canada; and Nan Meltzer, private human resource consultant.

For all the pleasure of developing and testing the ideas, writing and rewriting remain hard work. My thanks to Lavina Fielding Anderson of Editing, Inc., for taking a sharp pencil to the manuscript when necessary, and to Gwen Luke of the University of Utah's Institute for Human Resource Management and Joy Sansome of Utah Power and Light Company for patiently typing draft after draft.

Finally, my most sincere thanks are but dim appreciation to my partner, Jill, and our children, Bentley, Danielle, Yvette, and Zachary, who sacrificed many hours of my time to this project.

Alpine, Utah   C. Brooklyn Derr
February 1986

Contents

Part Three: Practical Applications

The Author

C. Brooklyn Derr is associate director of the Institute for Human Resource Management and associate professor in the department of management at the University of Utah, Salt Lake City, where he conducts classes and research in career management. He received his B.A. degree in political science from the University of California at Berkeley (1966) and his Ed.D. degree in organizational behavior from Harvard University (1971).

Former academic appointments include research associate at the University of Oregon, assistant professor at the Graduate School of Education, Harvard University, visiting assistant professor at the Graduate School of Education, University of California at Los Angeles, as well as four years in the department of administrative sciences at the Naval Postgraduate School, where he also studied career orientations in naval officers. From January to August 1985, Derr was visiting professor and research associate supported by the Raoul de Vitry d'Avancourt Chair at the European Institute of Business Administration, Fontainebleau, France. Here, in addition to conducting classes in career management and executive development, he researched career management practices in Europe.

Together with Edgar H. Schein, Derr codirected a seminar in 1978 at the Massachusetts Institute of Technology that helped initiate investigation of a new aspect of career dynamics and from which emerged his edition of *Work, Family and the Career: New Frontiers in Theory and Research* (1980). Derr's publications include three books and numerous chapters, articles, and technical reports. He was one of the founding members of the careers division of the Academy of Management, which began as an interest group in 1979.

Managing the New Careerists

*The Diverse
Career Success
Orientations
of Today's Workers*

 ONE

The New
Career Success
Orientations

I recently did some consulting with Bill, the thirty-eight-year-old division chief of a booming California computer graphics company that was founded about fifteen years ago. Bill, whose background is in engineering, had come to a workshop I was teaching because he needed help in managing his subordinates. The discussion of career orientations clicked with him, helping him to understand several of the areas where he felt pressure and giving him some options for dealing with tricky personnel cases. "We spent the first ten years growing like crazy," Bill assessed. "If we had a problem with someone, we just found a place to stick him. But now we have to tend to management." This company recruits at top engineering schools across the nation and turns its bright young people loose on a smorgasbord of tempting design projects. The early career is demanding but fun. The regular promotions and bonus system keep most of them coming back for more. At midcareer, however, problems sometimes develop, and the company has lost several people that it considered candidates for top management. It wanted to know why.

Bill told me about several cases under his supervision. He was surprised by their diversity, but I was not. It reflected a pattern that was repeating itself all over the nation, as companies were discovering five distinct career success orientations among

1

their employees: (1) getting ahead—making it to the top of the hierarchy and status system; (2) getting secure—achieving recognition, job security, respect, and "insider" status; (3) getting free—obtaining maximum control over work processes; (4) getting high—getting excitement, challenge, adventure, and "cutting edge" opportunities; and (5) getting balanced—achieving a meaningful balance among work, relationships, and self-development, so that work does not become either too absorptive or too uninteresting.

For instance, Bill was unstinting in his praise of Garth, a thirty-three-year-old design engineer who had been with the company eight years, steadily created dynamic new programs, and even made significant contributions to the hardware end. Within five years, he had zoomed to the supervision level and had begun managing several projects that included people senior to him. In a company of 5,000 employees, he clearly stood out as a "comer." In the career management business, I would call him a "getting-ahead" type.

"His success is part of his problem," Bill said. "He's probably after his boss's job." Rex, Garth's security-oriented boss, is "nervous as hell" around him, finds him pushy and aggressive, and complains that "he doesn't really have any loyalty to the company." Bill is sympathetic. "In another four years, he'll be after my job, too. Maybe we shouldn't try to keep him. He's always lobbying for more projects, more people, more budget. Well, dammit, so are other divisions. Even if we could give him everything he wants—and it would probably pay off for us—I still feel that we're just helping him get a great resumé together for his next company." Is Garth a sneaky or disloyal employee? Absolutely not, Bill asserts. But Bill feels personally responsible for the problem Garth represents, because he has sponsored several of Garth's important projects and admits to basking in the reflected glory when they have paid off big. Bill also considers himself ambitious and aggressive, but he feels helpless about the management problem. Part of that problem is mediating between Garth and Rex.

Rex was in on the founding of the company and is Garth's immediate supervisor as coordinator of design projects. It is a thankless job, requiring endless follow-up on deadlines, correspondence, and revisions to keep track of where three dozen projects are at any given moment. Rex, however, loves filling out charts and carries a lot of the company's history around in his head. His loyalty, competence, and devotion to the company are unquestioned. J. M., the boss, frequently has him speak to the staff at special events to remind employees about the tradition of excellence established in those first rocky months. Rex thrives on the personal attention, and Bill has learned a lot about how to manage a getting-secure employee by watching J. M. and Rex. Still, it is Rex's very loyalty to the company that makes things difficult for Bill. "He runs on applause," says Bill, "and I'm running out of things to reward him for. He'll do anything he's told, no matter how long it takes, but you have to tell him first. And his first reaction to a new project is always, 'That's not the way we used to do it.' His conservatism is driving the kids crazy."

With another employee, Elizabeth, Bill has a still different problem. She is a brilliant technician, but, unlike Garth, she does not seem to be after anybody's job. She is a getting-free type. Married and the mother of three children, including a year-old baby, Elizabeth negotiated for an at-home work station during the last pregnancy. She still uses it at least part of each week. She worked part time even during maternity leave. When she has had to cut back for a few days, she has always made up the time. She seems oblivious to much of the company's friendly esprit de corps, concentrates on her work, fights like a tiger for technically challenging projects, and comes through superbly. But she has also refused two or three promotions that would have made her a supervisor over groups larger than two- or three-person teams. "I don't want to spend my time managing," she explained in a shatteringly unconscious insult. "I want to spend my time working."

Bill's dilemma? How to manage someone who does not like anyone looking over her shoulder. When he tried wandering by with a cup of coffee in his hand, she met him standing up, rattled off a progress report that was a haze of technical terms, and firmly ushered him out. "She knows budget, technical specs, and deadlines," says Bill. "She's come through 100 percent for the last five years. But I have this uneasy feeling that there's going to be blood all over the wall some morning, and I'm not going to have the faintest idea how it got there."

Part of his nervousness comes from experience with several others who sought autonomy. One of these had also hated anyone looking over his shoulder; and Bill, respecting his wishes and track record, had backed off, only to discover six expensive months later that he had been going down the wrong road. At least two other "hands-off" workers, after three or four years of excellent production, had quietly given notice and left to set up their own companies. "I don't mind competition," Bill lies stoutly, "but they were some of our best people. In fact, it was when they left that J. M. decided we should get serious about management. How could we have made it possible for them to stay?"

For a long time, he had the same feeling about Casey, again a bright project manager at midcareer; but the pattern here seems to be different. Personal freedom does not seem to be the bottom line for Casey. He appears more obsessed by the details of his craft, insatiable about learning all he can, technically sophisticated, always pestering Bill for state-of-the-art equipment or permission to go to a professional meeting. "He's probably accounted for more technical innovation than any other four people, but I have two problems with him," Bill confessed. "I'm not sure that he's loyal to the company. If he got a more challenging offer, I'm sure he'd be off like a shot, even if he had to take a pay cut to do it. Then, too, how do I get him to do the dull work? He's a genius at debugging a program, but he won't take the time to tidy up the loose ends afterward because he bores easily."

The company also recruited several dual-career couples just out of college about six years earlier, "and for the most part, it's paid off." Don and Doris, who work in different branches of the company, seem to manage their three children and home life in a way that does not impinge on company time, "but they're just not available, either." Both of them worked hard during the first six or seven years, even while the last two children were coming along; but after they were promoted to a certain level, they seemed to "settle down." They do not refuse demanding projects, but it is clear that work does not always come first. "Don came in on Monday, tanned and bright-eyed from a weekend of hang gliding. Doris's chamber music group gave a concert the same weekend. Everybody else was red-eyed and jittery with caffeine overdoses from working on a big project and being up three nights running. It wasn't their project, but it wasn't really not theirs, either."

It is not unusual for managers even in a small to medium-sized company to deal with this variety of career success orientations. As a manager, Bill must find a way to match the company's needs with Garth, who wants opportunities to advance and get ahead; with Rex, whose orientation is toward company loyalty and long-term career security; with Elizabeth, who desires autonomy and control of her work situation; with Casey, who wants the kind of challenging and exciting tasks that will make his adrenalin flow; and with Don and Doris whose game is trying to balance their personal and professional lives. It is highly unlikely that a manager in the 1980s will go through his or her entire career without encountering career-oriented workers who define success in this whole range of ways.

A career is more than a job. It is more than a long-term sequence of jobs. A career is also more than luck or happenstance; it may be permanently altered by fortune, but it has a sense of direction that comes from the individual careerist. Furthermore, a career, because it is long term, must acknowledge and respect aspects of personal life that have an impact on work life. Career success is being able both to live out the subjective and personal values one really believes in and to make contributions to the world of work. When these directions are thwarted, many careerists resort to career politics to ease the tension between what they want and what the organization will allow. They try to achieve their own personal definitions of career success while still doing their work at some acceptable level of performance, looking as though they fit within the organizational culture, and paying their dues. At most, they match their needs with the opportunities that exist at work. At the least, they do not get fired. The challenge for managers like Bill is really three-fold:

1. As a manager, he is also a careerist, acting on his own defi-nition of career success and trying to maximize it. Increased understanding increases his ability to manage his own ca-reer successfully.
2. His subordinates have career success orientations of their own. If he can identify them, he can understand them bet-ter and try to match their needs with the organization's. If he can give Elizabeth what she wants, Elizabeth is much more likely to give the organization what it wants. Even if there is a mismatch, good management can prevent subver-sion, "dirty" career politics, and sabotage.
3. Peers and superiors also have their own career agendas. To be organizationally and personally effective in working with them, Bill needs to understand their career success ori-entations.

Understanding Career Diversity

Academic awareness of diversity among career orienta-tions developed in the early 1960s, when Edgar H. Schein of MIT, for example, began studying forty-four MIT master's de-gree graduates (Schein, 1978). He interviewed them six months and one year after graduation and then sent them questionnaires at five-year and ten-year intervals. He found that, between five and ten years after graduation, these forty-four—who had all ini-tially thrown themselves at various career ladders with equal en-thusiasm and had swarmed up them with equal speed—started looking a good deal more diverse. With real-life work experience, feedback from peers and supervisors, and the emergence of their own perceived talents, people sorted themselves into five groups: (1) "managers," who kept clawing right up the ladder with un-diminished zeal, (2) "technicians and specialists," who settled down happily to pay attention to the details of their craft, (3) the "security oriented," who discovered that promotions were rewarding largely because they meant that the company prized them and wanted to keep them, (4) those with high "autonomy" needs, who found ways of carving out their own space in large organizations or starting their own companies, and (5) "entrepreneurs," who also ended up starting new ventures, products, and services to meet their needs to be creative and to reap the benefits of their labors.

Since Schein's initial efforts, he has identified several other basic career orientations (Schein, 1982), which he terms "anchors." One of these orientations has to do with service or dedication to a particular cause (such as world hunger), client group (such as women), or ideology (such as better medical service for the aged). Another is a "pure challenge" anchor he has found among high-powered consultants who love competition, seek out high-risk situations, and thrive on adventure. This category is similar to the getting-high "warriors" I found in my navy study (Derr, 1980, 1982c) who clustered in the fighter pilot and fast-attack nuclear submarine communities. They had an insatiable need for adventure, thrived on being at the center of the action, and were almost universally regarded as "crazy" by their colleagues. Schein also found a "life-style" anchor—part of a balanced perspective that certain careerists maintained between their professional and private lives. The resemblance between this group and my getting-balanced people is obvious.

Michael Driver (1979, 1980, 1982) has also published important work on different career self-concepts. He surveyed business executives and staff specialists in a variety of companies and formulated from their self-perceptions a quartet of definitions of career success: (1) some defined success as a spiral, as continued growth and self-renewing experiences (getting high); (2) some steady-state individuals wanted long-term stability and a relatively unchanging work identity (getting secure); (3) still others were transitory—they saw a successful career as having a variety of very different experiences (getting free); and (4) the linear people saw success as upward mobility to the top of the organization or profession (getting ahead). Driver hypothesized that these career concepts grew out of the habits of thought, motives, and decision-making styles of individual careerists, becoming the foundation that guided a person's long-term career choices.

Bailyn (1982) reported that only 29 percent of her sample of 1,351 MIT alumni engineers had traditional high-success aspirations. Instead, many were security oriented, others wanted increasing technical challenges, and still others spent their psychological energy on activities outside work. Holland (1973) also formulated a theory of diverse personality orientations and their impact on work as he studied six different career environments. By seeing the environment, rather than the internal aspirations, goals, and talents, as the most important dependent variable, Holland raises interesting questions about the interaction of the internal (individual) career and the external (company) career, which will be discussed in more detail in Chapter Three. The ultimate sources of individual career diversity lie beyond the realm of this book in the deeper reaches of psychology. No doubt, family upbringing, educational and institutional experiences, socioeconomic class, racial/ethnic/religious cultural diversity, and gender differences all play a role. Whatever the sources, we carry around with us different ideas or cognitive maps on many subjects—not the least of which is our work.

Some people might argue that these different orientations to career success have always existed and that the contribution of scholarship on the subject has simply been to catalogue and label. While it is impossible to know for certain, it also seems likely that the different dreams, assumptions, and expectations concerning work have developed out of more basic societal trends. For at least the past 200 years, upward mobility in the United States has been both a desirable and an attainable goal. An increasingly diversified economic and educational system has supported this goal. In our own decade, this societal pattern has produced increasingly diverse career success definitions, made possible in large measure by past economic success.

Pluralism in Our Society

Internal career diversity among employees is not just a fad that will quietly disappear. It reflects the greater political, social, educational, and economic pluralism of society at large.

In the last couple of decades, a greater value has been assigned to diversity. Daniel Yankelovich and John Immerwahr, participating in an examination of work in the twenty-first century, hypothesized that the two greatest forces extending into the future were "the increase in the amount of control or discretion that jobholders have over their work and the emergence of a new set of work place values which we call the philosophy of expressivism. The task of integrating these two trends will be one of the central tasks of managers and administrators" (Yankelovich and Immerwahr, 1983, p. 34). Because of the shift to an information society, professional, technical, and managerial jobs—precisely those portions of the job market with more discretion than blue-collar and manufacturing jobs—have mushroomed. Forty-nine percent of all white-collar workers say they have "a great deal of freedom" to perform their jobs; only a third of blue-collar workers make the same claim (p. 35). Furthermore, high-tech jobs are those in which the routine work is done by machines—unlike the situation during the industrial revolution, when unskilled laborers could do most of the work, because it required little judgment.

"Expressivism," which these two authors define as internal and highly personal values—"fulfilling one's potential as an individual" (p. 36)—has already, they claim, transformed the marketplace. Sensitivity to nature and community and greater emphasis on autonomy and freedom of choice have transformed work. Whereas, earlier, the paycheck was king and people who wanted to change their work had to change their jobs, the new expressivism simply assumes that work will provide not only basic survival needs but a steadily increasing standard of living. Thus, work becomes important for "personal growth and self-development." Half of the work force they surveyed say their parents worked to survive; 5 percent say their parents worked primarily for self-development. When these respondents speak for themselves, survival as the primary motivation drops to 38 percent, and the number who work for self-development—17 percent—more than triples (p. 37).

Not surprisingly, education is a direct predictor of how likely a person is to have expressive values. Since education has been steadily on the rise, expressivism is probably a trend of the future. These authors also predict a "best scenario" and a "worst scenario," both, they point out, depending "on the ability of American managers to respond to the new conditions" (p. 38). In the worst scenario, work will not be sufficiently engaging to satisfy workers. American jobholders will show up and do what is required but find their real fulfillment in other activities. Given the insecurities associated with an uncertain economy, these workers will not quit their jobs; they will probably do just enough to avoid being fired and invest their creative energies elsewhere—in hobbies, community service activities, moonlighting, or frankly hedonistic forms of escape. Nearly half of all current jobholders already admit that they do not do much more than is required. Another study shows that the amount of time employees spend actually working dropped 10 percent between 1965 and 1975. In high-discretion jobs, this lack of commitment could be crippling. In the best scenario, expressive workers will find an arena for their self-expression in their work. In one survey, 52 percent of jobholders said they "felt an inner need to do the best job possible" (p. 38). An effective manager in an effective organization will find a variety of ways to match such people to job and career opportunities at work. Expressivist jobholders want more freedom in how they do their work and are more concerned with creativity. If these demands can be met, they will make strong commitments to their jobs.

The old contract of exchanging money for time is passé, Yankelovich and Immerwahr claim. Instead, the new contract for workers in the twenty-first century will need to appeal to expressivist needs for "autonomy, creativity, community and entrepreneurship." Structure and hierarchy are out. Teamwork, individuality, and community are in. An adversary relationship between unions and managers is out. The value of nonmonetary rewards is in. Technology that tries to bypass human beings is out. Systems that "take advantage of and reward people's needs for self-fulfillment" are in. It is an exciting picture and one that is borne out by other researchers as well. Gunther Klaus (1983) asserts that "corporate pyramids" are being replaced in the best companies by horizontal organizations where literally no one is the boss, because everyone is. Isaac Asimov (1983, p. 42) claims that "the concepts of work and fun" will be blurred by new technology, leaving creativity as "the most important human activity" in a future he describes as one of "incredible excitement and precious little boredom."

Naisbitt (1982), in his best-seller *Megatrends,* also claims that large organizations are becoming more decentralized and deinstitutionalized, regrouping into smaller operational parts. The computer is helping coordinate small groups of horizontal, innovative task forces and entrepreneurial operations. Moreover, Naisbitt maintains that decision makers of the future will have to use right-brain intuition and creativity more effectively, that corporate cultures will be less "macho" and more androgynous, and that there will be greater emphasis on quality and qualitative information, rather than mere number crunching. He, too, believes that the work force will be more pluralistic and require more diverse options.

Toffler (1981) claims in *The Third Wave* that a technology-centered future will emphasize customizing for diverse tastes, life-styles, and preferences rather than standardization. Some people will work at night, and many will work part time. Vastly new work schedules and senses of time will evolve. In many of the new research park facilities springing up around the country, employees already have very flexible working conditions. They can work at home on their computers. They dress for comfort rather than "success." Offices are airy and architecturally pleasing but casual. Impressive recreational and leisure-time facilities are part of the parks. So are luxury apartments, located nearby for more intense work time when this is required (Guyon, 1981).

According to one prediction, professional and technical workers will increase by 30 percent between 1980 and 1990 (Gottschalk, 1981). And this future is almost upon us. In 1983, for the first time, more people were employed in services than in industry. The population is also growing older. The baby boomers are graying, and longevity is still increasing. Workers expect to work longer, have second and third careers, and experiment with diverse skills. Large numbers of women are in the

work force, bringing with them different sets of values, orientations, and skills that are just now coming under scrutiny. As
Gilligan (1982) and others (for example, Gottschalk, 1983)
have pointed out, many women reject the corporation and are
starting alternative companies. There are greater demands from
ethnic and racial minorities for their special needs to be recognized.

   The glut on the labor market is obviously only a temporary phenomenon. Those born during the baby boom that began in 1936 and peaked in 1964 are now surging forward
toward midcareer. The midcareer, traditionally a time of pla-
teauing as opportunities tapered off, has the potential for trans-
forming the workplace by sheer numbers; the midcareerists are
increasing twice as fast as the rest of the labor force. One difference has already become apparent. The information economy
will require an educational system that prepares workers to
function in the electronic society. Two decades of the "me generation" have already redefined education, not as a segment of
the life cycle but as a part of life itself.

   Another difference is in mobility. For a quarter of a century, 20 percent of the people changed addresses annually. Suddenly, in 1976, this percentage dropped to 17.7 percent. Two-
career couples, attached in different ways to their work and to
their communities, are staying put. And in 1979, 52 percent of
U.S. marriages were "two paycheck," up from 46 percent just
four years earlier. Geographically, the two-century-old tradition
of urbanization is ending, and the trend is toward moving out—
to smaller towns and rural areas. The center of population mobility is also shifting, from the Northeast and Midwest to the
Southwest and West, under its new name of the Sunbelt.

   Demographically, as the baby boom rippled out, it left a
population in 1979 with the median age of thirty. By the year
2000, the median age will be thirty-five. In 2025, 20 percent of
the population will be over sixty-five, and the median age that
year will be 42.4. The 1980s will see a 20 percent jump in the
number of workers over the traditional retirement age, and experts are already predicting the dropping of mandatory retirement. Nevertheless, many older workers are accepting "early

retirement" and engaging in second careers and new part-time jobs. Between 1980 and 1990, as the baby-boom generation hits midcareer, there will be a 42 percent increase in thirty-five- to forty-four-year-olds—that is, those who will be ready for prime midcareer plans on a middle-management career ladder.

By 1990, people may wonder what the controversy over women in the work force was about. Two-thirds of all women may be working by that time. As early as 1980, women got 60 percent of all new jobs. Overall, women accounted for two-thirds of the labor-force growth in the 1970s. And, while more than half of all women workers are still in traditional clerical and service jobs, the U.S. Department of Labor estimates a 21 percent increase in the number of woman managers between 1975 and 1985. The 1979 figure that located 25 percent of women in management was up 15 percent from 1965; interestingly enough, only 17 percent of them were in the private sector in 1978. The census bureau, looking ahead to the year 2000, predicts that women could outnumber men by 7.2 million and that 45 percent of the U.S. work force will be female. As of 1981, about three of every ten women worked part time, and about 4 percent were said to "moonlight" outside their regular jobs. There are no firm data on women starting new businesses, but in a year as unexpansive as 1981, 80 percent more businesses were started than in 1975.

All of these factors affect the family. In 1944, women averaged 2.5 births. By 1977, this figure had dropped to 1.8. Two out of five mothers with children under the age of six were working by 1980. Many adults—a large proportion of them divorced single parents—are moving back in with their own parents. Moreover, it is estimated that about half of all working women leave their children with relatives (often grandparents) while they work. Divorces are up 96 percent since 1970; ninety of every thousand marriages end in divorce. Only 60 percent of American households in 1981 included a married couple, and only 26 percent of all working women with children were part of a traditional nuclear family in 1984. By 1978, there had been a 37 percent increase in women between the ages of thirty and thirty-four and a 22 percent increase in those thirty-five to

thirty-nine giving birth to a first child. Even younger women
seem to be postponing childbirth. In 1960, only 24 percent of
women between twenty and twenty-four years of age had not
yet borne a child. By 1982, 43 percent of the women in that
age group had not yet had a child.

No one factor can explain this diversity. And no one approach is going to satisfy all the diverse elements of this pluralism. Part of the breakup of the monolith, not unexpectedly, is
taking place behind the door of the executive suite.

 TWO

New Challenges for Managers

For decades, the image of the manager has been of someone thinking through long-term goals for a company, making plans to implement those goals, then mobilizing the resources of the company to carry out the plans. Managers are the planners, co-ordinators, and controllers. They make strategic decisions; they delegate, oversee, and control. The image has been cerebral, intellectual, quantitative, and often remote.

Recent research on the nature of managerial work paints a different picture. Henry Mintzberg (1973) did an in-depth field study of five chief executive officers using an anthropological research framework. He found that they worked in a scenario characterized by variety, brevity, and fragmentation. Their activities are measured in seconds and minutes, not hours. Information often comes from gossip and hearsay, not from formal meetings, research, or reports. The pressure of the job encourages the development not of a planner but of an adaptive information manipulator who works in a stimulus-response environment and who favors live action. The manager spends more time in meetings, phone calls, and informal drop-ins than in any other activity. In those meetings, both formal and informal, strategies are plotted and decisions are reached. Managers are the neck of the hourglass between their own organization and the outside world. Subordinates take between half and a third of their time; superiors take relatively little—about 10 percent. Far from carefully thinking through issues and mapping out

15

quantitative approaches, they deal with a chaos of drop-in visitors, phone calls, lunches, and short encounters. And they like it that way.

John Kotter's (1982) study of fifteen managers from nine corporations across the United States identified their six key challenges: (1) setting basic goals, policies, and strategies in the face of uncertainty; (2) balancing scarce resources and not letting short-run interests dominate those of the long run; (3) keeping on top of many activities—identifying problems and solving them quickly; (4) getting information, cooperation, and support from superiors without being perceived as overly demanding; (5) getting corporate staff and other groups to cooperate in resisting red tape and formal lines of authority; and (6) motivating a large and diverse group of subordinates. For them —and probably for most executives—being effective depends, in large measure, on getting a lot of things done through a lot of different people despite having little control over most of them. In other words, the reality of management is that much of it operates on instinct and experience, not on careful cogitation. In such a setting, there are several reasons why understanding how to manage the new careerists in the 1980s makes sense.

New Tasks for Managers

Although managers spend most of their time working with people, that is not the goal in itself. Getting the work done is the goal. Mobilizing people to get the work done is the manager's problem. Every manager discovers that his or her time goes into coordinating, putting out brush fires, preventing end runs, building bridges, and mending fences. But the work still has to be done. Evenings and weekends are not long enough. Every manager needs to have good people working away on the projects that need to come through. No manager can succeed in the long run unless he or she can effectively manage subordinates.

No matter how formal the structure of a given organization, what managers really do is exchange information quickly and informally in an unstructured, unplanned world. How managers and those around them acquire, hoard, and manipulate scarce information is a critical variable. Personal and information skills are important. Understanding the diversity of the work force and the external environment, therefore, means possessing an important informational resource.

All managers have their own careers to manage, have to deal with superiors or peers who are competing for the same promotions or new assignments, and have to understand how to work within the organizational constraints to make every move count. The managers of outstanding companies are those who treat people effectively and give prime time to their employees, treating them as individuals and adults. Peters and Waterman's (1982) *In Search of Excellence* underscores the point in a dozen ways: many critical organizational problems are solved by solving people problems. As a result, many companies are asking managers to be career counselors. Exxon and IBM, as well as some other productive companies, have a place on the manager's performance review to rate how well that manager is developing his or her employees. Mentoring, in short, is seen as much more important in a manager's job description than ever before. In some companies, managers must develop two or three potential successors before they can move on. Unfortunately, many of these systems concentrate on looking only for getting-ahead future managers rather than developing ways of maximizing diversity in companies, but it is only a matter of time before the link with productivity is made.

On the negative side, mismanaging diverse employees can have serious effects on managers' careers. Managers need to understand the sources of possible conflicts, be wary of active and passive resistance, and even be prepared to stop actual attempts to sabotage a plan—for when people's expectations of their work are not satisfied, they may engage in activities more damaging than just loafing on the job, complaining, or gossiping. The most difficult kinds of conflicts to resolve are values conflicts. It is important to understand what really motivates subordinates to work in the first place. What are their long-term career success definitions? How can a manager make the best match between the needs of an internal career and the conditions of the external career? When that match cannot be made perfectly, how can a manager help minimize the negative consequences?

Modifying Career Orientations

The concept of career success orientations is seldom useful in motivating young employees. Schein (1978) found that it usually takes between five and ten years of on-the-job experience and feedback to establish a good sense of work identity. Nearly everyone in U.S. companies understands the getting-ahead ethos. They start out determined to climb the ladder. They covet labels such as "hard-charger," "fast-tracker," "front-runner," and "high-potential." They will discover their internal career somewhere about the fifth to eighth year of employment, and part of that discovery may be that the ladder no longer looks good.

A career success map, though deeply influential, is not a straitjacket. People can modify their career orientations, given enough motivation and information about options. A getting-ahead person may choose to back away from being totally absorbed in work and adopt a getting-balanced orientation after a family crisis or a heart attack, for instance. Suddenly, the executive suite is just not worth it any more. Or if a personal situation changes (for example, someone becomes a single parent), your seventy-hour-a-week employee may quickly become a strictly nine-to-five person, more interested in flexible work schedules than in spending whatever time it takes to do the job.

Managerial Ethics

As a corollary, some good workers simply are not work oriented. They do not have a career in the sense of the word that I am using. Other careerists will be in transition or searching for a new career orientation as a result of a major life event, such as an illness or a divorce, while still others may have discovered the discrepancies between what they thought they wanted and those insistent internal messages saying "something else." They will be searching, without a clear career success orientation. A general guideline is that a managerial goal should *not* be to coax, bribe, or threaten everyone into being the type of workaholic, advancement-hungry overachiever that businesses have often thought they could not get enough of. Although certain types of businesses do seem to need more of certain personality types, any business needs variety—creativity, not clones. All career types have their strengths and their place in a successful ongoing organization.

Most of us are products of various religious value systems and cultures. Built into those cultures are strong ethical propositions: What constitutes honesty? What is a fair day's work for a fair day's pay? What tactics may you use to make a sell? How do you report situations to your advantage and yet remain honest? Where does looking out for your own interests end? What does being loyal to an organization mean? What types of motivation are legitimate? All of these questions ran into the national wave of narcissism and self-indulgence in the 1960s and 1970s that had the good effect of making people realize that they were responsible for their own happiness and the bad effect of increasing selfishness. In fact, the line between the two frequently depends on one's point of view. This new awareness—which legitimates seeking personal happiness in a way that might have been termed "ruthless" by another generation—is precisely why managers must be prepared for the negative consequences of career politics if legitimate avenues for diversity are not available.

For managers themselves, the ethical considerations can become quite complicated. Not only must they make decisions about managing their own careers within ethical guidelines they feel comfortable with and within the ethical limitations of their profession, they also must consider the ethics of their management practices. Where is the line between motivating an employee through promising honest rewards honestly earned and manipulating that same employee by promising the most attractive combination of circumstances even when it is unclear—or downright improbable—that the manager can actually deliver that reward? Should a manager try to speak getting-secure language to a getting-secure subordinate on Monday and getting-ahead language to another on Tuesday, or is it the employee's job to adjust to the manager?

A manager might think it in the company's best interests to use the career success orientation instruments in this book to "sniff out" the employees who have "undesirable" orientations and get rid of them. This approach has several dangers. First, your diagnosis will probably be incomplete, perhaps even inaccurate. Even though these instruments explain and make comprehensible the diverse range of strategies, motivations, and tactics that modern managers must deal with, no single diagnostic instrument can fully capture the complexity of human beings.

Second, professionals in the assessment business are consistently less dogmatic than amateurs, because the professionals have developed a certain amount of humility about the capability of one label to cover an entire person. For instance, an interesting part of the workshops I run are the "microlabs" where I ask people to assess themselves on several dimensions and then make some conclusions about how this information affects their career orientation. After a brief theoretical discussion, I ask people to analyze their learning style, their birth order in their families, their life stage, and their relationship with partners and children—both current and as projected into the future. For another dimension, they analyze what has significance to them outside work: sports, hobbies, and recreation; religion; community service or politics; and so on. Still another dimension is special status (being handicapped or being a member of a minority group). As people discuss their self-perceptions with others who put themselves in the same groups in these microlabs, some interesting information about their careers develops that does not emerge from a more direct approach. They also see their careers differently depending on which aspect they happen to identify at a given moment in the exercise.

Even with the carefully designed questionnaires I use, I find that people frequently lack clarity about their motivations. This kind of information comes out in "triangulated" interviews with them and one or two significant others, and then in a second interview, where I feed the information back to them.

This method is extremely useful but almost impossible to apply without some training. In short, managers who read this book and try to divide their employees into categories with the intent of getting rid of everybody in the nondesirable categories probably will be making decisions on the basis of inadequate information.

Beyond the practical problems of attempting to make decisions on the basis of inadequate or inaccurate information, the ethical question remains. Even if your ability to categorize workers is accurate, is it fair to get rid of people without giving them an opportunity to change their behavior? People can modify an internal career orientation to make a better match with the requirements of the external career. Furthermore, so major a change may not even be necessary. Specific feedback about particular behaviors that are inappropriate or ineffective will usually produce changes that will greatly enhance a worker's productivity and a manager's reputation as effective.

A further consideration is understanding how career politics works. Playing career politics well involves achieving as much as you possibly can, given the realities of personal constraints and the conditions that exist within your organization. At the same time, you must attempt to minimize unintended negative consequences. Attempts can backfire. Also, a career is a long-term proposition. Even a highly desirable promotion is not worth it if you have to cash all your social chips and incur universal ill will to get it.

Although politics-playing careerists may not act in the company's best interest, it is important to understand that career politics is not in itself a dirty or Machiavellian operation. Politics has to do with getting things done. It involves paying attention to how the system really works (including its informal dimensions) and how to make use of that system to accomplish meaningful objectives. Wheeling, dealing, and politicking are part of a manager's life; but managers are usually able to define their own best interests to correspond with those of the organization. Career politics become damaging to the organization only when management does not recognize and allow diversity. If employees feel that they must "disguise" themselves as getting-ahead or getting-secure types no matter what their real orientation is, the politics will simply move to a deeper level, with more subterfuge, more sabotage, more surprises. When employees feel that they have no alternatives, they use methods that are personally painful to their integrity and usually damaging to the organization.

Skillful managers, on the other hand, recognize that career politics is a dynamic way of managing mismatches that keeps worker satisfaction high and enhances productivity. A good manager knows and communicates that a worker will not always feel perfectly matched and that the organization will not always be able to offer a perfect set of alternatives. And that is okay. Cooperative career politics minimizes negative consequences for both the organization and the individual. By supporting career politics, a good manager keeps it from going underground, which is the only alternative as long as the employee stays with the organization.

 THREE

Assessing
Career Options
and Constraints

In some ways, the problem of management can be explained historically by the free-labor-market model. Business has needed certain types of talents. It has decided how badly it needs them (how high it is willing to bid to get them) and how easy it would be to get and retain them (how low it can pay and still get and keep them) and then has made its offer, selecting what it wants from the candidates who have applied. It has assumed that people work for status, job security, and money. Although some lip service has been paid to the importance of "challenging" and "fulfilling" work and the opportunity to grow and develop, that has been seen as essentially the employee's problem. What the enterprise could offer was cash in return for services. In other words, the *external career* (the combination of opportunities and constraints existing in a given occupation and organization) was the sum total of career expectations: the organization's needs and the realities of the labor market dictated what the individual did.

What managers must now also deal with—a task requiring considerably more sophistication and expertise—is also the *internal career* of its workers: that internal and subjective career success orientation, those unique personal career definitions, hopes, and plans. You may have an employee seeking autonomy, but your organization may need, want, and reward only loyal and conforming people. What can you do? What is the context within which your employees act out their internal career plans? From a manager's perspective, what are the critical aspects of the career development system with which you must deal to productively direct the internal career energy of these diverse employees? How do you provide reasonable options and opportunities for various kinds of people in an attempt to match their needs with those of the organization? How do you narrow the gap between the internal and external careers?

Three components of the external career are important for both individuals and managers. They are the major career backdrops against which all scenarios for internal career success must be tested. They are also the major contextual levers of intervention for channeling and directing diverse careerists. These are (1) the corporate culture, (2) the important variable of timing or phasing, and (3) the kinds of career development policies and programs that are available.

Corporate Culture

The culture of an organization is the most important contextual variable in the external career of its employees. Culture acts as the backdrop to everything else that goes on, as Deal and Kennedy's (1982) insightful *Corporate Cultures* first brought to national attention. Bridges and roads are not part of a nation's economy, per se, but they have enormous impact on it. Culture acts as that essential infrastructure in organizational life. As Schein (1985) has amplified, culture is a manifestation of "deep," perhaps even unconscious assumptions, values, and decision-making styles—difficult to identify, difficult to change, but essential to understand.

For instance, in some organizations, first-naming the boss is taboo. In other organizations, *not* first-naming the boss is taboo. Playing career politics is successful only within the limits and parameters of your organization's culture—those myths, legends, values, taboos, norms, roles, coalitions, and networks that must be understood and used effectively. In all likelihood, if you are successful as a manager, it is because you learned these lessons well. Employees who do not understand them make mistakes, look clumsy or opportunistic, or get a reputation for "playing dirty." As a manager, you are responsible for representing the culture in general and for steering neophytes through its rapids.

Every organization has its own culture, as does every industry. You do not normally find the same game in a university as you do in a bank. You do not use the same tactics in a hospital as in a computer company. IBM and Digital Equipment Corporation (DEC) are in the same industry but have very different cultures. IBM has the reputation of being efficient, understated, neat, and tidy, while Digital Equipment has the reputation of being creative, loose, messy, and ambiguous. Not all corporations have strong cultures or communicate expectations clearly. Deal and Kennedy (1982) and Peters and Waterman (1982) insist that successful companies do. If companies really do have very definite norms and easily identifiable patterns of expectations and rewards, employees have a clear choice: there is either a match or a mismatch between their own internal career orientations and the external career realities. On the other hand, companies without such fixed cultural parameters may permit more flexibility and more diverse opportunities for the various kinds of careerists—especially for those who have internal orientations difficult to match in the world of work. We present here some questions to help you identify career-related aspects of your particular organization's culture. First come some questions about history and traditions.

1. What was the role of the founders? What legacy did they leave this enterprise? In any organization, even top management can move only so far before running into the inherited cultural tradition. Organization specialists claim that it is impossible to read the culture from the statements and actions of people who articulated the direction for the organization early in its history. Many assert that it is impossible to have a pronounced culture without strong leaders in the early days of the company. Their statements become myths, slogans, and legends.

For instance, Henry M. Lane and Eileen Morley (1979) in "Neiman-Marcus" point out that Herbert Marcus, chief executive officer of the organization from 1907 to 1950, set a strong tradition that his son Stanley, president from 1950 to 1972, amplified and strengthened. As far as quality was concerned, Herbert Marcus wanted to sell the finest and most fashionable merchandise in the world. He also wanted the selection to be unique. Stanley Marcus referred to this selection as "editing": "The quality that makes one paper like the New York *Times* really stand out lies in the editing. One paper features its foreign news on the front page, another buries it . . . inside; one plays up violence . . . the other relegates [it] to its local news section. So it goes with stores. Essentially all of us buy in the same market but we select differently" (Lane and Morley, 1979, p. 158).

At Neiman-Marcus, exclusiveness meant more than sole representation and reliance on manufacturers' workmanship. It included the improvements in style and fabrication that Neiman-Marcus buyers insisted on and paid extra for—such as silk instead of rayon linings and handmade buttonholes. It also meant always to improve the merchandise, never to reduce its quality in order to decrease costs. Herbert Marcus held actual price to be a poor indicator of value. Whether merchandise cost $5 or $50,000, he expected it to represent a true value to his customer. Despite its image of catering only to the very wealthy, the store always carried popularly priced merchandise. Stanley Marcus called it "a store with a split personality," selling fur coats or jewelry items at $50,000 but also doing a large business in $50 dresses.

Customer satisfaction was Herbert Marcus's final maxim. He believed that there was a right customer for every piece of merchandise and that a merchant should match customers and goods, even if this meant losing a sale rather than selling a customer an inappropriate garment or product. Stanley quoted his father: "There is never a good sale for Neiman-Marcus unless it is a good buy for the customer." His comment became the Neiman-Marcus "Golden Rule" (p. 159). Stanley Marcus also considered beautiful, spacious, uncluttered store interiors and attentive personal service highly important contributions to shopping pleasure and satisfaction—at a cost that the founders judged worth while. "We want to sell satisfaction, not just merchandise. . . . This may prove expensive to us and a few may take advantage of this policy unfairly but we are convinced that adherence to this policy will cement our customers' loyalty to Neiman-Marcus" (p. 159).

These two men illustrate the role of a company's founders. Assuming the stature of heroes, they embody a philosophy that shapes the decisions and directions of a company. You must know about your company's history to understand an important part of its culture and communicate it to the people you supervise. In fact, the culture is inextricably linked to the company's evolutionary history. Older organizations have a richer culture (and one that is more definite if they have had strong founders and leaders) than do younger ones.

2. Who are the cultural heroes? Who are the deviants? Usually, the events that created the heroes started out as history. Something happened, and someone made a huge contribution that also had symbolic importance. One of the things a strong leader understands is how to create heroes and how to check deviants, thus setting the parameters of what is acceptable to the company. For example, I once consulted with a small chemical company in which every executive had a truck driver's hard hat as part of his office decor. At one point in the company's history, the truck drivers had worked around the clock for about a ten-day stretch, delivering explosives to save a mining contract of such crucial importance that the company might have gone under without it. The president made truck drivers cultural heroes, communicating the expectation that "in our company, we come through."

An example of an acceptable deviant is an employee of a conservative Canadian banking company who turned around its whole data-processing system in a brilliant way. He was a genuinely eccentric person who once showed up to work wearing one bright blue sock and one lurid green. On another occasion, he drove from Montreal to Ottawa for a meeting, could not remember when he got there what the meeting was for, and returned without attending it. People loved telling stories about him, and his eccentricity was part of the company's total personality. In contrast, a deviant in a federal agency pushed company tolerance too far. He was a badly needed crackerjack computer operator who espoused a form of meditation that involved chanting. When he chose to do it in the company lunchroom, he had gone further than the organization would allow. The story continued to be told, years after his departure, as a means of instructing the young about what kind of people worked for this government organization.

3. Are there any other important legends or myths that are part of the folklore? What are they, and how do they affect work life? The story is told of a defense-related contracting agency where one of the bosses, working late at night to get out a proposal for a government contract, came rushing out to the photocopy machine, made his copies, and was starting to rush away when a secretary, who was also working late, reminded him, "Hey, you forgot to sign for your copies." This legend gives a couple of clear messages: (1) You work until the job is finished, and (2) at this company, no one is exempt from the rules.

Now come some questions associated with informal organizational structures.

4. What "tickets" do you need to punch to get ahead in this organization? What positions, education, experiences, and slots does it take to get to the top? What formal and informal patterns do you need to understand to work the political system? You most often learn these by precedents and past case histories, from mentors, sponsors, and peers. It is essential information, but it is not in the company personnel manual. Even when an organization has a career track spelled out, the real route to the top will not often match what is written. Your subordinates will look to you for information about which jobs lead to various career paths.

5. What is the dominant professional group in your organization? Is it the engineers? the managers? the marketing people? What are the most powerful units in your organization? In many organizations, strategic planning is very powerful, because it has the ear of top management, while in other places, it is the kiss of death. In some organizations, marketing holds power. In others, human resource management is a very respectable if not powerful function—okay but a dead end.

6. Are there any powerful factions or ongoing coalitions that have important effects on decision making or decision implementation? You probably know several people in your organization who can accurately predict whether a particular idea will make it, depending on what units—and also what strong personalities—will either move a decision through or gang up to kill it. In one government agency, for example, I was told that a pending program did not have a chance because two directors were opposed to it. There were seven other directors, but these two were the key players. When they united, that was it.

7. What informal networks—social or collegial—wield power? How do you become a member of such groups? Women at CBS complained about being excluded from a stag poker game, even though it did not take place during work hours. The men protested: "Can't you even choose your own friends anymore?" The women pointed out that it was hardly informal friendship when people were flying in from St. Louis and San Francisco just for this poker game. Furthermore, the top managers had consistently come out of that poker group. The men protested that they never talked business. The women accurately pointed out that it did not matter—the creation of networks, the critical information attainable through networks, and the informal support developed in such groups meant that women were being excluded from consideration even before consideration began (Moyer, 1981).

Traditionally, it has been very difficult for minorities and women to break into similar groups. "Nancy Brandt," a case prepared by Arva Rosenfeld Clark (1977), identified a dinner group of executive husbands and their wives who would meet on the weekends. Clearly, the husbands had a lot of useful information Monday morning. Nancy, herself an executive, called the head executive wife and asked to be invited. The woman was reluctant: Nancy would be the only unescorted woman. Nancy countered by saying she was dating an account executive who would fit in beautifully. The invitation was cautiously issued. All went well until after dinner, when the men retired to the sitting room for brandy and cigars while the women went to the kitchen to do the dishes and talk. Since Nancy had come for the male group interaction, she went to the sitting room, and her date went to the kitchen. She was not invited back.

Sometimes these groups are car pools, sports-related groups, drinking buddies, or luncheon friends. Sometimes an organization does not have them. But if it does, how do you use them, maintain them, and build them?

8. Are any organizational slots reserved for special categories? Some positions in a company are for heirs apparent. They are usually visible positions that require a lot of decision making and can be closely monitored. If you go for such a job and get it, it means you are on the fast track. In contrast, the equal opportunity officer for some organizations is nearly always a woman (formerly a black person), and this position is nearly always a dead end. In the chemical company I consulted with, we were supposed to put together a new organization design, but we were not to touch the marketing department. Why not? That position was always reserved for a member of the originating family, and the real marketing was done in purchasing.

9. Are sponsors available? In most organizations, people cannot get ahead without at least one and preferably two or three important sponsors. By virtue of being a manager, you have the potential, at least, of being a sponsor. How well do you use that power? As a sponsor, you can help your candidates understand the informal structure, go to bat for them to see they get the right job, and introduce them to the right informal networks. Sponsors are important for people of all career orientations, not just for those who wish to get ahead. Some organizations put their best employees in supervisory positions so they can sort out and nurture high-potential future managers. In others, there is a strong executive club that is hard to break into, especially for women and minorities. A California bank and other companies have actually assigned mentors or sponsors to incomers, but the available research indicates that this system has not met initial expectations. In addition to their organizational roles, sponsors and neophytes also have to like each other and get along. If a manager does not see ways that a young executive can help with his or her work and does not see

this junior as loyal and capable, the manager really has nothing to gain from the sponsorship.

The next questions help us get at the nonstructured informal fabric of an institution that serves mainly to justify, symbolize, and sustain or constrain the ongoing culture.

10. What are the taboos, the "thou shalt nots" of your culture? I once did a conflict management workshop between some top administrators of a large city school district and the deans of local colleges of education. I had collected some data to help the discussion focus on certain points of conflict, but the discussion ran into a brick wall of silence from the associate superintendents: no comments on the data; no confirmations that they were correct; no corrections noted for invalid sections; no advice about how to work on a problem situation. Finally, I called a break, got to the superintendent, and asked, "Why aren't your people addressing the data?" He explained, "We've been burned so many times by academic types or interviewers who then splash the story all over the newspapers that we have a kind of rule about not washing dirty linen in public." With this information, the workshop could deal with the need for confidentiality and then get on to conflict management.

11. How strict are the requirements for travel and relocation? The U.S. military, for instance, makes it explicit that career success is tied to one's willingness to move every three or four years. IBM employees joke that the initials stand for "I've Been Moved." Some "big eight" accounting and management consulting firms tell their executives that if they are not traveling 70 or 80 percent of the time, they are not making money. True, this kind of mobile life-style is slowing down somewhat. It gets too expensive, for one thing. For another thing, employees are starting to negotiate for a more stable life-style. But it is still an important consideration in many companies. Is it an apprenticeship that you served or are serving? Or is it one of the tasks of top-level management?

12. What are the norms about time? At one company, if you are not at your desk by 7:30 A.M., you are not serious about your career. It does not mean anything, though, when the early-bird executive leaves at 3:00 in the afternoon. One Boston

consulting company assumes that you work until 2:00 P.M. on Saturday. Do you work through the lunch hour? Do you take a vacation? If you take one, how long is it? Do you check in with the office? How often?

13. What is the dress code and how important is it? At one large marketing-oriented company, you wear white shirts, conservative ties, and suits for headquarters visits but slacks and sports coats in California, while marketing representatives wear pastels to call on fashion-conscious clients, and those in Florida blend in with their clients by wearing shorts. At one small western computer company, a polyester sports coat is considered high style, and a three-piece suit would bring suspicious looks. A dress code may not be important, but, if it is, you had better know it, follow it, and communicate it to those you supervise. When I was called to consult with a forestry products company in Idaho, I showed up in slacks and a sports coat. I did not realize that the top management viewed themselves as transplants from the Ivy League and considered three-piece pinstripes to be their personal statement about how they viewed their company. I felt inappropriately underdressed and did not make that mistake again.

14. Is there a corporate sport? or several? Are they important? In some places, golf is the sport, and one must learn how to play if one wants to make contacts and be well regarded. Tennis, squash, and softball have also been mentioned by various aspiring executives as important activities in some corporate cultures. IBM's "Watson Trophy" winners come up through formal sports leagues that are an important part of the company.

15. Are there certain symbols (gold pens, lapel pins, blazers, desk computers) that are important to keep in mind? What do they mean? I was once at dinner with an executive of a major oil company and pulled out a Hallmark wood-tone pen to write something down. "Hmm," he observed. "If you were with us, I'd know a lot about you." Intrigued, I checked out the information. Wood tone meant up and coming in this firm, walking-on-water executives got silver pens, and the heir designate got a gold pen, said my informant. A divisional vice-president of a large consumer products corporation on the East Coast flew

to headquarters on the West Coast for a meeting, bringing with him the handsome set of luggage he had been given by the just-departed chief executive officer (CEO). His reception was distinctly chilly. A colleague explained after the meeting that the new CEO had specifically made negative comments about the luggage his predecessor had typically used for a reward. The savvy executive spent his lunch hour shopping and came to the afternoon session with an acceptable new briefcase.

16. What is the organizational language pattern? How important is it? At one company I consulted with—not a legal firm—the CEO frequently used the phrase "make the case for." It was a clear signal to his subordinates that he wanted a certain type of presentation and was predisposed to consider such types favorably. At a large western religious bureaucracy, the stamp of approval is "appropriate," meaning "effective" or "good," but also with strong moral overtones. "Inappropriate" means not only "it won't work" but also "you are embarrassingly gauche and naive to have suggested it." You probably use the company lingo by reflex, but you might consider what importance it has in dealing with the people you supervise. Do you watch to see whether they pick it up on their own, or do you deliberately teach it to your high-potential candidates? Do you consciously use it with your peers but not with those you supervise? Would making some explicit explanations help you or hinder your work as a manager?

17. Is there an ideal family or relationship situation in your organization? Usually, this is a factor that works against women, since many of these assumptions are still loaded in favor of a male careerist with a supportive wife and well-behaved children. The Nancy Brandt case made this point. However, in Susan Nero's (1984) phrase, a currently popular countertrend is the "bride of the corporation." She uses it to describe the childless and unmarried woman who is completely mobile, completely committed, and completely competent. Single men are also highly valued by most companies unless they seem to be gay (still a widespread informal taboo) or if they seem to be unstable. Women with children can overcome this stereotype, but usually at the price of putting their careers first and letting live-

in help, a more flexible partner, or a good day-care center take primary responsibility for their children.

18. Are there some "hideouts" where people meet to socialize? A lunch spot? a bar? a gym? How about on-site meeting and socializing spots? Would it be advantageous to your career plans to join the group that goes to one of these rendezvous spots? What might you learn? What contacts could you make?

19. What is the most advantageous place to have your office in the building? On the top floor? the bottom floor? If the company has several offices, is the one in Denver or the one in San Francisco the real headquarters? Do you need to spend a part of your career at one of these locations?

20. Are there any company rituals that exist to sustain the culture? Company picnics for the family, yearly managers' meetings, annual performance reviews, or ritual aspects of regular meetings all play this role. In one particular squadron, navy fighter pilots who get their wings have to go through a hazing ritual that is probably more dangerous than anything they do in a plane. After a ritual amount of heavy drinking at their favored bar, the other pilots pour beer on the bar, pick up the new pilot, and skid him down the bar on his abdomen. The trick is for him to stop before he crashes off the end. This is called a "carrier landing." Then they break some glass along the bar and do it again for a "dangerous carrier landing." Full acceptance comes only after this part of the ritual.

The preceding questions have been aimed at identifying three important parts of any corporation's culture: the history and traditions from which key values have emerged, the informal structures that control success within the company, and the mechanisms that sustain the culture. Strong cultures also share values and beliefs that are important to understand for career success, and the final questions deal with these aspects of organizational culture.

21. What are the dominant themes of your organization? In many firms, it is possible, without much analysis, to articulate the company way or what makes it unique. By using a logo or motto, an employee can quickly tell you what the organization stands for. These themes serve as powerful philosophical

guides, and much has been written in the culture litera
about the need to have a clear and guiding statement of mi
or philosophy. For example, Mary Kay Cosmetics representatives are supposed to tell customers about the bumblebee,
which, though aerodynamically unsound ("people will tell you
it can't be done"), manages to fly high and well. It is not supposed to, but it does. ("We're the odds-upsetters.")

22. Does your organizational leadership or the majority
of its members share a common political, religious, or life-style
ideology? The tea company Celestial Seasonings is reportedly
held together by counterculture-, ecology-, and health-oriented
leaders and workers. One Salt Lake City company with which I
work is considered a Mormon company because many of its top
leaders are visibly active and committed Latter-day Saints who
often hold high ecclesiastical positions. Interestingly enough, a
few decades ago, it used to be referred to as a Masonic company.

Timing

Any politically astute player has a good sense of timing.
Any employee who understands his or her culture but acts pre-
maturely or "out of synch" will be viewed as clumsy, pushy, or
gauche. How can you smooth the way for promising employees?
Such scholars as Edgar Schein (1978), Gene Dalton, Paul
Thompson and Raymond Price (1977), and Douglas T. Hall
(1976) have written knowledgeably about the importance of
time or stages in the career. Daniel Levinson (1978) has probed
adult developmental stages. In a political perspective, timing refers to appropriateness—making the right career move at the
most timely career and life stage. A typical linear career goes
through four stages.

The Getting-Established Stage. From the ages of about
twenty-two to twenty-eight, most of us establish our adult identity, where much of who we are depends on our work. We invest ourselves intensely at work to become identified as an engineer, a manager, or an accountant. This period usually coincides
with the early career, generally an apolitical period where we
concentrate on learning the ropes, learning our group's culture,

paying our dues, and establishing and refining our technical expertise—in short, acquiring the tools of the trade. In many respects, we serve an apprenticeship and slowly, under close supervision at first, get additional assignments that require us to demonstrate the range of our abilities and our capacity to acquire new skills. It is a hard-work stage that usually requires extraordinary amounts of effort and time.

Out of this stage emerges the potential for political action. As we understand the cultural fabric, line up sponsors and mentors, and become identified as bright young stars who can enhance the work of a sponsor, we acquire a sense of which jobs are important, which jobs we should stay away from, the amount of effort involved in certain assignments, and what the company will reward.

The Questioning Stage. Toward the end of the early-career stage and in the early middle phase, organizations start to identify their high-potential employees, lining them up for special training and special privileges. Nearly everyone tries to qualify for this group, partly as feedback to themselves ("I can make it, too") and partly so as not to cut off options. There are frequently some political tests. You are invited to dinner with your spouse so that he or she can be checked out. You are screened to see how well you have absorbed the culture. You now have enough experience and feedback to make some realistic appraisals about preferences and abilities. Your internal career success orientation becomes clearer.

Somewhere along in this stage, typically at about ages twenty-eight through thirty-three, comes for many the first questioning period of adult life. ("Is this what I really want?" "What have I bought into?") Many people sense the first serious imbalance between their nurturing and their achievement sides. They begin to want to spend more time with their children, working in the community, or developing an avocation. For many, these questions come up only to be tabled. The organization does not want them to stop and deal with personal issues, and they may not want to, either. After all, the breaks are just starting to come. People who postpone now, however, are usually grade-A candidates for a major midlife crisis later on.

The Midcareer Stage. Between the early thirties and age fifty, the midcareer develops. Ideally, a match between internal and external careers means a period of high productivity and great personal satisfaction. In less than ideal circumstances, this period involves working on the mismatch between internal and external careers. People who have resolved the initial questioning phase (or who have successfully postponed it) sense a new stability, a settling in, a focusing of energy. There is either a new sense of purpose about the original career or a strong redefinition of career success and a new burst of creative energy. This period is politically highly charged. In fact, more political issues and opportunities probably develop during this time period than at any other point. It is the time for getting where you are going.

This career stage usually lasts until about the mid fifties, but it can hit a serious snag about the mid forties if those life questions that came up earlier have not been successfully resolved. A lot of things are up for grabs. It is no longer possible to ignore the demands of the emotional and nurturing self. One forty-five-year-old executive in a large eastern corporation found himself barely able to avoid weeping in meetings and struggling to concentrate while dictating a memo. His wife had once again threatened to leave him, "but she wasn't as serious this time as she had been before. *I* was the serious one." He had handled earlier crises by throwing himself into his work and working around the clock. "But I can't do it anymore."

It is also at this midlife, midcareer crisis stage that we need to come to terms with our own mortality, health, and body changes. There are probably fifteen or twenty working years left, but most of us will not have made the great contributions or achieved the pinnacle of success that we envisioned when we were starting out. It is a time for sifting illusions from reality and coming to terms with the reality. For those who deal with this stage successfully, the fifties and sixties can be exceptionally productive and happy years.

The Late Career Stage. In the late career stage between ages fifty and seventy-five, personal career ambitions have been satisfied or dealt with. Our energy can turn toward nurturing and fostering those coming along. We can prepare to disengage from the organization or launch a second career. However, as retirement approaches, the issues of health and economic security may intensify, along with an identity crisis triggered by the fact that a long-term work relationship will be phasing out. Late career is usually a somewhat less political phase, but it may involve the sometimes painful process of giving up or transferring the reins of power. Some do not retire gracefully and keep on playing hardball politics right up to the time they separate from the organization. If you have nailed down the kinds of benefits and security you want, there is usually an implied contract with the organization about moving to a comfortable position to finish out the last few years or making certain types of contributions in return for security. It is a time for transferring power. The most successful people find a way of doing it gracefully, assuming the position of senior statesperson for their organization. As a manager, where are you? And where are those you supervise?

This congruence between life stages and career stages does not always work as smoothly as the model. A frequent clash between age and stage develops when a careerist, for some reason, is early or late. Women who are re-entering the work force in their thirties after spending a big chunk of time focusing on responsibilities as wives and mothers frequently feel, as one put it, that "my nurturing side was overdeveloped and my achieving side was underdeveloped. I felt an urgent need to prove that I was good at something else, too." While this shift in balance may come at exactly the right time in their personal lives, nearly all of the career development literature would see them as delayed—out of synch with the schedule of most organizations.

The same pattern also shows up with nontraditional students who are getting a second degree or finally tooling up after a long absence from college, a stage in the military, or something else that has "interrupted" the tidy American pattern of graduation from college to job. "These graduates are in their early to mid thirties," one career counselor observed, "terrific workers, mature, and dazzling in interviews. They're easy to place, but then they don't go anywhere in their jobs. How come?" One reason is that many companies do not know what to do with them. Usually, a manager in his or her early thirties knows what to do with an apprentice and knows what kind of work an apprentice does—not necessarily fun but important to the organization. Scott, a manager at midlevel who is thirty-five, explained his dilemma: "I can't use them. Sure, they look great on paper, but they just don't work out. Look at Lynn. She came in here three months ago with a new M.B.A., very bright, very capable, exactly my age, and ready to go for my job. She doesn't want to be an apprentice. No, she hasn't spent ten years in the business, but she's spent ten years doing things she thinks are just as valuable, and she wants credit for that life experience. Also, she just isn't interested in staying up all night to get a presentation ready every time I need one. But somebody's got to do it. *I* did it when I was just starting out." Scott's confusion and resentment as a manager can block his ability to use re-entry workers effectively unless he finds a way of dealing with his feelings.

A related problem for a manager is the dual-career couple who hit graduation and are off and running. Both of them invest major time in their careers for five to eight years. Then, according to their game plan, it is time for a family. They are secure and cannot simply be fired out of hand if they want time off or even drop back to half time or, most frequently, level off their performance for a while. But from a manager's point of view, they are just hitting their stride professionally. No matter how affirmatively a company talks about its family-oriented values, in practice it is usually less willing to act on them. It takes managerial skill to use these people effectively and creatively.

Career Development Options

Most managers have a good sense of the internal gyroscope of their employees. Where do they think their best career placement moves will be? Up? Out? Sideways? Down? And when? When the economic picture is bleak, movement slows down. Employees would rather have a less-than-perfect job than no job. This makes your task as a manager both easier and harder—it is easier to keep people but harder to get turnover when you want it and harder to move your own career along.

Career development is a term that is sometimes applied to two very different set of activities. If a company supplies resources to help employees achieve their own career objectives, then it is engaging in career enhancement. If the company focuses primarily on its own management needs and recruits, develops, and moves its employees according to those needs, then it is engaging in career management. Obviously, the benefits of career enhancement for a company show up in terms of long-range productivity, not necessarily in the short range. Here is a list of typical career enhancement programs and career management programs.

Career Enhancement

- Self-assessment
- Education and training opportunities
- Career counseling
- Career/life planning
- Individual development plans
- Variety of individually tailored developmental benefits
- Flexible scheduling
- Facilitation of movement between positions and career paths
- Career opportunity information
- Job matching and posting

Career Management

- Orientation and early socialization programs
- Performance appraisal and information systems
- High-potential employee selection and development
- Training of supervisors in counseling and coaching
- Human resource strategic planning and future-trend analysis
- Succession planning
- Career profiling
- Development of career paths (including lateral movements)
- Managing the midcareer plateau

- Managing retirement and utilization of senior employees (including downward and part-time options)
- Related training events

Most companies will supply information on benefits and job openings, but there is a crucial difference between encouraging employees to explore options and simply leaving job listings on the bulletin board in the employees' lounge. And certainly, whatever a company's long-term plans, the realities of a sagging market, a buy-out by a larger competitor, or expansion into international fields can drastically change personnel policies.

In summary, before you can discuss strategies for maximizing an internal career with those you supervise, you have to understand the context formed by the external career, especially the company's culture, the sense of appropriate timing, and the options for career movement. You need ways to communicate your view of individuals' limits and constraints. You may need to fine tune your own sense of what the company regards as appropriate timing. As you attempt to counsel and coach diverse career types under your direction, you will do better at matching their career agendas with the various career development opportunities available in the organization.

We have not stressed other critically important external career factors here (for example, the job market, demographics, obsolescence) because, while very real and important, they are not often manageable by either the individual or the administrator. Culture, timing, and options are. As a manager or as a careerist yourself, you can use them to implement a better match between the internal and external careers. They exist and must be taken into account, but they can also be skillfully used to change your career condition.

Career politics, the subject of the next chapter, is the dynamic game (frequently played against managers) of finding equilibrium between internal and external career needs. To be effective, you must understand what diverse careerists are experiencing and attempting. As a manager, you cannot avoid career politics. But you can help to better mesh the needs, talents, and desires of your employees with the requirements of the organization.

 FOUR

The Politics
of Managing Careers

As diversity proliferates in internal careers, external careers are becoming increasingly constrained and tight. Wausau Insurance now has salary reviews every eighteen months rather than annually, merit increases have a ceiling of 4 percent rather than 6 percent, and the company's officers took a 5 percent salary cut in a recent year. AT&T announced plans to cut 11,000 jobs by the end of 1984 and also offered voluntary early retirement to most of its 60,000 service technicians, repairpeople, and managers. Chase Manhattan announced its own plans to eliminate 2,000 jobs by the year's end. Armco Inc., the fifth largest American steelmaker, slimmed its corporate headquarters staff down by 10 percent. Western Electric has laid off 16,000 workers since 1982. Du Pont has maintained an early retirement program (McGinley, 1984). As Yankelovich (1981) put it: "We have moved from an uptight culture with a dynamic economy to a dynamic culture set in an uptight economy" (p. 43).

How does this open-closed dilemma get worked out? Through career politics. Career politics occurs at the point of discrepancy between the aspirations of the internal career and the realities of the external career. It is a strategy for easing that pinch without threatening job security, a deadly serious game plan for maximizing the internal career orientation over time while minimizing unintended consequences.

42

Formulating a Political Strategy

A career success map—the internal career orientation—is a unique, personal theory of action. Getting-free careerists, for example, will naturally try to gain more autonomy. If you do not understand what they are doing, and if they cannot fit their moves into your company's plan, you may lose valuable employees. Schein (1982), in his discussion of career anchors, maintains that organizational leaders often seek uniformity and conformity from their employees yet feel free to change the rules and opportunities to meet business demands. Individuals often find parts of themselves at odds with their employer, perhaps as a result of a change in policy, perhaps as they become more sure of their career identities. Sometimes the strategies for coping with those dilemmas lead to changing jobs or even careers. More often, nowadays, employees play organizational politics.

Robert Dahl's classical definition of organizational power is the capacity of an individual or group to modify the behaviors of other individuals and groups in a desired direction (Dahl, 1957, p. 201). Emerson (1962) maintains that, along with other ingredients, power depends on the intensity of one's needs (or the will to use resources to attain a position), and French and Raven (1968, p. 259) ask two critical questions of power holders: "What determines the behavior of the agent who exerts power?" and "What determines the reactions of the recipient or target person?" Any student of organizational power and politics will immediately recognize these theorists as key figures in the field. The significance of their concepts here is that, as Virginia Schein (1977) points out, you have to understand intentions before you can understand tactics. Identifying the internal career, in a political sense, corresponds to the question "What does he or she really want?", or "What are his or her underlying (even hidden) agendas?" You need to know the answer before you can logically develop strategies and tactics for matching up the internal and external careers—or at least for coping with mismatches. Furthermore, as a manager, you have your own set of political values.

Some factors are givens: you and your subordinates have to perform at a minimum level of competence or you will be fired. You have to observe basic norms, values, and attitudes important to your corporate culture. You have to be willing to pay dues and earn tenure. You have to exert whatever effort and skill are required to remind your organization that you are valuable in spite of your idiosyncrasies. You also need to remember that implementing a political strategy takes place over time. Employees will readily make short-term sacrifices for long-term gains. A getting-high person can put up with working to please as much as a getting-ahead person if, at the end of five years, he or she will be in a position with a lot of leverage to choose more stimulating assignments. As a manager, you can make that happen more easily.

Another important part of any political strategy is to minimize unintended consequences. Politics is a game everyone plays, but the person who plays it awkwardly, blatantly, or badly could get hurt. Most often, bad political players get caught and are branded as "politicos." Such people are consequently viewed with suspicion, and their career opportunities are limited. Some of them are moved out or down in short order. As I have already discussed, for example, timing is an important part of any political move. Such a move is inappropriate in the early career, when a careerist is still getting essential work experience, paying dues, and lining up sponsors. It is sometimes inappropriate in the late career, too, when the careerist may be seen as trying to throw around weight that he or she no longer has. If you are managing someone in that position, you can provide a useful reality check that may otherwise be missing.

Be aware of your own political options as a manager. Politics is a game both sides play. An organization is dynamic. It generates changes. It responds to changes in the market and the economy. It can—and does—make a careerist jump through a lot of hoops in the early stages; but it becomes morally difficult to fire an employee once those initial stages are past. When the environment forces a major change in direction for the company, it is difficult for your getting-free employee to discover the external game shift. It is equally difficult when your company retrains a getting-ahead executive because there was such a good person-organization fit, only to find out once she gets tenure that she has very different goals.

Even if someone does not hand you a difficult problem by revealing a career success orientation different from what you thought you were buying, you still have to face what happens in late midcareer to many of your employees. They are no longer the up-and-comers. They are simply the solid citizens who have done good work and to whom the company owes much. Some companies are ruthless about dumping people who have plateaued, but most of them realize that such an action is bad for morale. If loyalty is valued in the company—and it is in most—your challenge in managing these solid citizens who may have another fifteen or twenty years to go is to use their considerable talents and experience without letting them retire psychologically or become deadwood. In a real way, both sides often try to find a way to ride out those last few years as gracefully and productively as possible.

This situation can certainly create a real waste of human potential and human resources. That is why allowing more definitions of career success than just getting ahead will help you find a way to capitalize on these solid citizens, not just tolerate them. That is also why providing more career development options (see Chapters Twelve and Fourteen) will help you better capture the energy and commitment of your diverse careerists. Ultimately, success is being able to live out what you really believe and make your personal contribution to the world of work. It is coming up with win-win compromises between actualizing the internal and the external careers. This is a goal that you and individual careerists should both be able to agree on.

Good political game playing varies according to the situation. A good strategy for a large corporate setting would not necessarily be effective in a small business or a professional milieu. You must clearly and accurately understand your organization's culture, acceptable patterns, timing, and career development options—the external career—before you can make any realistic strategies for yourself or your employees to realize internal career orientations. A crucial part of that understanding is realizing that not everyone is working for the same reward. Managers need to believe this maxim: "They wouldn't do it without the money, but they're not doing it just for the money." When you can identify the "something else," you are on the way to understanding how to manage the new careerists.

Most of your political resources, whether you are acting for your own career or as a manager, are generic, although some resources seem to fit certain career agendas or contexts better than others. The following are generally applicable resources:

1. *Use of information.* Try to acquire scarce knowledge or important data that will help an organization reduce uncertainty in decision making. This information needs to be critical to and supportive of the core functions. It must also be accurate.

2. *Use of office or position.* You can use official information, rewards and punishments, appointments, access to other officials, and legitimacy to keep or build a better position.

3. *Personal image.* It is extremely helpful to be articulate, to look official and appropriate in dress, speech, and mannerisms, to obey the norms and espouse the values of the company, to develop and "sell" your unique abilities and characteristics, to develop charisma or attractiveness, and to cultivate respect for high standards among peers.

4. *Control of valuable resources.* Among the most valuable resources to control are necessary knowledge, needed expertise or technical skills, discretionary budget, time and human resource commitment, energy, and information.

5. *Manipulation of cultural symbols.* It is tricky but important to use and selectively abuse the rules. Use norms, values, rituals, language patterns, dress codes, symbols, taboos, traditions, time, and space to your benefit and to the detriment of an opponent.

6. *Acquiring autonomy.* By gaining expertise in a critical function or by hoarding and controlling expert knowledge in that area, you become "indispensable." This allows you

to redefine the rules to exercise more control over work rules affecting life space.

7. *Gaining informal influence.* By becoming part of informal networks, building power coalitions, developing reciprocal relationships with influential sponsors, exchanging favors and socially indebting others, or becoming an important team player, you move yourself into a position where you are visible and available for more important assignments.

8. *Increasing authority and position.* Closely related to the previous point is the ability to get good jobs, get good performance reviews, move up (or toward the center) every three or four years, and act like a future member of the executive club. An important strategy is to arrange your life so that you are available (mobile, free to work long hours and weekends, able to travel).

9. *Opponent analysis.* Who are your chief competitors for a promotion or resources? What are their long-term agendas or self-interests? How do these conflict with yours? How can you block or thwart them in areas of importance to you where your interests conflict?

10. *Sabotage or use of negative power.* Although you will get in trouble if you use these strategies inappropriately, every powerful person must learn how to draw effectively on such resources as selective compliance, negative timing, psychological withdrawal, secret active campaigning, blackmail, the legalistic use of various policies and rules, a show of force (group opposition), information manipulation, and open confrontation. Be wary and restrained. The best political strategies look unobtrusive, subtle, rational, and supportive of organizational goals. Making obvious waves can easily swamp your boat.

Limitations on Playing Politics

It is clear that career politics is an inevitable, universal, and usually very effective way of bridging the equally inevitable and universal gaps between the demands of the internal career and the exigencies of the external career. Almost everyone plays career politics. Some people do it better than others. However, there are limitations built into the political game. The best political power players, as Kotter (1977) points out, are sensitive to what others consider legitimate behavior in acquiring and using power, they are intuitive about appropriate uses of power in various circumstances; they have a wide repertoire of options and skills at their disposal to be used as circumstances require; they are good career planners and seek positions that allow them to successfully use and develop their power; they use their resources to develop more power; they have a sense of the limits of power and temper power plays with maturity and self-control; they are comfortable influencing others; and they take responsibility for their actions.

Competence. There is no substitute for competence and no adequate excuse for lacking it if you want to get very far. This is a hard reality. Political savvy does not even qualify as a substitute. Without basic—even superior—technical competence, you simply are not a candidate to play politics. Yes, there is a form of political gamesmanship that does not rely on competence; but careerists that play this way end up with the kind of crony fellowship and master-of-ceremony bonhomie that enhances only company loyalists. And, yes, it is certainly possible to have pure competence in staff, technicians, and even managers that is not worth a plugged nickel because these dazzlingly competent people do not have any political savoir faire. The goal of competence and politics combined is to influence events, people, and organizations to get a certain job done. Part of that job is meeting your own needs.

Of course, there are always times when we coast, when we are between specialties, or when we are simply not performing up to our capabilities for one reason or another. But I am talking about long-term laziness, lack of judgment, or lack of skills. People in this situation are in danger of being fired or at least of being permanently shunted to the sidelines.

Paying Your Dues. Power, as Korda (1975, p. 30) observed, lies in the production of intended effects. The trick is to "make people do what you want them to and like it, to persuade them that they want what you want." You simply cannot do this without an apprenticeship phase where you gain the experience necessary to identify the goals of the organization, information about people's personalities and motivations, and the sheer nuts-and-bolts understanding of how the business works.

If you do not have the reputation of being a "good citizen"—of being loyal to your occupation or organization—you simply do not have the acceptability to exert much influence on it. As Moberg (1977, p. 3) observed, political behavior in organizations is the attempt "to effect a relative expansion of [your] power base in ways which are not clearly attributable to a self-serving intent or political motives." In short, the best political power does not look political. Careerists who are openly and obviously using the organization to meet their own needs at the expense of the organization damage themselves politically.

For example, one of my former students did not want to pay her dues. She was thirty-five; she had raised five children, helped her husband manage his career, and served as an executive in Girl Scouts and in various church and community projects, and she just plain wanted it "to count for something. I don't have time to play around for five or ten years." She negotiated hard during job interviews for midmanagement positions and landed a very good job with one of the top financial brokerage houses in the country. This company rewards aggressive, competitive people, but it has a clear apprenticeship phase in its career track. Callie was not willing to do jobs that she felt overqualified for. Her manager remarked that she "wasn't salvageable," in terms of the company. She was too pushy, was too aggressive, and played dirty. She was told to look for another job and moved out after two years.

Cultural Margins. In any organization, there is a "deep culture" with strict rules. Top management follows those rules to rise to the top, and you can tell future members of the executive club by the way they share basic assumptions and profess similar values, by the opinions they hold, and by their position in intricate friendship and political networks. Probably only getting-ahead people need to pay close attention to that deep culture. However, within every company are wider cultural norms that must be met for minimum acceptability. Certain norms and values, formal and informal rules, rituals, symbols, and customs must be recognized and accepted at some level. Politics is often played at the margins of such cultural norms, but it is played *within* them. Outlaws have little organizational power.

It is by playing within cultural margins that we earn the credits, or organizational scrip, with which to negotiate our own agendas. Part of using power effectively to further your own ends is making it look as if your internal personal causes are "pure" or as if your behavior is due to external situations beyond your control (Moberg, 1977, p. 12). Thus, you will not "contaminate" your power with the charge of self-interest. Meanwhile, you can proceed to establish and increase power in the usual ways: instilling a sense of obligation in those you work with and for, proving your expertise and becoming "indispensable," establishing a reputation for good judgment so that your opinion becomes influential and even, in some areas, decisive, getting others to identify with your vision and ideas, and fostering feelings of dependence in others by controlling resources and rewards (Kotter, 1977, p. 30).

Luck. Luck is one of those wild cards that has to be acknowledged but cannot be totally counted on. Many articles in such popular publications as *Forbes, Business Week,* and the *Wall Street Journal* contain profiles and interviews with executives who proclaim that career planning is silly because what career success comes down to is being prepared to grab the opportunities when they come by—being in the right place at the right time. Career planning experts take reports such as these with a grain of salt. Yes, luck is important; but their research shows that people who have succeeded—not just getting-ahead careerists but those with a variety of career objectives—are invariably good career planners. They have a clear sense of what they want to do. They have one-year, five-year, and ten-year plans. They also have contingency plans that are sometimes four levels deep. These people may have to modify their plans or use career politics to get as much of their agendas met as possible while still maintaining some sort of influence and power within the organization. But they are not going to be tripped up as easily by bad luck as those who have no career plans.

For example, one of my students taught in a Boston college for three years after graduating. He liked teaching but switched careers to join a Utah firm as a management consultant. It was a promising beginning, but, after five years, he was facing a dilemma. It was obvious that the firm was being outpaced by its competition and would soon fold or be sold. He had been away from academic life too long to move easily back into it. Specialized jobs in his field were practically nonexistent in Utah. Yet sticking with the company and hoping for a miracle would be wishful thinking. He had not thought ahead beyond a vague "maybe I'll go back to teaching someday" and felt stranded, out in the cold. Another person I know was director of a medical supply company that was bought out by a company whose policy was to bring in their own people for jobs above a certain level. Her choices were to take a demotion or look for another job. Again, she had never thought of career alternatives and was doubly at a disadvantage, struggling to cope simultaneously with the psychological adjustments and the practical considerations.

All of these conditions—basic competence, the ability to fit into the organization, hedging against bad luck—are tickets that get you into the game of playing politics. Staying in depends on your ability to use organizational power and personal strategies. But an important and little-considered limitation on the game is your ethical code.

Ethical Restraints. Most of us have some fairly clear concepts about how far we are willing to let a team take us before we feel that we have abdicated personal responsibility and individual integrity to a sort of group mentality. Similarly, most of us have equally clear concepts about how far we will push our own self-interests if doing so will cause our organization to suffer. Some professions—such as law and medicine—have clearly spelled-out professional expectations that the individual members are supposed to internalize as personal codes. These codes are policed by peers, and there are legal and professional consequences of breaking them. These ethical limitations, whether personal or part of the profession, are real and need to be allowed for in any working system of career politics.

The problem with ethical limits is that they are ultimately observed on the individual level. Organizations and professions might spell out requirements in the employee handbook, but they are still subjectively interpreted by individuals. Everyone may know, for instance, the rule on expense accounts; but everyone also "knows" that no one really checks too closely as long as you do not exceed certain margins and as long as sales figures look good. In another business, managers are endlessly willing to help people whose technical abilities might not be up to snuff but they will fire people for fudging on their lunch hours, not signing for personal photocopies, or showing up to work late all the time.

Considering the enormous and complicated ethical problems posed by the use of organizational politics, the lack of research and reporting on the subject is surprising. Cavanagh, Moberg, and Velasquez (1981) point out this lack in an important article that creates a decision-making tree. According to their model, the choice of a given political behavior must pass three screens: (1) "Does it result in the efficient optimization of the satisfactions of interests inside and outside the organization?" If it does not, "are there overwhelming factors that justify suboptimizing these goals and satisfactions?" (2) If the answer to the first question is yes, does it "respect the rights of all the affected parties?" If the answer to this question is no, one must again ask if there are "overwhelming factors" to justify violating those rights. (3) As a third screen, does it "respect the canons of justice?" Again, if it does not, are there "overwhelming factors" that could justify such a violation? If the proposed action can pass the three tests of meeting organization needs, respecting the rights of individuals, and being "fair" to all concerned, then it is an ethically appropriate decision. If it cannot, and if there are not "overwhelming factors" to justify the violation, then it is not an ethical decision.

The failure of most books and articles dealing with political strategies to consider ethical consequences leads to a kind of default end-justifies-the-means moral code. Decisions are made according to the desirability of the outcomes, not the quality of the behaviors. Cavanagh, Moberg, and Velasquez provide an example:

Lorna is the production manager of a non-cohesive work group responsible for meeting a deadline that will require coordinated effort among her subordinates. Believing that the members of the work group will pull together and meet the deadline if they have a little competition, Lorna decides in favor of a PBA [political behavior alternative]. She tries to create the impression among her subordinates that members of the sales department want her group to fail to meet the deadline so that sales can gain an edge over production in upcoming budgetary negotiations.

How might we evaluate this PBA? Management theory tends to focus our attention on consequences. One might argue that if it works and Lorna's group pulls together and meets the deadline, it's okay. Or, a more critical observer might argue that even if the objective is accomplished, an important side effect could be the loss of a cooperative relationship between the sales and production departments. What we tend to lose sight of, though, is that "creating an impression" is a euphemism for lying, and lying may not be ethically acceptable in this situation [1981, p. 364].

Other Restraints. Even in terms of self-interest, some constraints are good business. If your organization depends on some sort of competitive advantage, you obviously cannot make political decisions that will lessen its ability to compete, or you will remove it—and your job along with it—from the marketplace. This is a natural limit to organizational politics. Productivity, good will, quality, and unity in goals can all be damaged by self-serving political actions; the political actor frequently bears the consequences of those actions. Sabotage seldom succeeds.

Another consideration is that blatant selfishness destroys a political base of power. Organizational politics is, by its nature, an unobtrusive, subtle game of image building or maneu-

vering in the American business culture, where "good" words
are *loyal, helpful, teamwork,* and *dedicated* and "bad words"
are *politics, self-interest, manipulation,* and *sharp operator.* It is
politically disadvantageous to appear to act in your own interest
at the expense of your organization or other people.

If your political game is discovered, you may not be
fired, but you will certainly be unable to keep playing your
game. If people know what it is, you are too easy to block.
Everyone understands that politics is pervasive in organizational
life and that you cannot get ahead without being politically effective. In fact, political skill is essential for organizational productivity. Everybody knows that. Everybody nods in concur-
rence. Still, politics is considered self-seeking. If you are brutal,
if you injure other parties or the organization, or if you go too
far, you are finished. People do not like your tactics or you.
You get a bad name. You lose political capital and, in fact, may
be in danger of being fired.

For example, Guy, a "shark" in an advertising agency
where there was intense competition to represent certain port-
folios or consult with certain companies, had himself on everybody's blacklist within a year by his unscrupulous aggressiveness. "He's a barracuda, a jungle fighter," the word went out.
People who ordinarily employed slightly underhanded tricks to
stay in the competition themselves were ganging up against him,
passing on strategic information to his opponents, and making
him look bad. He had violated the ethical norms in a company
where the ethical codes would already seem shockingly loose to
many observers.

Another example is a professor who was obviously a getting-high careerist. He had a good reputation in his field and
made sure everyone knew whenever he had an interesting new
project, got a new grant, or had an article published in a prestigious journal. But his name was mud in his department. He
was constantly gone; he complained about having to teach routine courses; he refused to serve on the workhorse committees
that kept the department running. Within a couple of years, he
simply had no political credit left. His opinions carried no
weight, because he was not willing to put in the minimal amount

of work required to be considered a member of the community. He seemed to be completely self-serving. Obviously, he was advancing his own interests at the expense of the department, and, even though he was tenured, he soon moved on, to the regret of no one—except perhaps his new department.

The next five chapters will examine the five career success orientations already introduced: getting ahead, getting secure, getting free, getting high, and getting balanced. In each chapter, case studies of typical workers with the given orientation will be presented, along with descriptions of strategies they use for maximizing their orientation, the rewards and costs of each orientation, and how each orientation can be most successfully managed.

 FIVE

Getting Ahead

I first met Nick when he was twenty-eight, the up-and-coming manager in a large food chain that has exploded into diversification with enviable success. Nick was taking an executive development course in career politics that I was teaching, but he could have written the course content himself. Nick loved challenges and went after promotions with a ruthless gusto that paid off for him again and again. He routinely worked nights and weekends. "The weekenders are part of the inner circle," he explained. "Some of the most useful conversations I've had with supervisors have been during those late-night sessions or over a couple of beers after we've put in an all-afternoon session on Saturday." He described a project he had been given recently and repeated the words of his godfather, "This is a tough one, but if you can pull it off, you'll be on the dean's list." He is not just thinking wishfully when he says he has been tagged as a rising star. And he likes having his hands on power.

Nick knows how his company operates, and he fits in flawlessly. He is learning golf (the company sport), drives a Ford without options (suitable for his career stage), and is planning to marry and move to suburbia, at least partially "because it's the right time to be doing something like this." He dresses conservatively but not too formally; and, as a serendipitous touch, he is Catholic (all of the top management in this company is also Catholic). In short, the red carpet is out—even though it goes over some pretty elaborate hurdles—and Nick is on it, picking up speed with every stride. "I'm executive material," he says without boasting. "I'll do a good job for them, and they know it. They're paying plenty to keep me, and I'm making it worth it to them—every penny." It is not absolutely clear sailing, of course, and he does not fool himself about the rough spots. "There'll always be competition. I'll have to fight for everything I get." But that does not bother him as much as some inner feelings. "I like living in the East; but until you're in senior management, you might as well pitch a tent at the airport. I don't like the travel," he sighs, "but I've accepted it."

A more serious problem is that Nadine, his fiancée, has already announced her plans to pursue her own career as an architect. "What can I do?" says Nick. "I believe she should. She's good and she's willing to be flexible while the kids are little, but what's the boss going to say? At the last company picnic, Bob's wife showed up, cute and pregnant and knitting a little sweater. Mr. T. saw her, and you would have thought she'd invented the wheel from the fuss he made over her. Top management *loves* the kind of marriage where the husband walks out the door and says, 'See you next Tuesday if we're lucky,' and she says, 'Okay, honey.' " Even more gloomily, Nick confides, "I love kids. I have a very close-knit family, and we all still get together at Mom and Dad's about every other week. I'm looking forward to children. But what if Nadine is serious about expecting me to help keep house and take care of the kids? I haven't got *that* kind of slack."

When we went over the results of some of Nick's career success orientation tests (Chapter Eleven), he grinned ruefully, "This is what I get for answering questions honestly. I *do* have a strong independent streak, and I want both things at the same time: to be independent and even a little daring and still advance my career. Is this the right place for me to be?" He also told of listening to the evening news with one ear while he was checking some sales figures and having the two sets of information "explode in my head. My parents have worked all their lives for people who've been given a raw deal. We grew up socially conscious. Here I am worrying about how many million paper cups we sold in Canada while a whole generation of children is starving to death in Africa. Am I crazy?"

Nick is still fairly young to have a cast-in-concrete career

success map, and he must work through the questions he is uneasily aware of: Will his career destroy his independence? Is this
company going to demolish his sense of social responsibility?
Can his own career handle a dual-career marriage? Still, his motives, values, and talents clearly reveal a getting-ahead orientation. What turns Nick on, keeps him up late at night, pries him
out of bed early in the morning, and keeps him revved up during the day is being part of the inner circle, competing successfully with his colleagues and peers, and winning—as evidenced
by concrete symbols such as promotions, raises, titles, and high-
status assignments. His life values up to age twenty-eight have
all supported this orientation. Furthermore, his track record is
impressive. He has a "high-potential" label on his file, has attracted the eye of the talent spotters in top management, and
seems to have the skills in dealing with people, working through
office politics, and analyzing the concrete needs of a situation
to keep coming through, time and again. He also works for a
company that likes what he can deliver. His timing is good, and
the company is expanding.

How to Get Ahead

There is room for many individual variations and strategies in any career orientation, but the literature is clear enough
on the much-studied getting-ahead types that it is possible to
make a checklist of what it takes to move on and up—fast.

Know Your Organization. Getting-ahead types are superb
at reading and understanding their organization's culture. Nick
knows without asking what kind of car he should be driving for
his rank; he also knows—although he would rather not—that a
nontraditional wife will be a minus, not a plus. Another example of such a type is Georgia, a thirty-four-year-old executive
in a large and extremely successful computer company that
prides itself on the kind of flexibility and autonomy that make
a cross section of an ant colony's tunnels look as straightfor-
ward as a tick-tack-toe chart by comparison. This kind of fluid-
ity would drown many executives, but Georgia is aggressive
enough to be seen as the chief competition of her peers, com-

fortable enough with the "old boys" on top to joke without losing her dignity, and considerate enough of her subordinates to
win their respect and loyalty—as long as this does not interfere
with the job. "It amounts to a sixth sense," says one of her colleagues enviously. "She can tell where the next coalition is
going to form, I swear, just by seeing who orders steak for
lunch."

This high-powered, fast-changing world values employees
who are always available, always productive, and always undis-
tracted. Georgia has been living with Paul for three years—which
is perfectly acceptable. "Easy come, easy go works out better
around here than paralyzing divorces," observes a colleague.
They have no children, no plans to encumber their relationship
with any, and no long-term commitments even to their relationship itself. Georgia exercises at a spa every other day, keeps no
pets, lives in a condo close to work that is "tastefully but im-
personally decorated," according to Georgia herself, routinely
works through her lunch hour, takes work home every night
and weekend, and keeps a bedside notepad to capture ideas in
the night. All of these personal elements are highly acceptable
to her company.

Georgia and Nick understand the deep patterns of their
companies' cultures and know where the margins are, how to
maneuver around hot spots, where the pressure points are and
how to trigger them, how to combine the formal parts, such as
regular staff meetings, with informal parts, such as collecting information from secretaries, to get results, and how to manipulate symbols. They speak the company language, but they are
not clones in the way a getting-secure person would be. They
know how to take a company slogan such as "service when the
customer needs it" and use it to spur innovation. They walk,
surefooted and quickly, that thin line between looking as if the
company owns them and looking as if some day they will own
the company.

Put Your Job First. If the research is unanimous about
one point, it is this one: getting-ahead careerists get there because nothing comes before the job. They may hold very sincere views about the importance of keeping close to a spouse or

lover, about spending "quality time" with their children, and about keeping in tune with nature or their inner self or God. But by any measure of time, energy, or emotional commitment, the job comes first.

A good but unorthodox example is Russell, a tenured professor of psychology at an East Coast university. For him, being successful is not measured by the conventional gauges of research, publications, and papers at conferences but by the even more competitive and ruthless standard of professional status—whom he knows and who knows him. The only son of Jewish parents who escaped from Nazi Germany and sacrificed unstintingly to put him in the best schools, he had a brilliant academic career at Princeton, Oxford, and Yale, always introduces himself as "Doctor" or "Professor," and has a phone bill close to $500 a month just from staying in touch with a complex network of topflight people in top fields. Although he is comparatively young and his own research, while promising, is only medium weight, he has an uncanny skill for wining, dining, doing favors for, and generally making himself useful to important people. "He's incredibly well connected," says a colleague who claims not to be envious.

Russell's career aspirations were clear and clearly handled. He first taught at a midwestern university, but "it was too far from the mainstream," he says. A prestigious appointment to one New England university brought him up against the fact that "I just wasn't going to make it publication-wise," so he switched to another university with a very good reputation but without the same requirements. He got tenure "because there was no way not to give it to him," according to another colleague. "His letters of recommendation were the *Who's Who* file for his field. And it probably didn't hurt that he car pools to the university with the provost and has intimate little dinner parties with him and his wife every few weeks." Although few of the letters of recommendation commented, except in the most general terms, on Russell's work (he often hires others to do his research), he has "served on every impressive committee, departmental task force, and association office that has any impact," most colleagues agree. "He's effective on committees, and he never drops an important detail. No matter what you say about his contributions to his field, he's made incredible contributions to his profession for a man his age."

The goal of Russell's career success map was not getting tenure, as it is for many academic people. Tenure was simply a necessary step in his larger career plan of living in the exact mainstream of everything important going on in his profession: a much more demanding and difficult job, which he obviously does superbly—and full time. He is not married. His friends are all professional associates. And his beautiful apartment also serves as the setting for gourmet dinners or dazzling cocktail parties.

Have a Career Plan and Move Quickly. Obviously, not every company likes getting-ahead types. A company that likes solidity rather than brilliance and prefers tradition to innovation gets very nervous with these "flash-in-the-pan" problem children. That is why getting-ahead careerists ferret out fast-track companies and then match their talents with the organization's needs to set up an exciting rhythm of assignments, promotions, and successes—one that puts them ahead of their peers. This "moving-up" style is not only compatible with their personality type, it is also essential to their image. As a result, they are easy to buy and, while the rewards are coming through on schedule, will sacrifice sleep and social life and do whatever else is required for their company. They are also ready to make geographical company and career moves when they sense new opportunities that match their aspirations.

But they do not stay bought. When their internal rhythm no longer matches the company's, their antennas, always out for other opportunities, start quivering. They need options for moving up. If they do not get them, they will make them or start looking for them. Almost invariably, people like this can tell you where they want to be in one year, in three years, in five years. They may not tell you, though, if it would give away important strategic information. And they will certainly not tell you about the contingency plans they have in reserve in case they run into a streak of bad luck or circumstances make it impossible to implement their chosen plan.

One prime example is Catherine, a thirty-five-year-old mother of three who returned to her university in Vermont at the age of thirty-two and dug with zest into a demanding program for an education degree. She chose education because "there are few women administrators. If I show myself as promotable, and with equal opportunity as a context, I think I can be a superintendent within a few years." She appears to be a "superwoman." She worked very hard in her graduate program while simultaneously maintaining "a good marriage and doing fantastic mothering," according to her physician husband. When she took some business administration classes, the awed professors said, "What's she doing in education? She's ahead of all our students." Her own college offered her an assistant professorship when she graduated. The flexible hours and proximity to home—they live near the university—would have been appealing to most, but Catherine refused the job because "it was too passive and specialized." Instead, she accepted a position as a principal at a junior high school in a small town fifty miles away. She slept four hours a night, drove two hours a day, and dealt with one problem after another in her "fairly turbulent" school. Her superintendent considered her "my star" in his district.

During her first year, while she was establishing herself with the teachers, parents, and students, continuing to maintain a high-quality relationship with her husband and children, and experiencing a long commute daily, she also maintained contacts at the university. At the end of that year, she shocked her superintendent by quitting and taking the assistant professorship she had earlier been offered.

"It just got too much for you?" asked a sympathetic friend.

"Oh, no," she said matter of factly, "but we're not likely to move out of state and I could see during this year that it's going to be harder to become a superintendent than I'd thought. I've got good sponsors at the university, and they're succeeding in recruiting a nationally recognized faculty. I think I can get more mileage out of this job—department chair, maybe, or dean." If her health holds up, no doubt she will.

Get a Sponsor. The research literature is absolutely clear on this point, too. Getting ahead takes at least one very influential sponsor, and two or three are better than one. This is not the parent-child, teacher-student relationship of the mentor—it is much more reciprocal than that, especially in the corporate world. In other words, competence in itself will not buy you a sponsor. Only a combination of competence, compatible personalities, and the sponsor's need for your service will.

The relationship clearly transcends that of supervisor and employee as well. Senior people in a company are typically getting-ahead types themselves. As they are promoted, they soon realize that they can no longer do all the work, even if they are willing to stay up all night. The only thing that will keep them looking good is bright young people who will invest time, energy, and talent in projects that the senior people can deliver to their own superiors. Furthermore, top-level managers have to look at their own future. What happens when they get to the top of their ladder? A getting-ahead company has little time or space for managers whose skills are obsolete, who do not understand that the business has changed, who did not shift when the power did. It is very much to the advantage of senior executives to bring along bright young people who will be indebted to them and then take care of them when they have reached their own positions of power.

For example, in a Canadian crown corporation that I worked with, the three most powerful men were all protégés of Jean-Paul, a ruthless and innovative man who had held the reins for a long time but was now in his middle sixties. The three were agreed: he was in the way, they needed his job, and they had the right candidate for it. But they spent anguished hours over how to make the move without hurting Jean-Paul, since they all owed him their jobs. Serge creatively took Jean-Paul out for dinner and for considerably more drinking than they usually indulged in. He came back the next morning hung over but exhilarated. Jean-Paul had revealed that what he really wanted was to live out his days in style in Montreal (his boyhood home), not Ottawa. He also wanted to continue to keep his finger on the pulse of the company and feel that he had some influence.

From that point, it worked like greased lightning. They increased his salary by ten or fifteen thousand dollars, moved him to an awe-inspiring office in Montreal, and set up a schedule so that, as a special assistant to the executive vice-president, he flew back to Ottawa two or three days a week for key meetings, where he performed highly visible and highly symbolic functions. Everyone was happy. From an organizational point of view, these actions communicated all the way down the line that important contributions continue to be rewarded, satisfied the sense of obligation that the three vice-presidents felt, and rewarded Jean-Paul with exactly what he wanted. Although no one knows ahead of time whether a protégé is going to be a respectful colleague or a backstabber, the company's own culture will usually teach the perimeters of what is acceptable.

Punch the Right Tickets. One of my most instructive experiences came as I watched a young man acquire a sponsor and go from there. Mike, one of my students at the Naval Postgraduate School in Monterey, California, was there because he had singlemindedly set his sights on becoming an admiral, and "I didn't go to Annapolis. Postgraduate school will help me get in the club anyway." In other words, his career plan was already outlined, and he was moving on it. He could identify which tours of duty he needed to undertake, which assignments would give him the most points, which kinds of experiences he needed in his portfolio, and which academic credentials would look best. Along the way, he had acquired "good officer-family material." Darlene was attractive, congenial, willing to take full responsibility for parenting their four children ("a good number"), and supportive of his ambitions. According to him, she would "go anywhere I was assigned, get along with anyone I needed to meet, and be sure that things hummed smoothly at home."

His next assignment, according to this game plan, should be in Washington, "so that I can get to know the right people and get the right kind of command for the next tour." When Admiral J., a topflight naval officer from the submarine corps, came to campus, Mike was ready. Although his rank was only commander, he openly contradicted a captain in J.'s presence and went on to give an impressive speech that caught the admiral's attention. Later, I saw them walking across campus together. As Mike explained a few days afterward, "I could tell that J. didn't like the captain. It was a chance for me to make points, and my network says that this flag officer is headed for the top."

Mike kept the contact alive with follow-up notes, relevant newspaper clippings, and Christmas cards. His next tour of duty was Washington, and he was assigned to J.'s staff. I saw him three or four years later in Washington, where he had clearly made himself indispensable. J. reciprocated by lobbying for him. Mike got the command of a new destroyer, got an excellent rating for that tour, and has now become a captain, while his sponsor has moved up to become one of the most influential admirals in the navy. It was in every way a mutually beneficial relationship. Mike later told me that Admiral J. had finally taken him into his confidence and told him what assignments he still needed in his experience portfolio to be considered for senior rank. Moreover, J. had used his influence on several occasions to see that Mike got the jobs that would give him the opportunity and visibility he needed.

In most organizations, it is important not only to perform well but also to occupy highly regarded positions. One role of a sponsor is to advise the protégé on what tickets to punch. The sponsor also helps the more junior individual get some key jobs. Few sponsors can get their protégés promoted to senior management positions unless they have performed well in key posts along the way.

Run On Challenge. Many people around getting-ahead types are appalled by the long hours, the stress, and the challenge. "That kind of job would be an invitation to a coronary," confides one executive gloomily. "Staying up all night to write a report and bounding in at 6 A.M. to be sure that the boss reads it first is not my idea of a good time." But for getting-ahead types, it is. Georgia discovered in college that she "liked competing, and I *really* liked winning." The oldest of two children, she says she was "programmed for success." Her father, a very successful lawyer, praised her most when she got good grades.

Her mother, who had dropped out of college to get married, groused about that choice in subtle ways and fed Georgia the message "Get where you're not dependent on anyone."

Catherine, during her first year as a junior high school principal, helped put together a new curriculum, served on several district committees negotiating employee benefits, and hammered out new budgets, in addition to settling into a new school and handling a faculty nervous about a new—and female —principal and a student body that hardly had education as its top priority. Nick's weekender schedule is tolerable now because Nadine thinks breakfast dates at 6:30 A.M. are charmingly offbeat, and his parents are delighted with two hours every other week. All of them genuinely thrive on what they are doing and genuinely do not want to change very much of it, even though they all admit to times when fatigue and discouragement make them mutter about "the rat race."

Benefits and Costs

Getting ahead has been the career model for so long and so intensively that almost every other career alternative has to dismantle it first. Getting-ahead people have been accused of being overly ambitious, money grubbing, shortsighted, selfish, and immature—"always expecting other people to pick up the pieces." From the outside—and from someone who defines success other than as getting to the top—some of these labels are justified. But, from the insider point of view, the panorama from the plate-glass corner suite is alluring. It is also rewarding.

Benefits. "Rich or poor," the saying goes, "it's nice to have money." Getting-ahead types do. They also have the things that money can buy—comfort (even luxury), convenience, personal services, and the best of whatever they happen to value. Catherine can drive away from her home every day with the confidence that a high-priced and highly educated nanny will care scrupulously for her children and that the housekeeper will have the lint out from under the beds and dinner started when she gets back. Russell lives in a beautiful twelve-room New York apartment, expensively furnished in antiques. He has flawless

taste in art and music, indulges both, and has a concert and gal-
lery schedule that boggles the mind.

Although none of them dislike money and none of them
would work without it, it would not be true to say that most
getting-ahead people are in it strictly for the money. Nearly all
of them genuinely love what they are doing. Action is "stimulating, not stressful," says Georgia. "I get more variety in my
work in a month than most people get in a year," says Nick
with real satisfaction. "I'm *good* at this," insists Russell. "It's a
real rush to feel a network come together and make things happen."

Bailyn's (1979) research noted that work-oriented careerists reported greater satisfaction with their work, greater satisfaction with their leadership ability, higher self-esteem, and
higher self-evaluations of their competence, problem-solving
skills, and creative abilities than those who put other considerations ahead of work. None of these results would surprise getting-
ahead types, many of whom quite sincerely find their greatest
happiness in their work. Most of them protest the "money-
grubbing" label as well. "Look at it this way," says Catherine.
"I'm making a real contribution to education in my state. It can
be a lasting contribution to my community. Sure I like it, I'm
rewarded for it, and it turns me on—but it's important that
somebody with my kind of talent (and I'm not overestimating
my ability) gives education some first-rate thought." For others, this sense of mission might be expressed as making profits
for shareholders, enhancing the modest investments of the common people of America, revolutionizing a staff area or process,
or making a better product for a consumer. Although some getting-ahead types will cynically say that they are in it for "what I
can get out of it," for very few does that tell the whole story.

Getting-ahead types admit that they are not always available to their families and friends but point out the positive side
as well. Thanks to Russell, his parents have visited Israel several
times, live in a comfortable home that their Social Security
benefits could not come close to paying for, and get to meet
interesting people. Mike's children go to school with the children of other upwardly mobile people. "They know what patri-

otism means, which is more than a lot of kids do today," he adds, "and Darlene has access to benefits through the officer's club and various recreational activities that my salary alone couldn't give her." Nadine adds another perspective. "Nick is a very interesting person. He's always been doing something interesting, has been in an interesting place, or has been solving a problem in an interesting way. I probably won't have as much of his time as I'd like after we're married, but there'll be a lot more of him than there would be with some of the architecture students I went through college with." Jean-Paul, the senior statesperson of his Canadian firm, has long been a mainstay of such cultural elements of the community as the museum and the opera. "He happens to like art and opera," one of his protégés said, "but if it hadn't been that, he would have done something else equally important—Boy Scouts, perhaps, or energy conservation, or higher education." Serge put it succinctly: "Money, influence, talent, and status—the ability to make things happen in many spheres. It all goes with getting ahead."

A recent *Wall Street Journal* and Gallup poll (Allen, 1981a) queried executive wives about the relationship costs and benefits of living with husbands who had made it to the top. Although 15 percent said that their children had suffered and 28 percent were not sure, 57 percent felt that their children benefited from their husbands' careers, especially in educational opportunities. Some of the personal rewards for these women were material possessions, travel, exposure to interesting people, being able to live with an exciting man, the status of being married to a respected professional, and being able to purchase a variety of helpful services. In other words, many of the wives saw their husbands' careers as their own, supported them in them, and participated in many of the benefits. Maccoby (1976) also found that many "gamesman" executives had wives who enjoyed winning the social game and had real talent at playing it. These women were competitive, success oriented, competent, and energetic. They raised their children to be winners. They liked entertaining, working on committees, and being involved in civic affairs. The families also reported playing lots of games together, focusing on having fun together in ways that built positive relations and good memories.

An interesting example of an executive family on the international scene is Peter and Maren, young Swedes who would be very much at home in any fast-paced company that prizes its getting-ahead executives. Peter grew up in a professional family with a business-executive father and a physician mother. At Stockholm, he graduated with an engineering degree and joined a dynamic multinational firm, a world leader in precision mechanical engineering and steel products. With 56,000 employees and offices around the world, it offers its young executives profitable and prestigious multinational careers. Company scouts spotted Peter's managerial promise. He did well on his first assignment as a supervisor, did equally well in management development seminars, and then went to the Netherlands office as an assistant director, adding Dutch to his fluent English. After two and a half years, he was ready for the Italian operation, and he knows he will move on within a year to Italian headquarters.

His wife, Maren, is a pretty former airline employee, fluent in Swedish, English, Dutch, German, and Italian. A skilled hostess and a charming conversationalist, she cheerfully mothers seven-year-old Lars and five-year-old Britta, enjoys international living, has adapted gracefully to an affluent life-style, and efficiently manages Peter's "showplace" home in Trieste and their summer cottage in Sweden. She plans to move into part-time work of an appropriate status once both children are further along in school.

Although most of these characteristics would be assumed prerequisites for an American executive wife, Peter is lucky to have her and knows it. He is lucky in the first place that she is willing to make his career her own, since dual-career couples are the rule rather than the exception in Sweden. Many of the Swedish women who are Maren's friends refuse to leave Sweden, making it difficult for their husbands to accept work assignments in other countries. (This is a frequent complaint of Scandinavian managers in general.) Peter works long hours and travels a lot. A devoted and affectionate father, he could not have the quality of family life he currently enjoys if Maren were less willing to spend a major share of her time on it. Peter is determined to do whatever is necessary to rise in the company,

and she is quite willing to support him in it. It is a real advantage for their children to be able to speak three languages and
move easily in international circles; but when they are old
enough for high school, Maren wants them in Sweden, making
the right connections and preparing to attend advantageous universities. Thus, returning to Sweden is a high priority for Maren,
and it is also a high probability, since Peter's career path will un-
doubtedly take him back to his company's headquarters within
ten years.

   Costs. One of the realities of getting ahead is that many
people start out with this orientation, but relatively few have
what it takes to drive on to the top. For many, at one point or
another, the game is no longer worth the costs to health, relationships, or self-development. The most obvious cost is what a
job-first commitment demands. Time spent at work cannot be
spent with a spouse or children or in sailing or stamp collecting,
even though it may make it possible to hire a housekeeper so
the spouse can go along on business trips or to buy the boat to
sail in. Nick faces his future with Nadine with some trepida-
tion. Georgia frets that "Paul may waltz out anytime. I don't
give him enough time and energy. I know it, and I long for intimate friendships—not just with Paul but with some of my wom-
en acquaintances, too—but I don't want the kind of drain
they'll be on my attention."

   The is-it-worth-it question comes up at different career
stages with different impact. Dennis is a getting-ahead executive who ran into the question hard. At forty-five, he is staff
vice-president of a consumer products corporation with multinational affiliates. The personal appointee of the company's
CEO, he is in charge of interactions with community groups and
government. As the only son in a family of two from a farming
community, he early learned the work-and-success ethic of his
parents and recalls his most persistent success fantasy as "getting off a private jet. A limousine and a chauffeur are waiting.
I go to a plush office with a silver water pitcher on the cre-
denza. I wonder what movie I got that out of."

   Although he grins about this youthful dream, his present
reality matches it. After getting his master's degree, he served

two years abroad in the Peace Corps, married, and began teaching in a community college, but "it was too abstract, unrelated to the real world." He and Leslie moved to Washington, D.C., where he got a job in a government office and began an extraordinarily rapid career. He has excellent administrative skills and political sense and a rare ability to make outstanding policy decisions and mobilize human resources. Fifteen years later, he was a powerful man. At that point, Leslie threatened to leave. Pregnant with their fifth child, she confronted him about the neglect she was feeling for herself and the children. Shocked and scared, Dennis gulped and re-evaluated. That was when the offer came from the consumer products company headquartered in Atlanta. Both he and Leslie saw it as a chance to live at a slower pace, spend more time with the children, and "catch our breath."

These expectations were accurate. The conglomerate offered a variety of opportunities, not the least of which was a chance to influence policy during a period of considerable government intervention. The company was actively expanding, and Dennis's gift for conceptualization produced a brilliant environmental policy that became a model for the whole industry. He helped in reorganizations, appointing his allies to key positions. But after three years, he had to look at a new set of cards. The president of the company and many of the line managers had come up through the production side. He had never been able to woo them successfully. As profitability slackened, Dennis had to face the fact that, when an economic crunch came, his sponsor, the CEO, would not be able to ride it out. The "exotic" staff work that Dennis was doing would be cut, and the business would be turned back to the operators. His own political credit had been extended about as far as it would go.

He contacted me for some career counseling. We looked at his options: Stay on and get demoted or at least have severely diminished influence? "No way; I'd be suicidal within four months." Invest in a shop in the village? "That's Leslie's choice." Become a professor and consult part time? "Too passive for me." Or spin off to another good position in a related industry or back into government? "And what happens to my marriage then?" For him, the family issue was a top priority. "We have a good marriage now. It's working. I want to keep it that way. I don't want to lose contact with my children again. But there's got to be some way to do it all. This job has looked great on my resumé, but I've known that I was stepping aside for a while. In my heart of hearts, I never meant to make it permanent. I always foresaw the day when I'd step back in." His final decision was to accept a new and exciting post as undersecretary in the government, with promises to Leslie that "things will be different." As the family left for the East, Leslie sighed, "I guess it really goes best when Dennis enjoys what he's doing. I enjoy nice things, too, and I know they're not free. Besides that, the children will be in college soon, and we have to plan for that."

Both are lucky—that Dennis prizes his family, that Leslie is willing to accept quality time instead of quantity time. For many getting-ahead careerists, a divorce would have been the answer, and many do not consider it an unreasonable price to pay for the success they want. Mike commented with regret about the number of colleagues who were getting divorces and taking to alcohol. (Sometimes one situation caused the other.) Both situations drew his contempt. "Two cocktails max. That's my limit," he announced. "And only on weekends. I can't afford to lose my edge." He also seemed to regard a good marriage as a matter of discipline. "Darlene and I are a team. We're both working for the same things. I'm on the edge, and she's the support system."

What if Darlene changed her mind? He laughed, then thought about it. "I'm not saying it couldn't happen," he said, "even though it's unlikely. It's possible that I could change my mind, too. But that is very unlikely. It's a much greater advantage to have a stable marriage than to have a divorce." But what if his military success turned out to be insufficient for Darlene? What if she wanted more? Mike was almost indignant. "You can't change rules in the middle of the game. She knew from the beginning where we were going and what it would take to get there."

Enzio, a well-to-do scion of a German family in Brazil, had worked for two chemical companies after obtaining his degree in business and a master's degree from the European Institute of Business Affairs (INSEAD). He had already been divorced once because his wife had not been willing to let work come first. His career plan included work in Europe with a multinational chemical company with American affiliates, followed by getting to the top in Brazil, before going into politics as a way of expanding his influence. He was interested in remarrying but was studying the literature on executive wives so as to avoid another costly mistake, partly because of the emotional pain involved but also because "it would slow down my career." Georgia pays the same kind of price in her personal life. "I worry that I'll burn out. In five years, will I just check out and have babies?" She is hypersensitive to the deadly judgment passed on women who are "not serious" about their careers: "She'll just get pregnant, so don't invest in her." She even admits to using it herself on one rival. But whatever lure domesticity and motherhood may have for Georgia, nothing in her current life accommodates such a pattern.

Additional research points to other dimensions of the time problem. A getting-ahead executive needs to work long hours, to travel, to be intensively involved with peers and senior sponsors, to be available to move with an opportunity, to fit into the corporate culture. The executive wives in the *Wall Street Journal* survey reported that their husbands worked up to seventy hours a week and came home exhausted. "There's nothing left for me or the children," was a frequent theme. Their own duties included hostessing, dressing appropriately, appearing at the correct functions, managing home and family emergencies, and being extensions of their husbands' careers (Allen, 1981a). Many of them liked it. Some of them, such as Leslie, did not. Nadine may not. Georgia's Paul has a minor social role in her company life, but his main job, she says, is to "leave me free." That is a double message when it comes to building relationships.

The personal consequences for getting-ahead executives must also be considered. "You get on the fast track," mused one, "and where do you end up twenty years later? The image is that you're rich, famous, and holding forth at an exclusive

cocktail party. Is that the reality?" Maccoby's (1976) "gamesmen" are chilling models for many in this twenty-year view.
They see work and life as a win-lose game and follow the rules
but are detached and depersonalized. If work is not challenging,
they become depressed and bored, dissatisfied with personal
relationships. The wife of an aggressive trial lawyer confessed,
"Will is hell to live with before and during a trial. Sometimes I
just want to slap him and scream, 'I'm not your opponent! I'm
your wife!' It's not that he goes into a blue funk and broods
for days if he happens to lose. It's just that he can't understand
why I can't take care of myself while he's setting up this courtroom in our dining room during every dinner. Sometimes he
treats our relationship as something he has to 'win at,' too, and
that terrifies me." Maccoby found that his "gamesmen" sometimes lack compassion, see winning as the only good, and see no
point in relationships for their own sake. As Russell revealingly
says, "I don't go out of my way to make enemies with the
junior faculty, but I don't waste much time on them either."

Nickles (1981) found that the pacesetter women in her
survey of 2,400 were well educated, self-confident, quickly decisive, goal oriented, career centered, and self-centered—only 16
percent felt they should help the less fortunate. A majority
were willing to sacrifice their personal relationships for their
work. The career women of the future, speculates Nickles, will
let nurturing fathers and day-care attendants raise their children—if any—and sexual relationships will be simple, quick-
pleasure experiences. Susan Nero's (1984) recently completed
research on Los Angeles women who were middle managers in
the $30,000–$71,000 range revealed another set of conflicts.
These twenty-nine women were between the ages of thirty-one
and forty, had master's degrees, and had no children, though
half were married or in long-term relationships. In general, they
reported little or no personal life outside work and complained
of stress and burnout. Single women spoke of their need for a
relationship. Married women brooded over whether and when
to have a child. Many of them admitted feeling that "something's missing" and further confessed that neither their work
nor their relationships were especially fulfilling, despite their

clear focus on getting ahead. Exceptions were the women with husbands or partners who took great pleasure in their careers and actively fostered them. These women seemed more fulfilled and contented, but their careers seemed to have taken the place of children.

In dual-career marriages where both partners have a strong commitment to getting ahead, the stress often spills over into personal lives. Children have to be "managed" so that they receive maximum attention but create minimum interruptions. Business talk dominates dinner-table conversation. Relationships between spouses are not so much tender or nurturing as they are practical divisions of labor. The logistical problems of simultaneously maintaining both the relationship and the position on the fast track are often overwhelming.

Managing Getting-Ahead People

In some ways, managing these careerists is easy, because they tend to manage themselves, especially in the early phases. If carrots are the going reward, they want carrots. They learn the culture of the organization, internalize its norms, obey its rules, and work hard to get a good performance record and establish a good image in the right places. They are reliable, responsive, and responsible future members of the executive club. What may be difficult, especially for larger companies, is managing their high-potential future executives during mid-career. It is very expensive to have an executive leave after a company's investment of years of training and experience; but if the pace of the rewards slows down, the executive might very well start looking elsewhere, badger top management for advancement that is simply not available, or become discouraged and depressed over being "stalled" and withdraw into some form of escapism.

Many upwardly mobile managers have an internal clock. If promotions do not come every two or four years, they do not feel successful. Dennis, recalling his early career, talks about "the fine line between being eager and being obnoxious, between being aggressive and being impatient, between pushing a manager for chances to show what I could do and being willing to go where the grass was greener, too." Business school graduates are taught to find jobs in companies with the potential for quick advancement. Unfortunately, this clock is no longer ticking in time to the national rhythm. A somewhat sluggish economy combined with the baby boom has created a midmanagement glut. There are more position seekers than positions. If patience and/or lateral moves are not acceptable, the only way up is out.

Thus, the problems in managing getting-ahead types may not show up until midcareer. A useful strategy is to share information with them early about the company's long-term plans, what the promotion potential is, and what the acceptable nonvertical options are. You can also try expanding their definitions of success. For some getting-ahead people, even being "number two" is seen as failure. Some managers have discovered that getting-ahead people will accept alternatives to the traditional up-the-ladder promotions that communicate the same message: "You're a member of the club. You're an insider. You're moving up." These "symbols" are sometimes as seemingly trivial as gold pens, sometimes as significant as bonuses, being sent to special training events, or being asked to help entertain important visitors. Getting-ahead careerists like lots of responsibility and authority and the opportunity to make a substantial contribution to the organization; promotion based on merit or results; pay that, including bonuses and options, puts them in a special class; lots of room for advancement and a rapid promotion schedule; enough money to purchase culturally appropriate housing, memberships in the right clubs, the right car, the right clothes, and so forth; power to move toward the "inner" circle; and lots of competition in test situations where they get information about how good they really are.

Almost certainly, some of your subordinates will be getting-ahead careerists. In your company's culture, where do they fit? Does it like them? Reward them? Get nervous if there are too many? As a manager, you are in a logical position to be a sponsor—to steer them toward the most productive assignments and channel their considerable talents to the company's profit. An effective, energetic subordinate will also help you look good. If you are a getting-ahead type yourself, you can probably have a very effective working relationship—for a time. You need to understand, however, that no alliance will be permanent. Most getting-ahead people are fair and willing to test themselves in any circumstance, but they are also competitive, detached, contemptuous of weaknesses, and very much in control of themselves. While you may see yourself as doing a favor for a getting-ahead junior, recognize that your own strengths and weaknesses are coming under cool scrutiny.

On the positive side for you, though, are some big pluses. Getting-ahead careerists may have demanding technical competences, but their major skill is in managing people. Kotter (1982) suggests that effective managers can operate very diverse and demanding businesses through interacting effectively with networks of people. Getting-ahead careerists have good generalist skills: planning, time management, a sense about costs and benefits, an ability to get along well with and motivate others, excellent analytical skills sometimes verging on the intuitive, and healthy emotional lives, including the ability to bounce back from defeats and to maintain high levels of enthusiasm and to manage stress. Any manager can use those abilities.

Getting-ahead executives have dominated American business to the extent that their ethic has become identified as the American way of life. "Do it faster, better, bigger," is their slogan. They have the intelligence, the energy, and the will to pull it off, time after time. They run on the pleasure of achievement—visible achievement that is recognized, appreciated, sometimes envied, and always empowering. Nearly everyone begins a career with this orientation, but only a few have what it takes to keep moving straight to the top. Those who get there report that the view is fine—most of the time. Some who drop out or find themselves sidetracked along the way label themselves as failures. Others who check out do so because they want to live their lives in other ways. For them, success has a different definition, even though it might not be something that the people around the boardroom table would value or even admit. These "other definitions" drive getting-secure, getting-high, getting-free, and getting-balanced careerists.

 SIX

Getting Secure

Leon recently celebrated his fiftieth year with the same organization, a large southern state agency where his grandfather had been employed a century earlier. In fact, his grandfather had first hired him when he was a teenager as a kind of low-paid private secretary. "That was back in the days before anybody was worried about nepotism," Leon recalls, "but he didn't want to show any favoritism. I got a dime an hour less than everybody else, and he kept me working straight through lunch for the first three years. I thought I'd starve to death." It is a source of considerable satisfaction to him that he is now managing director, a higher rank than his grandfather ever achieved.

His branch of the agency is responsible for historical records, and he has frequently been criticized by his subordinates, most of them college-trained archivists or historians, for his complete lack of historical awareness. "He doesn't know what records we've got, he doesn't know what's in them, he doesn't know how to use them himself, and he's always deathly afraid whenever anyone else wants to use them," snorts one archivist. His frugality with the agency's funds is legendary. At one point, he searched beneath the telephones of all the employees to see whether any stray paper clips were there, thus creating what one sardonic employee dubbed the Leon L. Goold Rusty Paper Clip Collection. He talks earnestly to new employees about "our look," by which he means the white shirt and pinstripe suit or equivalent. He reminds male employees to get their hair cut when it seems to be getting a little "shaggy around the ears" and has been known to tell woman employees to keep a spare pair of stockings in their desk so they can immediately change if they get a run.

He runs a weekly staff meeting at which he reads announcements about steak knives being offered by the employees' credit union, regulations governing the use of the parking garage, and the fact that employees who are ill the day before or after a holiday must have a note from their doctor substantiating their illness. Attendance at this meeting, which begins fifteen minutes earlier than the usual commencement of the working day, is mandatory. To many of his employees, he is out of date, a fussbudget, and almost paranoidly eager to please his superiors. All of them agree, however, that he works long hours and has identified himself completely with the agency's values.

To his superiors, Leon is invaluable. "Around here," drawls one, "change comes two ways: very slowly and not at all. I know those bright young kids we've got in the archives want to be doing outreach programs and lecturing to county historical societies about how to use the tax records and are agitatin' to get every musty old militia roll microfilmed. We've had some bad experience with publications out of the university and had some legislators asking why taxpayer money was making things like that available. Around here, we see our first responsibility as acquiring the records—and there's a lot of them, more now than ever before. Our second responsibility is to preserve 'em, and publication is way, way down on the list."

Obviously, one of Leon's jobs is to watchdog the records and to screen access to them, to preserve them but not necessarily to see that they are made easily accessible. He fulfills this function admirably. In his role as a division head, one of his chief responsibilities is to attend and to hold meetings. With at least four or five hours a day given over to committee meetings, department meetings, individual meetings with staff members, weekly meetings with his own supervisor, and informal meetings to prepare for the meetings, he often has to stay late, come early, or come in on weekends to catch up on his correspondence, prepare the budget, stay current with recent acquisitions, and "do my reading." He faithfully reads the employee newsletter and considers himself personally responsible for knowing every item in the policies and procedures manual.

He is a bright man, capable and energetic in committee meetings and endlessly willing to follow through on assignments. His staff is correct about his lack of expertise in historical or archival matters, but he perceives his job as managing the records, not understanding them. He religiously attends a professional meeting of archivists every year, but this reflects a policy of professional development for division directors, not his own preference. He has one hobby, collecting Civil War souvenirs, "but I haven't even had time to do that recently," he confesses. "Nose to the grindstone." He could retire within the next two years but says modestly, "I don't think I could do that. My health is good, and it's hard to find an experienced manager these days. As long as my boss is around, I'll probably stay on, too." Radiating through every word is his sense of being needed and appreciated.

Leon is a classic getting-secure type. He represents someone who has bought his secure position not with expertise or good ideas, although he is lacking in neither, but with his undivided loyalty. He is the kind that it is impossible not to promote simply because he is completely there and is so completely identified with the agency's interests. Ironically, managing his department is the only job in it that he is currently qualified for because of the new educational requirements he himself worked to institute as part of the overall upgrading. Several men and women in his department share the same career orientation. They are willing to work long, work hard, and perform completely any task assigned to them. They like the agency because "the pay is good, the raises are regular, and the benefits are excellent." They face with comfort the prospect of thirty years at the same desk. When promotions come, they will turn their attention toward learning the new task with the same fervent attention to detail and the same emphasis on doing a good job that they give their current work.

The Getting-Secure Personality

A clear pattern of assumptions and obligations shapes the approach a getting-secure careerist takes to work. These people feel that there is an open giving and receiving of contractual relationships—of rights and responsibilities—whether they exist legally or not. Psychologically, the employee guarantees loyal, dedicated work—lots of it—in exchange for lifelong employment and a secure career identity, predictable career progression, relatively stable work circumstances, respect and recognition (though not necessarily fame and glory), and an opportunity to make contributions to the institution that will be valued. Thus, it does not matter whether raises come infrequently as long as they come predictably. It does not matter whether the pay begins lower as long as both parties assume that the commitment is for the entire career. And it does not matter whether another company flashes a bigger paycheck or a more attractive wad of options; the loyalty is fixed.

There has been some tendency to think of "good ol' Charlie, forty years with the company," as admirably loyal but fairly unimaginative and unambitious. We explain such long-term commitments historically—that Charlie grew up during the Depression, for instance, when you would hang on to any job you could get. Although tight economics may make security look like a promising career map, this view ignores the psychological drive of some employees to belong and their willingness to exchange their physical efforts and psychological commitments for that sense of belonging. Some workers, particularly the getting-free and getting-high types, might be driven to distraction by the very things that provide such a solid and rewarding sense of satisfaction: stability, predictability, routines, clear-cut roles, a sense of place, recognition and appreciation, and a long-term employer commitment. Schein (1978) interpreted this phenomenon partly as a geographical attachment. He maintained that some security-oriented individuals need to feel rooted and settled in a place. Perhaps their security came as part of their being linked to family or lifelong friends or as geographical attachment. DeLong (1982) found that regional attachment and job security may be quite different aspects of the security career orientation, even though they may occur in the same person. The psychological need to belong is different from the common need to feel secure before moving on to higher-order needs. For these careerists, getting secure *is* the highest

psychological need. It must also not be confused with the career
stage of getting tenure and paying dues in an organization as
prelude to pursuing your real job orientation. We all have some
need for basic job security. For these people, getting secure is
an end in itself.

In a different culture, it is easier to see some of the positive aspects of this career success orientation, even though, in
American terms, the disadvantages are still there. Kenji, a Japanese executive, was one of my most interesting students at the
European Institute of Business Affairs and an example of how
national culture modifies, perhaps even dominates, personal career orientations. By every standard, he should have been a getting-ahead person. Bright, competitive, ambitious, driven to
achieve, and extremely able, at age thirty he already had five
years of experience with his company as an international bank-
.ing expert specializing in Euro-Asian business relationships and
stood on the threshold of a brilliant career.

Yet there were some anomalies. He wanted top positions;
but during interviews and career counseling, another theme
sounded repeatedly. Loyalty to the company and outstanding
performance on its behalf were bedrock values for him. He
wanted to achieve—but for his company. He wanted top positions—as a way of belonging more firmly and more surely to the
company family. His definition of career success was "lifetime
employment, the rewards of money, status and exciting jobs,
good health, being seen as loyal and hardworking, and good
relations with colleagues and peers." Having a successful family
life was the last item listed. Were there personal constraints that
would affect his availability to the company? No. If he were
sent abroad for a three- to five-year tour, he would take his wife
and children only if the company approved and only if they
were not needed to care for his parents. He had come to get a
degree at INSEAD and "learn the European mentality" for his
company. If they had instructed him to stop and return, he
would have obeyed at once. To some, Kenji would have been
seen as a pure getting-ahead type. In reality, he was a getting-
secure careerist with a strong secondary orientation to getting-
ahead.

He works six days a week. He leaves home at 5 A.M. and returns at 11 P.M. Religiously, he sees good service to his company as an actual means of salvation, not only for him but for his wife. He carries on the first page of his appointment book the company chants. The first son in a very traditional family, he saw his father, a top-level executive in a chemical company, follow the same schedule and act out the same devotion to work that Kenji is following. His mother would show him his father's study, hung with awards, and hold up for him the prospect of the same glittering future if he worked hard in school. He worked very hard and got into the best grammar school and then, with even more prodigious effort, into Tokyo's best high school, where his classmates were of similar class, backgrounds, values, and contacts. Together they now form their generation's network of power people. He graduated with honors and went to the bank, where he met his wife, Teruko, an employee. She willingly left work to devote herself to running the household, caring for their parents, raising their three children, and providing a supportive atmosphere with few emotional demands on him. She did not accompany him to France, accepting the ten-month separation with equanimity.

His fears were all work connected. Failure, to him, would be somehow to "lose face" and fail the company. One fear was, of course, making a serious mistake on behalf of the company. Another was becoming old, losing his edge, and being transferred to a customer company, even at a highly respectable salary and with a good title and even real work to do. Equally shameful would be to be retained by the company but given the lavish office, high title, and honorific functions that communicated respect for someone who could no longer make a real contribution. Senior executives removed in this way from the mainstream of company life were referred to as "sitting by the window."

People with a getting-secure career success map, according to Maccoby (1976), center their world around a company to which they have pledged their allegiance, as Kenji clearly had done. The expression "married to the company" hints not only at the depth of the commitment but also at the real psychological bonding of affection, affiliation, and identity that occurs. Maccoby's "company men" constantly monitored themselves in a given situation or a new job to find just the right image to fit in. They were determined to become part of this new extended family, assuming responsibility for its demands and conflicts much as they do in their own family situations. By equating their personal interests with those of the organizations, not unexpectedly, they take on the organization's worries and goals as their own. In addition to their often-secret fears of failing some sort of test, of being displaced by a powerful rival, or of being victimized by external circumstances, they brood over a new product that seems shaky, fret over the problem-ridden regional office in Kansas City, and feel defensive if someone criticizes the design of the logo. They also derive extraordinary satisfaction from the firm's achievements, speak with real pride of a record-breaking quarter, or bask in a positive magazine article on the success of the company's product in Hong Kong. Sometimes they will lapse into military metaphors, seeing themselves as soldiers on the front lines of the company's vital interests and being surprisingly willing to sacrifice their own interests. They are not infrequently hero-worshipers, highly attached to authority figures within the firm.

Another factor in the psychological profile is a smaller share of the aggressiveness, decisiveness, tenacity, and sheer drive often taken for granted by getting-ahead careerists. Getting-secure careerists are frequently as competent, likable, and bright; they understand the politics and strategy and may be extremely shrewd observers of the internal scene, but they bow out of the competition—sometimes because they do not want to commit their energies to such projects, sometimes out of fear of failing, sometimes out of fastidiousness, but mostly because they view self-interest politics as disloyal.

While fast-breaking rough-and-tumble situations that need aggressive leadership and quick decisions handicap such people, periods of retrenchment, amalgamation, and slow, steady growth see them coming into their own. They provide consistent leadership in such situations, are able to convey confidence and appreciation, set up workable routines, and put enormous efforts into keeping things moving straight ahead. They tend to see their roles as maintaining a working system with minor repairs and reforms. Another great advantage that these workers have over some of the other types of careerists is that they are able to adapt to company demands. Their skills are usually broadly based, and they tend to be sufficiently detached from the craftsmanship aspect of a job that they will take any position that the company needs filled and give it a good try. If they happen not to like the particular tasks that come with an assignment, they waste very little time fretting but simply accept the conditions and get on with it.

Getting-secure types, though some rise high in the organization, tend to cluster in good, solid positions in middle management, where their tenure is assured and where their presence is recognized. They are the guardians and solid citizens of the corporation, who form the alliances, coalitions, and treaties that allow some getting-ahead executives to succeed and block the attempts of others. As a manager, you can appreciate these qualities. You can also be aware of potential problems. Getting-secure people would definitely fit on the "local" side of Alvin Gouldner's (1957–58) continuum of "locals" and "cosmopolitans." "Locals" are not only extremely loyal to a particular organization; they use their peers and supervisors in the company as their reference group and view with suspicion people who import too many ideas from the outside. Cosmopolitans, on the other hand, are more loyal to their profession or occupation than to their employer and use their occupational peers, no matter what their current affiliation, as their primary reference groups. As a result, they disregard many of the cultural norms and shibboleths of a given company because of an overriding concern about the views of their self-chosen peer group. Conflict between getting-secure locals and these more mobile cosmopolitans is almost guaranteed when work brings them into close contact.

One of the difficulties of working with the getting-secure career success map is that hardly anybody wants to claim it. Since the dominant image of a successful career in America today is the getting-ahead type, getting secure looks like the

antithesis and, hence, like failure. Getting-ahead success stereotypes are particularly damaging to getting-secure people. Even
the language sounds demeaning: "need for security," "golden
handcuffs," "large corporations and government agencies,"
"organization man," "company joe," "dependent," "willing to
do whatever is asked," "solid citizen." All of these can seem unglamorous, dull, passive, and negative. "How can you have any
integrity," asked one of these people angrily, "when you just
sound like a blackboard for the company to write on?" Since it
is important to getting-secure careerists to perceive themselves
as valuable and contributing members, they "resent . . . the
overwhelming negative implications" of their very solidity and
dependability and "also wanted credit for their contribution to
the organization" (Maccoby, 1976, p. 67).

The problem is partly historical, too. Alexis de Tocqueville ([1851] 1945), over 100 years ago, observed that fierce independence and competition were part of the American cultural
fabric. In a territory with unlimited natural resources, the rewards of competition are much more obvious than those of cooperation, and the "good terms" in our work culture often im-
ply the opposite of security: *aggressive, industrious, self-reliant,
unique, challenging,* and *innovative.* The shame and guilt associated with this negative labeling may remind some of the civil
rights movement and the women's movement and their attention to how we use language. Studies reveal that getting-secure
workers are by no means a negligible segment of the work force.
Maccoby found that a majority of his middle managers were
getting-secure people. Of the 15 high school principals Derr and
Chilton (1983) studied, 13 were clearly affiliated with this career success orientation. Thirty-five percent of the 727 engineers Bailyn (1982) studied had basic security orientations.
Twenty-five percent of the 44 panel members Schein (1982) researched were anchored by a security need, as were 29 percent
of the 28 program managers in an aerospace industry and most
of the production managers in that sample. Twenty-five percent
of the 20 women vice-presidents in one large bank identified
their orientation as security. Only 16 percent of Derr's (1980)
124 high-potential naval officers had this career success map;

but, of those who did, 25 percent were in the Civil Engineering Corps and 23 percent in the Supply Corps. Thus, among widely divergent occupations and within many hierarchical positions, a significant proportion of employees really work for security.

Perhaps a third factor in the resistance to identifying oneself publicly with this career success orientation is that the external environment has supreme importance. Internal feelings of success for getting-secure people depend mainly on remaining in one particular setting for many years and matching requirements. The broad base of the work contract carries with it some fears of being seen as "too adaptable" or not having character, values, motives, or talents of one's own. "Unprincipled" and "wishy-washy" are some of the negative ways such accommodations can be viewed.

Although large, stable corporations are a good place to look for people with getting-secure career success orientations, they are not the only place. Emily graduated from Stanford with a brilliant record in engineering, then got her doctoral degree in the behavioral sciences and counseling. She had two reasons: she wanted to get insight into herself, and she wanted her "union card" into university teaching, in case she felt she needed to use it. Her first successful venture was as marketing vice-president with some Stanford colleagues who had created a technology-based invention. Emily sold it to a large corporation at a profit that made her financially independent overnight. She followed it up with a string of other successes. Typically, she will be hired at a fancy salary as vice-president or executive officer of a small start-up firm, which will be sold for handsome profits when it is off the ground.

However, Emily is conspicuously different from the other technical entrepreneurs and venture capitalists she pals around with. She is not willing to put personal capital into these enterprises. She frequently refers to her doctorate as "unemployment insurance." Her husband is a social worker at a very modest salary, but she likes that, because "someone in the family needs to make a steady income." Although they have been married eight years, their plans for children are a vague "after we get established." When things are going well, she flaunts her money and status, brags, and comes on strong. When things look uncertain, she becomes depressed and paranoid, overreacts in bizarre ways, makes odd economies, and sues for fees that, by contract, are supposed to be paid on a different schedule. Although she looks like an entrepreneur, she shares few of the characteristics of a getting-high career success orientation. What drives her into ventures that scare her to death is her inordinate need for "enough money."

It would be interesting to know whether a higher percentage of women than of men have getting-secure orientations. Statistics show a high percentage of women careerists in government service, banks, utilities, and other traditional bastions of security. But which came first—the need for secure employment that drew women to these settings, or the invitation to women from these stable organizations that early adopted equal opportunity guidelines and submit willingly to close regulation?

Another interesting factor is that many women have identified themselves as oriented toward security but have added, "I have no choice." They then list the personal constraints that put regular paychecks at the top of their employment needs. The greatest number of single parents are women. They must often support themselves and their children while they simultaneously acquire the skills to do so—either through on-the-job training or through carrying the double burden of employment and schooling. Thus, steady income, ongoing raises, and comprehensive benefits look better than gambling on a more interesting but less stable job. Furthermore, as one bright and articulate woman who is a manager in a government post pointed out, women have a stronger inclination than men toward investing in long-term relationships and working hard at them. It is easy to transfer this inclination to an organization and make it part of their career strategy. America is just now experiencing its first whole generation of employed women. A cautious consideration of security may simply be part of a developmental step for that society as a whole, roughly comparable to the "will they like me?" stage for any individual careerist just starting out.

A further constraint on women is the geographical link: a spouse's work, a child's school, a helpful neighborhood situation. They are less willing to move or to travel extensively.

Friendship networks and such personal growth activities as education, recreation, artistic development, and community service
may also make it easier for women to ask searching questions
about the price required to play the getting-ahead game. Many
women in large organizations have an unsentimental view of the
politics required to get to the top of a male-dominated hierarchy and decide early which directions they consider more rewarding.

How to Get Secure

Despite its bad press, getting secure may be the dominant
anchor for the greatest percentage of the American work force
and is certainly a fallback position of choice for many whose
primary anchors may be something else. Thus, it is important to
understand how the profile works. Here is a guide for maximizing this career success orientation.

Find the Right Company. Much of the time, locating the
perfect company can be done by observation. IBM and Hewlett-
Packard both have a reputation for providing lifelong and secure
employment. So do the utilities, government agencies, such
Japanese companies as Honda and Nissan, and many religiously
affiliated institutions. Ouchi (1981) discusses various American
firms that fit this mold, organizations he calls "Theory Z" companies. Personnel officers in an interview will talk about "company loyalty." They will be able to tell you what percentages of
the employees have been with the company for five years, ten
years, twenty years, and thirty years. Look for organizations
that have predictable and safe patterns of upward movement.
If this predictability and safety come with the pricetag of slow-
ness, that is all right. The British civil service has long been the
archetype of an ideal home for getting-secure people. You are
almost guaranteed a career ladder and a calendar as long as you
do not make a serious blunder. Exceptionally meritorious service may help you move a little faster on a couple of steps, but
continuing to forge ahead at a fast pace would be frowned on
by others in the organization and would also seriously disrupt
the organizational norms.

Getting-secure people not only are willing to pay their

dues but are anxious to move through a predictable routine. Although they would feel hurt if they "missed their turn," they see career progression over time very comfortably as part of a pattern controlled by senior people. I recently consulted with Lewis, a junior high school principal who was one of the finalists for a high school principalship that was opening up. All of the finalists were getting-secure people and very qualified, but Lewis explained, in total sincerity: "I won't be devastated if I don't get the position this time around. I understand that I came in through vocational education and that it'll take a number of years for me to be ready to run a whole ship. But I'm going to feel really betrayed if there isn't a principalship for me within the next ten years. My peers are starting to get them, and I feel I have been as loyal and hardworking as anyone and that the system will owe it to me." This statement clearly reveals two strong characteristics of getting-secure people: their willingness to wait their turn and their clear internal map about where they want to be and when. Although getting-ahead people have the same clarity about their maps, a getting-secure person such as this principal defines his or her map in terms of the top. There was no hint anywhere in the interview with Lewis that he aspired to anything beyond a principalship or that he considered switching fields from education.

   Study the Company Culture and Fit In. Since organizations that are appropriate for getting-secure people prize competence, loyalty, conformity, trustworthiness, and affection, you will solidify your position if you can internalize and communicate these values to your superiors. One woman I recently worked with in Washington, D.C., was a public relations officer for a large company headquartered in the South. Lucybeth had launched her career at the age of thirty-eight after raising her family and was very anxious to prove herself valuable to her new company. As part of orienting herself in her job, she had worked nights and weekends for almost eight weeks reading everything the company had ever preserved in its files about its public relations efforts. She had scanned miles of microfilmed newspapers at the university library to document the ads that it had used and joyfully shared her discoveries with her supervisors, who were pleased at her obvious interest and commitment, even though there did not seem to be any immediate use for such information. In workshops, Lucybeth seemed unable to detach herself from her company's perspective or to differentiate between its values and hers. In exercises requiring personal information, she seemed to reflexively answer with phrases like "My company thinks . . ." or "Here's what we do in my company." Needless to say, she was also completely faithful about carrying out assignments, meeting deadlines, and coming prepared to meetings. Her only hobby was going to the symphony, but work assignments frequently took precedence. She seemed to have transferred the same assiduous, creative, capable care she had given her family to her company; and her supervisors, pleased with the reputation she had established in the eighteen months she had worked there, predicted a long and happy career.

Getting-secure careerists understand the culture of their corporation. They know where the margins are, what the rules are, what you can and cannot do, and what will be rewarded or punished. In this, they are like getting-ahead careerists. Unlike getting-ahead careerists, though, they do not push these margins or bend the rules. They have a respect for the rules that, in some cases, borders on the superstitious. In one organization with a strong conservative dress code, a manager called in his executive assistant, who was wearing a three-piece navy blue suit and a pink shirt, and seriously told her that she was "too colorful." Getting-secure types would not consider missing a meeting, whether the content of the meeting was important to them or not. As a result, when these same loyal employees rise to managerial status, they can be baffled—and even a little horrified—at a suggestion to eliminate a custom or tradition that has outlived its usefulness. They can be thrown into a tailspin by the suggestion that the Friday morning staff meeting be changed to Thursdays for the benefit of those in the organization who do a lot of weekend traveling.

Put the Organization's Needs First. As with the beginning stages of any career, whatever the orientation, the needs of the organization must come first. For getting-secure people, however, that can mean deferring their own interests, needs, and abilities, or even changing directions several times during their career.

Scott, a tenured professor at a medium-sized southwestern university, had begun his career by straining every nerve to achieve tenure in his field, administration-management policy. He correctly saw tenure at his university as the key to orderly progression, good benefits, an ample salary with regular though small increases, and lifelong employment. Once he achieved tenure, however, he did not suddenly feel free to relax or pursue more personal interests. Instead, he clearly felt that, since the university had recognized and rewarded his ability, he owed it redoubled loyalty, and he threw himself with renewed zeal into the work of running the university. "He's the workhorse of every committee he's ever been on," said his appreciative department chairperson. Scott is willing to help set up student programs that other faculty members shy away from, programs that are important to the students but are administrative headaches and very time consuming as far as the other faculty are concerned. He volunteers for tenure review committees, offers his assistance with curriculum review committees, and consistently ends up with a significant share of the legwork in putting the budget together. Completely loyal to the university, he is the first to leap to his feet in faculty meetings when someone says something critical about the college, always countering with "We've got the best students at the university," and citing statistics about enrollment, the international makeup of the student body, and their successful placement records, all of which happen to be true.

He can usually be found in his office or in a nearby meeting any weekday starting at 7 A.M., an unusually early and consistent schedule at the university. In recent interviews, his children said that they respected and admired him, "but he was always gone. We don't really feel we know him." His weekend time is now spent establishing with his grandchildren a relationship he never had with his children. Respected by his colleagues, he will be sorely missed when he retires in three years and others will have to pick up the burden he has so cheerfully shouldered for the past thirty years of keeping the college and university running.

Try to Become a Member of the Inner Circle. Utter respectability and trustworthiness are the keys to the getting-secure inner sanctum. It is important not to violate norms and taboos in areas of procedure, dress, or speech, never to betray confidential information or try to play one faction against another by trading information. There is usually a place for noncompetitive affiliates in this circle. Within it, it is essential to maintain complete confidentiality and loyalty. To some extent, this will involve doing favors for peers and supervisors, helping them look good, and making public gestures that are seen as supportive.

The case of Robert is instructive. A local executive and manager in a large utility firm, he was attracted by the protected environment of these quasi-public, quasi-private organizations where, as he cheerfully admits, you "really have to screw up to be fired." However, loyalty is the ticket into the inner circle, and Robert, who has a strong getting-secure anchor that is partially linked to his love of the Northwest, has acquired a bad reputation. Comfortably situated at a midmanagement level that he can handle easily, he had a lot of surplus time and energy. A few months ago, he tried to put together, with his wife, a consulting operation on the side. Even though nearly all of the actual office work would be done by his wife as the active partner, with Robert playing largely a weekend accounting and investment role, his superiors were outraged when they discovered what he was doing. He has now been branded as doing something disloyal—as not giving all of his time and energy to the company. He came to me for counseling, shocked and hurt. "It's just not true," he protested. "The company has all of my attention it can use. I'm a loyal employee, but they've put me on the shelf." He has about twelve years to go before retirement and thinks seriously about finding another job, but his demands are steep: it would have to match his current pay, provide equivalent benefits, and also be in a secure environment. "I'd change in a minute if I could find it," he says, but he is not willing to accept anything less. A big factor is his home.

From boyhood, he has longed to live in the exclusive lakeside district of his hometown. After the children were in school and his wife began working, they could afford the payments on a house there. They have lived in it for five years; and, although he is sensitive about "boring" others by talking about it, it is obvious that fixing it up, buying things for it, keeping it in good repair, and tending his fabulous rose garden are prime considerations for him. Any employment option that might require moving or selling this house is simply not even going to be considered.

Decide Which Promotions to Go After. You want security, respect, and access to influential sponsors. For most getting-secure people, a comfortable and risk-free level of management about midway or slightly above the middle is best. Except in the most stable and hierarchical of organizations, a getting-secure person will not be successful at the highest levels because of the requirements for political skills, public relations, and risk taking. The case of Max T. demonstrates the trade-offs in career choices. A middle-level manager in a state agency, he moved very fast in his early career, which he began in the forestry service. The pay was good. There were good benefits and lots of challenges. But when he and Karen had four children and their schooling became a prime consideration, Max transferred to another department, one that required almost no traveling. He moved straight across with little loss of pay or status, but he now finds himself stymied. Most government bureaucracies have a long midcareer plateau where people must be content to stay for ten or fifteen years. Max feels not only plateaued but unappreciated, cut off from his early sponsors and isolated, in Idaho, from other sources of influence.

When he came to talk to me, he was frustrated and dissatisfied with his work situation but unwilling to change jobs. "I've been offered a job if I'd go to Washington, but I couldn't consider moving away," he said. "The pay is good, the benefits are great, and I have lots of free time here to spend on community service and with my family. I'd be crazy to leave." Sorting through the options helped him understand that he really wanted the security, not the constant string of promotions that would make up a getting-ahead pattern that he had identified with as a younger man.

Build Up Social Debts. Ron is gifted, talented, elegant—and aging. He made his reputation in sales and marketing, where he showed a genius for making the product look glamorous—something his supervisors prized—and conveying an image of service—his own goal. Strongly motivated by Christian principles, Ron is striving to integrate these principles with corporate growth, not always an easy task. In his company, most of the senior directors of departments are getting-secure types who have been rewarded as much as possible for their loyalty. Ron's job is also secure with the company as long as he is there, but he realizes that he has reached the top of his ladder. He lacks, he says, the "ability to be nasty" like the people at the very top, whom he sees as "liking nobody and being cordially hated in return." Ron makes an exception for Tony, his mentor. As long as Tony is executive vice-president, Ron will be protected. It is not that Tony respects Ron very much or even likes him as a friend. Rather, Ron was instrumental in helping Tony get where he is today, delivering much of the work that made Tony look good. What is more, two more junior vice-presidents also owe much to Ron, who mentored them early in their careers. So Ron's place seems secure, at least in the foreseeable future.

Ron has developed an ulcer but tries to remain serene about being "appreciated but eased out." In a different company or in one where his service record was less distinguished, Ron might very well have been completely out of employment. His social debts saved him.

Take Your Place. The great strength of getting-secure people is their stability. Other people come and go, but getting-secure people are with a company for the long haul. They are the company's memory, its living embodiment of norms, cultural requirements, and history. In a comfortable and natural way, they should exercise that prerogative and responsibility by reflecting past decisions, mentoring the young, and supplying precedents. In times of crisis, they hold down the fort. When they see an emergency coming, they realize that everyone is going to expect them to be there, even if it is not their own emergency. Being indispensable means that they do not have much flexibility about checking out, either physically or emotionally. Long hours in the office—not just working in other locations—go with the territory. In some ways, this means that they do not have the freedom of other types of employees, but it also means that others will turn to them in crises and count on them to keep routines running smoothly. That is their place. It is appropriate to claim it and use it.

Benefits and Costs

A getting-secure career orientation defines success by the context of work rather than by the content or process of the work. Although such people can be workaholics—and often are during crises—usually they are "steady-state" workers, taking a mild pleasure in work routines regardless of the task itself. The importance that work and work relationships assume for getting-secure careerists also has a negative side. Maccoby (1976) discovered that his "company men" often avoided deep relationships with others, had few friends outside of company "cronies," and tended to feel insignificant and lost when separated from the organization. The positive side of this equation is that, once in a secure place and feeling relatively unthreatened, security-oriented individuals are unusually cordial and helpful, particularly to peers in other areas or to young workers coming up. Similarly, their personal relationships outside of work can flourish when they feel relatively relaxed and unburdened by conditions at work. As their years of dedicated, loyal, and competent service pay off, their families and friends will also share in the genuine appreciation, status, economic benefits, and clear identification as contributing members of society that come to the getting-secure careerist.

Getting-secure employees, however, have their eggs in a basket someone else is holding. They are vulnerable to external change—to a dip in the market, to a change of top management, to a stockholders' takeover, to a series of bad years. They reflect this by worrying. They fear radical changes and the inevitable impersonality that comes from major changes in leadership and power relationships, all logical accompaniments of innovation and improvement. In the span of a whole career, it is unlikely that a given company will escape unforeseen change with its accompanying trauma for getting-secure careerists.

Martin is currently caught in this bind. An energetic and hardworking high school principal, he has poured his lifetime's energies into his work and now, at age fifty-five, is feeling unappreciated and betrayed. The last superintendent stayed in for nineteen years, his predecessor for fifteen. Martin felt very comfortable with their educational philosophies and styles and, from the beginning, felt trusted and appreciated. Now a new superintendent has arrived, with radically different educational philosophies. One of his most drastic moves was to use all available payroll funds to increase teacher salaries. No administrator got anything. This was just one move in several to turn the spotlight on classroom performance. Morale has never been higher among the teachers, but several of the principals, nurtured, like Martin, in the old system, are confused and unhappy. "Loyal service should be rewarded," Martin insists. "My two assistant principals are both terrific, but neither one of them is going to be a front runner for my position when I retire. And that's another thing. I won't be able to get the benefits I'm entitled to, because this new guy is channeling the money elsewhere."

What are Martin's options? Not many. Although, on a values inventory, he said that his wife and his children were his most "cherished possessions," his life-style belies this. He has always put in nine- or ten-hour days, frequently has night meetings with parents and community groups, never turns down an invitation to speak, and faithfully attends every state and local educational conference. He says that golf is his hobby but seldom plays more than once a month. Even his reading is confined to professional and business matters. His wife and children report that he is concerned and loving but largely absent. Raising their six children was Marion's job. Martin's weekends are given over to a time-consuming volunteer assignment with the local congregation of his church. Here he follows the same pattern of hard work, long hours, and faithful service for the rewards of visibility, appreciation, and respect. He is withdrawing now, prepared to "wait it out" until retirement. The new superintendent is sympathetic about Martin's changed position but resents his unwillingness to change. His teachers, who report him as somewhat manipulative, capricious, and undemocratic, are solidly behind the new superintendent.

Another example of getting-secure individuals' vulnerability to external change is the breakup, as a result of an antitrust suit, of the Bell System. Initial reactions to the situation by getting-secure careerists can be discerned in this *Wall Street Journal* report:

> Before "Fateful Friday," a Bell manager was assured slow, steady advancement through a company legendary for not firing managers even during the Depression of the 1930's. For top-flight managers, a larger career path was clear: job moves at local phone companies, a tour of duty at AT&T headquarters, back to the field to eventually head a phone company and then a shot for a top AT&T slot. Under such a system, a former splicer's helper in Grand Forks, N.D., is currently an AT&T vice chairman, and a former Hartford, Connecticut, equipment-maintenance man is the chairman.
>
> "The Bell system has an aura of certainty and fairness about it that hasn't caused a lot of us to think about the future," says William Burns, an executive vice president of the New York Telephone Company and a 28-year Bell employee. "There is a lot of emotional, nonobjective assessing of the future going on right now."
>
> For their part, traditional Bell managers fear that more outsiders will bring in the same arrogance and insensitivity that they saw in the first wave of newcomers. "Is AT&T going to be able to have the same concern for employees?" worries one AT&T executive. "Can you play competitive hardball and still be honorable?" [Bralove, 1982, p. 26].

Although some of the negative labeling attached to the getting-secure career success orientation is clearly unfair and denigrates genuine contributions, another cost to this career anchor is that the person may remain psychologically and emotionally undeveloped. The desire to "be taken care of," though a deep and fundamental human desire that must be met, can lead to damaging dependency and prolonged childlikeness. Part of growing up is learning to live with some degree of ambiguity and also learning how to meet one's own needs. Argyris (1964) has documented the fact that large organizations tend to treat adults like children—overprotecting them and overregulating them into conformity and compliance where these traits are not necessarily best for either the company or the individual. Maccoby (1976) found that his "company men" were chameleon-like, willing to assume a new personality if it seemed appropriate to the situation, constantly comparing themselves to the latest organization fashions. Schein (1978) also found that such individuals, more willing to accept decrees than challenge them, usually assumed that they "had no choice" when given a new assignment, travel responsibilities, or changes in work conditions, even when these changes created personal unhappiness.

Though getting-secure careerists seek relatively stable environments where they can be more productive, their very success may prevent them from finding the inner strength and sense of identity necessary to minimize the inevitable stress of a rapidly changing environment. Getting-secure careerists who continue to insist that they have conventional getting-ahead orientations are at high risk for stress, since they are denying their own strong sense of values, motives, and talents. An "irresistible" job offer may find careerists "knowing" that they should accept it and unable to come up with any good reason for refusing except that "I really don't want it." In such circumstances, they may question their own character and integrity unless they have come to peaceful terms with their own need for security and exchanged loyalties. Knowing how this career success map works is also helpful in circumstances where an internal shakeup alters the comfortably stable "understanding" about how things are. Grief and resentment are natural emotional results, even though they may seem extreme to observers who do not understand this orientation. Retirement can also be extremely difficult emotionally.

Managing Getting-Secure People

Getting-secure careerists have a genuine harmony of interest if their supervisors are also getting-secure people. They know how to wait their turn patiently and feel quite comfortable with orderly progression and seniority. One of their real challenges is working with peers or subordinates who are getting-ahead types who will not wait their turn, are pushy and aggressive about demanding promotions and rewards, and do not match the loyalty of the getting-secure people.

Getting-secure people, oddly enough, actually get along very well with getting-ahead supervisors. Everybody who is moving fast needs loyal, competent subordinates who support performance but do not go after the boss's job. The one potential problem is the built-in personality clash between a getting-ahead supervisor and a getting-secure employee. Although a getting-ahead person needs someone who will make lists, follow up on details, and track projects meticulously, these very characteristics can also irritate a getting-ahead person. Also, the getting-secure careerist is seriously disturbed if the getting-ahead manager seems to be bending and even breaking the rules. In other words, they can easily get on each other's nerves, because they are basically not compatible. That is an uncomfortable situation all around, especially for the getting-secure person who genuinely needs to feel respected by his or her superiors.

Getting-secure people are usually terrific at reading the company culture but tend to deify it to the point where they become company clones. This can cause problems for supervisors trying to make changes, since the getting-secure careerist may be confused about whether to protect old culture and traditions or cooperate with the new. To get the most from these solid citizens or at least prevent some of them from turning into deadwood, a manager needs to address the needs of their internal careers. Communicating a strong culture, clear rules, and clear rewards is a good step. Since these people often express their security needs in altruistic terms, such as the need to provide for their family or the desire to serve others, a good manager will help them align their own interests with values of the company in socially accepted terms. Pleasant work conditions, good hours, agreeable relationships, and a comfortable office are usually more important to them than exciting work, because these all provide a feeling of appreciation and long-term identity with a company or a primary group, probably the most important personal needs that are met by work. The fact that pay, regular raises, and promotions are also extremely important may confuse the manager who thinks of this motivation as primarily reserved for the getting-ahead careerist. It is really not. Pay and raises are important as signs of appreciation and job security, not as primary motivations in themselves, and a getting-secure employee will pay much more attention to benefits than a getting-ahead person will. Also, the predictability of a pay raise may be more important than the amount. Praise from superiors and "tokens" of appreciation such as pens, new office furniture, or a reserved parking stall all speak to their need to believe that they are valued and that their loyalty and steady performance make a real contribution. In exchange, they are willing to work incredibly long hours and put the company's needs first.

They are also adaptable and competent employees, often willing to work just as hard at a job they do not like as at a more desirable position. They accept criticism well as long as they sense that they are still valued and as long as the manager can communicate in detailed and explicit terms what needs to change. But maintaining their sense of order is crucial. These are not good people to upset, because they take it personally. Being asked to engage in ambiguous assignments or to weather some crisis or change often can be very difficult for them. So can changing some of the basic policies of the company. A betrayed getting-secure employee can become angry, even vicious, feeling morally justified in sabotaging people who they feel have "stabbed the company (meaning themselves) in the back."

Thus, it behooves a manager to make expectations clear and then to insist on periodically renegotiating so that flexibility becomes part of the expectation.

In summary, most young workers begin with some feelings of job insecurity: Will they like me? Can I cut the mustard? Am I going to make a fool of myself? And if I get fired, where could I find another job? This kind of insecurity, focused both on the job and on money needs, is common across the board to beginning careerists. Once they have "achieved tenure" by proving they are basically competent and compatible, most careerists are in a position to define their internal career aspirations in a variety of ways.

For getting-secure men in this era when dual-career relationships increasingly free them from the burden of being the sole provider, it may be possible to share the achievement of long-term security with a careerist spouse. If so, a getting-secure careerist can still have all of the advantages of being secure while shifting to a getting-balanced career success orientation, an undiluted plus in letting getting-secure people work on some of the psychological developmental tasks necessary to full personhood.

 SEVEN

Getting Free

Chip is a legend in the intermountain West. At the age of sixteen, he started work in a printshop, and he has had ink under his fingernails for forty years. He has worked for some of the biggest presses in the area and is an awe-inspiring, award-winning typesetter in the almost-obsolete field of hot-metal type. "It's an art," he says proudly. "Anybody who can type can run a photocomp machine, but you have to know what you're doing to use hot metal." Sprawled at the keyboard and feeling the rhythm of each individual letter falling into place, line by line, he seems in a trance. "I can tell by the rhythm if it's the wrong letter coming down," he says without boasting. It is probably no coincidence that the favorite recreation of this trim, mustachioed man in his fifties is dancing. Editors pay tribute to his skill. "You can count on the fingers of one hand the number of genuine typographical errors he'll make," says one, "but he's hell to proofread. When he makes a mistake, it will still look right—like *mountain* instead of *maintain.*"

He works out of the basement of his home in a modest neighborhood, setting type and composing pages for prize-winning books. His garage is full of cannibalized parts from old Linotypes, stockpiled against the day when he can no longer get parts for his working museum. He has no assistants. He scrubs his own type, pulls his own proofs, and melts his own lead. No press could attract him permanently or hold him for long. "I'd spend all day bucking their rules and all night doing my work," he confesses. In a short-lived partnership, he recalled, "that jerk never got anything done for telling me how to do *my* work. I can't stand someone looking over my shoulder. I got out. I want to work, not argue. And I want to do it my way." A hard-core, dyed-in-the-wool individualist, he has the corner on a small market—presses and editors who want the indefinable beauty of a hand-composed book or journal.

The Getting-Free Personality

Chip is the triple-distilled essence of a getting-free careerist. They are hard to work with, impossible to work for, slippery as eels to supervise and manage, and infinitely resourceful at getting their own way. Everybody likes some independence in their work, but the getting-free careerist ranks it slightly above eating and sleeping. They are not the ski bums who put up with driving tour buses all summer to finance a winter in the snow. Work is important to them as a career. They are usually dazzlingly competent, willing to work hard to become experts in a valued specialty, and skilled at bartering their expertise for their freedom. For a long time during the fifties and sixties, they looked like a dying breed, until the dropout culture of the same period ironically got translated economically into a wave of small-businesspeople who like it and are willing to pay their dues to make a go of it.

One of these new entrepreneurs on the international scene is Grant, an Australian studying at the European Institute for Business Administration. He did not even interview with European companies, because he had his sights set clearly on venture-capitalist firms in Australia. He had a master's degree in chemistry from an Australian university and had worked in a chemical company where he had been given many opportunities at the managerial ladder. He hated it. He could not stand the rules, the structure, the confinement. He wanted to own his own business, not because he wanted the thrill of entrepreneurship but because he wanted space. He rapidly acquired a reputation as a love-'em-and-leave-'em charmer who established intimate relationships quickly but moved on with equal speed when they became too intense—"smothery," as he put it. He wants to be a small-businessperson with a lot of control over his own turf with the right to spend time snorkling and surfing. He saw his life as clearly divided into spaces—work time, family time, personal time. But he was not a getting-balanced man. What seemed to motivate him was control, not balance.

Autonomy may be the most important emerging value among workers in the 1980s. Recently, Schein (1982) found that 20 percent of the consultants he studied put autonomy at the top of their values list and that the percentage went up as the sample became more diverse. Yankelovich (1981) reported that the late 1970s saw more than seven of every ten Americans claiming that personal freedom was an important part of their success formula. Guyon (1981) documents the move of many new high-tech research parks toward highly individualized dress patterns, telephone directories that list by the first name, flexible scheduling, leaves of absence, sabbaticals, and at-home work stations. It is not clear whether the new companies are fostering this work pattern because they have found it more productive or whether they are altering traditional work patterns to attract the kind of worker they want. In either case, the institutionalization of such support systems is usually sufficiently appealing to careerists that they will probably spread them wider by bargaining for them in new job settings. This all goes along with the argument in Chapter One that the work force is also becoming increasingly pluralistic.

Getting-free individuals are definitely cosmopolitans, just as getting-secure persons are definitely regionalists (Gouldner, 1957–58). In many ways, they are polar opposites, but both share a career success map that focuses on the context of work, one that supports their deep-seated psychological values. Getting-free individuals share with getting-high careerists an insistence that work be challenging and interesting, but they would not sacrifice their personal liberty for exciting work.

How to Get Free

Choose Your Work Setting. It goes almost without saying that managers and getting-free careerists have a built-in conflict. Managers want to manage. It is their nature. Getting-free career-

ists want to avoid being managed. That is *their* nature. It is a
kind of elaborate cat-and-mouse game where the rules are always changing. Finding a work setting with autonomy built in
will save a lot of grief from the beginning. Going into business
for yourself is one of the ways of solving the problem. Chip's
decision to move into his basement ten years ago probably limited the area of his influence, but it certainly gave him clear
boundaries of control. He was in charge there. Large corporations can also handle some getting-free people. For example,
Digital Equipment, known as loosely structured and ad hoc,
would have a lot of advantages for a getting-free person that another company, such as IBM, with its clear hierarchy, company
goals, and unified supervision, could not offer. Legal firms, universities, and medical institutions may have very tidy flow
charts, but the real organization may be as complicated as a
plate of spaghetti, with each meatball representing a private em-
pire. These "organized anarchies" provide a more or less stable
structure with highly trained professionals working as private
contractors within them.

Organizations that are loose structural confederations of
people and units seem to be more appropriate for people with
this internal career success map. It is easier to find a niche in
which to become an indispensable expert when the whole enterprise is loosely coupled than it is when it is tightly coordinated. It is easier to redefine fewer and more informal rules to
meet your own needs than it is to find ways around a host of
bureaucratic constraints that are rigorously enforced. Likewise,
those companies that must depend for their existence on uncertain information will usually require experts to produce,
manipulate, and interpret such data. These so-called knowl-
edge-based enterprises will probably have greater tolerance for
getting-free careerists because of the value they attach to such
knowledge and their dependence on and experience with professional norms and values. It will also be easier in such settings
to find and develop an area of expertise.

Another area that attracts people with this career success
orientation is the "semiprofessions," identified by Etzioni
(1969) as public school teachers, social workers, nurses, and

engineers. They occupy a halfway region between the person whose expertise must be respected and accepted because it is basically incomprehensible and the domain of public information, where the layperson generally understands the knowledge base and procedures. Semiprofessionals' knowledge is not extremely specialized or extremely systematic. Their codes of ethics are not as distinct as those of professionals. They do not enjoy as much authority over clients or have as many "class" privileges. Most importantly, they can be managed, while professionals are subject to peer review rather than rules and regulations.

"As long as I turn in X number of billable hours a month," says Martine, an attorney, "nobody asks me whether I'm at the library, the courtroom, or the golf course. Only secretaries know who goes on vacation when. About six of us get together for lunch regularly and hash over cases, but I'll swear I've read in the paper about three members of the firm that I've never seen at the office." Karen, a French teacher, finds the same freedom once she walks into her classroom. "I sit in a faculty meeting on the point of dropping over dead while we're hassling through lunchroom duty or discipline problems or something else like that. I wish I had more say in selecting my own curriculum materials and could get more budget for computer tutoring programs. I also wish the principal and central-office specialists would stop trying to impose their schedules and programs on me. But I'd never consider leaving teaching. When it's just me and twenty-eight students and French, I can fly. It's my world. Summers off are pretty nice, too."

Other companies, particularly those depending on accurate state-of-the-art information and expertise to survive, woo the best and wrap the organization around them. I consult with an innovative computer company that has set the ambitious goal of recruiting the top 10 percent of the nation's graduating engineers and computer experts and retaining the top 10 percent of their employees with handpicked rewards, dazzling retraining opportunities, and all the new toys they can play with. A research-centered university will "buy specialists" for its faculty, give them their choice of ivory-tower accoutrements, and expect them to become the world's greatest in their field. A teaching university, however, with less emphasis on research and publication, will supervise its people more closely and not give them the same latitude in setting up their own work conditions.

Pay Your Dues. Proving that you can do the work and perform to specifications is an absolute prerequisite to any kind of negotiating leverage. This means getting the right kind of training and early job experience. Usually, people who sense their needs for space and solitary expertise begin in childhood the pattern of choices that enables them to live out their dreams. Rene, a future French executive I met in my career management courses in INSEAD, comes from a bourgeois family. His father is in business, and his mother teaches mathematics in a secondary school. He launched himself well with a highly marketable engineering degree from a prestigious secondary school and came to INSEAD for an even more marketable M.B.A. degree. His family, though not religious, had stressed that good work is always rewarded, that the family must remain close, that one should try to solve one's own problems, and that one should not judge others. It had been a quiet and sheltered life for him and his one sister, very much centered in their comfortable Toulouse home within its walled garden. "Until I was fifteen," he recalls, "my parents had almost no contacts outside the extended family. Life consisted of work and quiet weekends with their children, when they either stayed home or had picnics, walked in the country, or drove to the sea." Rene liked solitude. He liked being first in the class, not because of the prestige but because it made him different and justified his solitariness.

Although he liked the humanities, he chose math and then computer science. Data processing was more than a technique to him. It had intellectual, humanist, and societal implications that he enjoyed. In ten years, he hopes to head up his own data-processing consulting company, one that is small (ten to fifteen employees) and on the experimental edge of developing new techniques and strategies. He also wants international exposure. His ideas of future home life (he does not plan to marry the woman with whom he is now living for another three years) mirror his past: two children, a house in a garden, a wife who has her own career, but one that is flexible enough to allow her to spend time with him. Balance and "harmony" are impor- ✓ tant principles, but he plans to build them into his work: rather than taking extended vacations, for example, he will schedule two or three days at the beginnings or ends of trips.

Paradoxically, considering his high autonomy needs, Rene also is attracted to large bureaucratic settings where the structure, title, prestige, and resources will give him a backdrop to play against. Perhaps he senses his own need for order and looks to an organization to meet it for him. His career success map is still unclear, but he represents a rare case of coupling getting free and getting ahead, in that order—usually these two orientations are diametrically opposed. The fact that his next-highest score after these two is on getting secure simply reflects these ambiguities. Although Rene's degree of self-knowledge and his considerable talents auger future success, there is always the possibility that real work experience will alter the degree to which he feels he can express these three conflicting orientations.

Another example is "Invisible Ivan," a man in his fifties with a prestigious appointment as a small-group specialist at a midwestern university. He racked up a star-studded academic career. His undergraduate and postdoctoral work were done at the best universities. His publications list goes on for pages. His university gloated when it was able to snare him and considered that he had repaid the very fancy salary they gave him by giving them an almost-instant international reputation. The nickname came later—after tenure, after establishment, after automatic name recognition. He never misses the faculty meetings, where his incisive insights and articulate analyses continue to make major contributions to the running of the college, but any attempt to appoint him to a committee finds him suddenly elusive unless it is a conspicuous project with a prominent payoff. "Just enough," one colleague observes, "to be sure we don't forget him." He is not above promising and then not delivering, making appointments and then not showing up for them, telling his secretary that he is in a meeting while he is really off on a private consultation. A junior member of the faculty complained bitterly, "I can't read the guy. He's supposed to be an expert in interpersonal relations, right? How can that be? He lies. He doesn't show up. If you ask him where he was, he dumps all over you. Sure, he's bright. Sure, he's competent. But you can't count on him."

The same junior faculty member was, a month later, dazed and dazzled by a typical "Invisible Ivan" performance. After missing committee meetings for almost the whole semester, Ivan had swept in, put his finger on an impasse that had stymied the group for three meetings, and suggested a solution "that was nothing short of brilliant. We'd been slogging away trying to shift around the pigeonholes that we had so they'd work. He showed up with a whole new system; and, even from the preliminary explanation, we could all see that it would work better than anything we'd been able to come up with in three months." Eventually, Ivan's department found that the best way to deal with him was to create a separate subdepartment just for him. The university still gets the prestige, Ivan still gets his space, but nobody has to take on the thankless task of trying to deal with him from day to day. This kind of consideration and reward does not drop out of the sky. Ivan gets it because he is good—very good. But he paid his dues to get there, and the university thought it was buying a getting-ahead type of the first order instead of someone who could cover his strategy so flawlessly.

During the dues-paying process, the getting-free career strategist puts together the perfect portfolio: the right publications, the right projects, the right recommendations, the right work experiences, the right skills and honors. It is this accumulation of skills and abilities that separates "he's a maverick but we put up with him" from "he may be bright but we can't afford his eccentricity."

Keep One Step Ahead of the Game. For the getting-free careerist, knowledge is power and expertise is freedom. That means that he or she has to keep one jump ahead of the managers who are hovering over their shoulders, trying to figure out how to "get my brain onto the computer," as one put it. Chip may be able to keep a monopoly on his art because it is not in high demand right now. In situations where the horizon of information is constantly being swallowed up by advances in the field, the careerist needs a long-term plan. "I need to know something nobody else does," one of them put it. "I've got to be the expert on something new."

"I made my reputation in economic history," one professor explains, "but that was thirty years ago. Since then, I've become the expert on the federal impact on the state from World War I on, and now I'm well established as a historian of the state's minority ethnic groups. Other people are doing significant work on the history of women in the state, but I think I've got a couple of new ideas to throw into the pot." That may be her next step.

Jay, an elementary school principal in a small western city, is, according to his superintendent, "one of the best administrators and instructional leaders in the state. As long as I keep my hands off." Jay explains, "I know the court and the rules. This city turned down the last three tax proposals flat, but it was willing to divert capital funds earmarked for buildings to an experimental year-round program. I mean, really experimental. There are only a couple of schools in the country with this kind of year-round program, and I've got people lined up to observe outcomes like vultures on the telephone lines. If I can pull it off, this school district is going to be known across the nation."

His superintendent spelled out "in excruciating detail" the objectives, the time limitations, and the constraints. "Now," he says, "my job is to keep out of his way and let him run his own show. I field questions and have this lovely little canned speech that views with hope the potential of this innovative blah blah blah but also has a serious paragraph about the potential consequences of failure. After all," the superintendent remarks with no trace of humor, "when this year is over, I might have to fire the guy." That is all right with Jay. "I like someone who is tough on results and loose on process." What if the superintendent is replaced by someone Jay cannot work with? He shrugs. "I'll just go back to my classroom. They can't touch me. The parents would kill them if they tried to tie my hands. I've had more recognized talent emerge from my classroom— well, out of my schools—than any place in the state."

Hoard, Control, and Manipulate Scarce Information. The getting-free careerist is in a privileged position. Colleagues do not like to see someone else getting the privileges, and organizations do not like to grant them. Whatever it is that makes you indispensable is the magic key you must never lose. Hank, a troubleshooter in an East Coast factory that produces top-of-the-line car bodies for one of the large auto companies, has it down to a fine art. A blue-collar worker from the assembly lines, he has a talent amounting to genius for being able to spot and innovatively fix assembly-line trouble spots.

"Not only fix," conceded his supervisor, "but move them a whole quantum jump ahead in terms of productivity. Look at these production figures for the last year. Headed straight for the cellar. And the factory was headed straight for the trash heap, our productivity was so low." He tapped the production chart showing a nosediving line and another one that took off upward at an acute angle. "This is where Hank took over. He didn't take his clothes off for three weeks. I never saw him asleep or talked to anyone who saw him asleep. He redesigned three sections and built half of it himself. We haven't been able to walk without clanking ever since from all the medals they hung on us. We delivered some great speeches about team commitment and mutually selected goals, but basically it was eyewash meaning Hank Furness."

What project was Hank working on now? The manager became very gloomy. Hank was off swimming with schools of porpoises. Fascinated by porpoise "language patterns," he also has a modest international reputation among marine biologists, has studied with some of the most important researchers, and has actually learned to swim with porpoiselike movements so that he can approach a school and mingle with them, listening for various sounds. "I keep leaving messages for him at this marina," says the manager. "He hasn't returned any of my calls."

Hank has acquired idiosyncratic immunity because of his

irreplaceable ability. In a conservative and formal company, he shows up to work—when he comes—in a beat-up Datsun pickup. Divorced, he moves from woman to woman, picking up speed if anyone begins to talk about permanency. He lives on the verge of being fired, but he has an uncanny intuition that governs his timing. He will return his manager's call just twenty-four hours before the manager would set the machinery in motion for an official reprimand. He will doodle, divert, and cause trouble for months, but then he will pull the chestnuts out of the fire. The managers must defer to his specialized knowledge, and he uses it to wring special privileges out of them. A couple of highly placed sponsors in the parent plant protect him from the hasty decision of a manager who might be exasperated beyond endurance. They know his record. They have seen the flying colors he displayed as he completed all of the troubleshooting courses they have come up with. They know how impressively he has performed in their weekend degree program. They have wooed him with promotions, raises, prestige. They begged him to write his own ticket to many managerial positions. None of it tempts him. He has what he wants.

Enlarge Your Peer Group. Another strategy that works well for academic or professional getting-free people is to acquire a national or international reputation, becoming a "cosmopolitan" rather than a "local." Such people show up in large corporations as well as academic settings. Their chief identification is with the profession (legal historian, for example) rather than with their institution, and they look to their peers in professional organizations rather than their immediate supervisors for guidelines, validations, and professional standards.

Christine is an associate professor of theoretical linguistics in Florida. Her ability to cultivate international connections paid off. "I got invitations to conferences in Germany, Scotland, Hong Kong, and Australia, all in the same year," she reported gleefully. "My department chair went exactly one place —to the regional meeting in Atlanta." It took some adroit balancing "to be sure the department knew that my activities were reflecting credit on them rather than that I was leaving them behind"; but, once that barrier was passed, she sailed through tenure review, and it was "somewhat taken for granted that I should have an easy classload to accommodate my research, writing, and conferences."

When the Chips Are Down, Come Through. You can be an eccentric and buck the system for just so long. When the pressure is on, you have to come through. This means that the bottom line for a getting-free person is competence, the capacity for hard work, determination, and, if at all possible, brilliance verging on the genius. "Invisible Ivan" is probably safe in his specially created department and his twice-a-year coups. So is Hank the miracle worker, although, ironically enough, if he improves productivity too much and the plant is no longer under pressure to produce, some manager, irritated over the edge by Hank's antics, is going to decide that he is dispensable.

Benefits and Costs

Benefits. Running a one-person show means that it can be the greatest show on earth—nonstop. "When things are working well," says Judy, a freelance writer, "I'm supremely happy, so happy I sometimes want to laugh or cry. If people were looking at me, I'm sure I'd be glowing like an electric light bulb. It's indecent to enjoy your work so much. I think of people trudging dutifully off at 7:35 to catch their buses, and I can feel the blackness just clamp down on me. I couldn't do it, not if I were starving to death."

Other getting-free people are equally eloquent about the pleasures of autonomy, the creativity of freedom, the exuberance of independence. Don, married to an architect who runs a one-person office, says, "Sometimes I worry about her because she works so hard, but her work makes her happy. It also makes her a very interesting person." Hank's associates agree. "You never know when or where he's going to turn up. If you want to give him a birthday party, you'd better keep the cake in the freezer, since he's likely to call you from Puerto Rico and tell you he can't make it. But when he's here, he's a great friend." The husband of one highly autonomous university professor reported, "I don't get to be with Sarah as much as I'd like; but compared to other women I know, she's worth waiting for."

Getting-free people, moving on the margins of their profession or deepening the refinements of their craft, are growing
people. They feel both challenged and satisfied by their work,
usually have the kind of stubborn integrity that comes with the
lonely independence they prize, and know how to motivate
themselves—sometimes a rare trait in a world that seems full of
manipulative rewards.

Costs. However, the spotlight never goes off on a one-
person show, and it is easy to turn into a workaholic. Martine's
husband observes, "When she's preparing a case, I never see her.
Even when she's home, she's not there. Her mind is still wrestling
through the problem. I've stopped taking it personally, but
being in the same room with her can be pretty lonely at times
like that." Furthermore, the freedom that getting-free people
work so hard for is its own greatest punishment as well as its
greatest reward. The need for personal autonomy is, in a sense,
antirelationship. Many getting-free people struggle painfully and
unsuccessfully with intimate relationships.

For example, Barclay, a movie producer in the unlikely
location of New Hampshire, operates out of a 200-year-old
country house. He keeps the blinds drawn on his south-facing
study—not because of the sun but because, one mile away, he
can see another house. "I need space," he says. "Lots of space."
Barclay inherited a substantial sum of money from his grandfather, a stockbroker, and it has underwritten his quest "for the
perfect vehicle to embody the perfect idea." His work is imagi-
native and daring: a teenager being lured into suicide by a cun-
ning and crazed stepfather, an Austrian countess who discovers
that she is the product of an incestuous union, a honeymooning
couple who discover that the husband will probably die of
chemical poisoning. In each case, he has written the script himself after monumental quarrels with a screenwriter. In each case,
the movies have been low budget, even though investors were
initially interested. "It has to be mine," says Barclay. "I can't
let other people clutter up what I'm trying to do."

He and his wife have been separated on occasion, because
Barclay periodically feels smothered by the demands of marriage and two children. "If I could be different, I probably
would," he says. "I love what I'm doing, but the price is high.

How long will the money hold out? How long will Susi and the kids be around? On bad days I'm haunted by the nightmare that I won't be able to hold out long enough to break into the industry in a big enough way to be taken seriously but that I'll lose everything else that I value while I'm trying."

Judy, the freelance writer, talks about the difficulty of creating a sense of identity. "Who are my colleagues? Who can I go to lunch with and talk about the rotten day I'm having? There's not even a category in the yellow pages for the kind of work I do. If I were to disappear, what could they put in my obituary that would make sense to anyone else? I know that I'd start feeling smothered if I had to show up to work on time and sit in committee meetings; but sometimes on a long project, I start feeling transparent. As if I'm not there."

For still others, the strain of having to continually acquire new expertise gets painful. "I burn out a lot," admits Adam cheerfully. Assistant professor at a prestigious eastern university and head of its achievement motivation project, he wrote his dissertation about a high-achieving tribe in an African nation who seemed to corner the nation's business. "But I couldn't take all the hoops I had to jump through to get tenure," he says. On the verge of what was, by every standard, a brilliant academic career, he checked out and, thanks to an influential mentor in Hong Kong, became a management consultant in international development. "The intellectuals come up with all these plans for developing nations," he says. "They look gorgeous on paper, but no one knows how to make them work. Well, Lyndon and I do." The clients come from the top: the Agency for International Development, the World Bank, developing nations. Thanks to his fluent Spanish, he consults frequently in Latin America and has a lot of contacts from a three-year stint in Managua during the Samosa regime. It was a highly profitable three years. With the proceeds, he and his wife, Micky, bought a beautiful canyon home in the California hills where they take their five children out for rides in the donkey cart at dusk.

He is gone for up to eight weeks at a time consulting and drags back, as he says, "with not much left. It couldn't work without Micky. She's incredibly bright and energetic, holds everything together, and provides the day-to-day continuity with the children while I'm in and out. And she's getting her own degree on top of everything." His treatment for his burnout is to putter around the garden, take over the meals, tune deeply into his children's lives, and "dust off the donkey cart." After a few weeks, he is energized again and ready to go. "It's lucky that I'm in high demand and usually can pick and choose jobs," he says soberly. "If I weren't so well paid, I'd have to put in longer stretches, and there wouldn't be enough of me left to scrape off the floor after a solid year of that."

Autonomy is on the rise nationally. In 1978, one opinion poll established that 60 percent of Americans considered marriage "temporary"; in the preceding decade, the number of unmarried couples living together in the United States more than doubled (Nickles, 1981, p. 18). Long-term marriages may be a national casualty if the trend toward autonomy continues. Carol Gilligan's (1982) work also indicates that men value autonomy more than women do, whether the reasons are biological or sociological. If this pattern is true, with women focusing on connectedness more than autonomy, the stage may be set for built-in conflicts to increase. An alternative pattern, both on the job and in personal relationships, finds both partners maintaining their own orbits with little overlap. Although such an arrangement meets the autonomy needs of both spouses/colleagues, it can hardly be called a partnership.

One of the undiscussed hazards of this career success orientation is that some people are not in a position to achieve autonomy. Rather than mobilizing their options and working toward the kind of freedom they crave, they fret away hours worth of energy in rebelling against their current work situation, a state of affairs that wins them no kind looks from their managers. Furthermore, rebellion, while barely tolerable in teenagers, is not endearing in adults. Another real disadvantage of an autonomous orientation at work is that it is hard to defend your territory when you are not present. Acquiring turf takes a lot of follow-through, negotiation, and bargaining. Ivan has probably passed his zenith of influence, isolated as he is in his own division. Hank needs to remain valued to keep getting those special privileges, but if he insists on being absent so much, sooner or later someone may find a way to displace him. And still another disadvantage of getting free is that, to the outside, you can look like a slave to your job anyway. I have a cousin in Idaho with an entrepreneurial bent who has parlayed his farm into an impressive agribusiness that grosses between five and six million dollars a year. He was one of the first to figure out how to turn dry farms into productive land and has patented several inventions and small machines. There is no question that he is in charge as the boss of his farm, the master of his life space. The disadvantage from my perspective is that it frequently takes him seventeen hours a day seven days a week to maintain it.

Managing Getting-Free People

People who like to manage and people who like getting free are absorbed in mutually incompatible activities. Performance reviews, regulations, check-ups, and check-ins drive a getting-free type crazy. "Invisible Ivan" deliberately keeps an erratic schedule around the office, shows up to teach his classes, and otherwise disappears for days at a time. Department chairs who try to involve him in the routine tasks of administration find their frustration levels climbing higher and higher. One approach that worked, however, was to nail him down on one megaproject that needed his exact set of skills, specify what needed to be done by when, and then watch the calendar as Ivan disappeared for a week, returning later with a wonderful tan and an ingenious proposal, which he single-handedly worked through the committee.

Chip, the bohemian typesetter, refuses to give any clues that will let designers or paste-up people schedule project hours. When asked "When will it be ready?" he invariably answers, "Oh, it's coming along." If pressed for a delivery date, he sidesteps neatly into complaints about how late the copy was delivered, what shape it was in, and who has required what number of unacceptable corrections, until the questioner is glad to escape. Experienced editors, however, know that he will then appear with a stack of galleys within twenty-four hours.

Hank's life-style seems enviable to many of his co-workers, but they admit, "I wouldn't even try to get away with what he does." Management has made it clear that he is a special case, tolerated but not approved. Thus, his "pollution" of the company's culture is minimal, and Hank does not become someone to emulate, even if the first reaction is envy. Furthermore, despite his contempt for the caution he sees as endemic in managers, Hank plays fair by his rules. He pushes the system regularly, but he has never broken his implied contract to come through in a pinch, no matter what else may be going on. Also, he has never allowed himself to be wooed away by other industrialists, aware of his wild talent.

French teacher Karen dutifully served her stint as chairperson for her high school's language department, a rotating assignment, but at a suggestion that she consider thinking about the principalship, which will be falling vacant in a couple of years, she stared at the questioner incredulously. "What would I want to do that for?" she asked. "What fun would *that* be?"

Getting-free types need to be cagey about being inveigled into commitments that get them overinvolved. Situations that require a lot of collaboration and dependency will make them ultraclaustrophobic, and they soon learn to avoid situations rather than accept commitments that they will try to weasel out of within a few weeks. It is relatively easy for them to say no to assignments that they see as "nice but not necessary" to keep their credit rating okay in their organization. It is also easy for them to turn down promotions and raises that would have the manager who is offering them slavering.

Managers with imagination could offer a getting-free person such attractive options as contract work or project work—both of which are one-time commitments rather than long-term relationships—merit pay, promotions that do not lead to encumbering jobs, and rewards such as prizes, medals, and recommendations that commend a project without requiring a future commitment. Another effective strategy in working with many of these people is to explicitly identify the objective along with the deadline, the budget, and the methods that must *not* be used (based on concrete historical evidence), and then leave them alone to figure out the way to meet the objective within the constraints. Most getting-free people consider the application of creativity, ingenuity, and what another careerist would consider inordinate amounts of hard work to be a price worth paying for the fun of doing it their way. Probably these employees are not going to identify their orientations early or explicitly at any point. The problems of managing someone who does not want to be a team player can be a real pain. Still, for the manager who is willing to find and feed them interesting projects and has the flexibility of allowing them to do it in their own way, the rewards are considerable.

In summary, then, getting-free people run on freedom and are willing to do almost anything to get it. Sometimes they can carve their territory out of a large corporation, holding off the demands of managers for conformity and compliance with a barrier of irreplaceable expertise. At other times, they can find their niche in medical or legal associations where it is assumed that each person will operate for himself or herself. Small businesses and crafts also draw people who have this tough streak of independence. They are good people to get to know—creative, growing, interesting, and in tune with what makes them happy. The problem is that they are sometimes hard to get to know. Part of their success orientation keeps them aloof from truly collegial relations, suspicious of collaboration, claustrophobic about closeness. Their personal relationships sometimes suffer, and they pay the price in loneliness.

Some people with this career success orientation can modify their craving for freedom and let getting balanced serve as a back-up orientation. They learn to cooperate and become competent at dealing with interdependent situations. Others fall back on looking like getting-ahead types until they are far enough along in the system to negotiate for more space. Michael Blumenthal, former chief executive officer of Bendix Corporation and secretary of the treasury, was probably reflecting this perspective when he declared: "Power is excelling in the use of my talents without any restrictions on them" (Korda, 1975, pp. 39-40). A lucky few can keep work and personal lives in separate compartments, playing their getting-free game at work and rejoicing in a rich relationship life off the job. Needless to say, however, this is a tough act to pull off. It takes a lot of energy to remain autonomous on the job, and few organizational settings encourage mavericks. It is even harder to draw a firm line between work time and relationship time. But for those who need the lonely space to create and cannot get enough of it, the satisfaction of contemplating what they have made and pronouncing it good is a sensation of success that they would not trade.

 EIGHT

Getting High

One of the most exciting people who walked into my seminar on career planning last spring was Gaye M., a rangy brunette with close-cropped hair, a spectacular tan, and a glowing smile. She was there as personnel program director in a large government agency. She had transferred from a position as a technical director in the air force because management of some of the newest aerospace projects had not come her way. An intermediate stop had been at the State Department, where she found that the Ivy League types had their own political ingroup. She was too impatient to pay the dues necessary to break into that group, so when a job in one of the intelligence agencies opened up, she jumped for it.

Among her conditions for taking the job were that she receive an agent's training and that she be considered eligible for missions as they came up. She had recently returned from a training mission where she had, she reported grinning in obvious delight, been helicoptered up the Amazon and dropped into the water. "I really got to test what they'd taught me in jungle and underwater schools," she said. "The only thing I've done recently that's been more fun was a nighttime mission over the North African desert, where we had to parachute in with our equipment. In blackface." This fascinating autobiographical information emerged out of a late-night conversation where she entertained a half dozen of us after class at her apartment. She had cooked a Javanese meal, demonstrated sufi dancing, and showed us two or three pieces of Etruscan pottery she had dug up herself on an expedition, delivering an impressive lecture on all three as she went. She also speaks three or four languages, climbs mountains, skydives, and hang glides and has recently taken up oil painting.

She was a stimulating seminar participant. She grasped the basic concepts almost before they were out of my mouth and offered some examples and insights in an illuminating exchange. But when one of the other participants asked for clarification and I needed to review some of the material, Gaye sighed, shifted in her seat, and began drumming her fingers on the table. Pacing the presentation to the rest of the group—no dummies but just not in her league—was a strain for me as a teacher. Allowing her to turn the seminar into a discussion of the idea and applications, while occasionally wonderful, was also problematical when she wanted to debate or discuss a new angle before the rest of the group had grasped the main point. She is a getting-high careerist, absorbed in the demands of her work, insatiable for learning new concepts and adding new skills. She thrives on interesting and exciting work, and when she cannot get her thrills at work, she flings herself into a new hobby or starts looking around for a new job.

The Getting-High Personality

Getting-high people often work in large firms, putting up with the bureaucracy of law firms or the military, because those places provide exciting work. That is their bottom line: exciting work. Yes, they need freedom for it, as do getting-free people, but getting-free people will not swap their freedom even for exciting work, while getting-high people will exchange large chunks of freedom for a great project.

Getting high is an addictive work drug that manifests itself in four main ways among careerists. Some, like Gaye, are absorbed by the techniques of their chosen profession. These technicians turn on by exercising their talents. They build their identity around their expertise and are endlessly fascinated with the content of their work. Shortcuts are unthinkable to them, and they are unsparing of colleagues who cut corners. If they cannot constantly refine their expertise and add new skills to their repertoire, they become bored and fretful.

A second group of getting-high people is the entrepreneurs. They share with the technicians a passion for the adventure of their work, but they are less enthralled with making a problem come out exactly right than they are with the thrill of the risk taking—the adrenalin rush of leaping into a new project and gambling that they can make it work. They are innovative, intuitive, and competitive. Colleagues and competitors complain that they have a sixth sense about creating a new product or a new market for an old product, for revolutionizing a production system, or for exploiting an old idea in a new way. Often they are small-businesspeople or in start-up companies. Sometimes they are in large organizations that have the vision and the resources to turn a gifted entrepreneur loose to make or break a division—a phenomenon called "intrapreneurship."

Someone whose career I will be interested in following is a former student at the European Institute of Business Administration (INSEAD) in France. George has studied economics and law at the University of London, a very good school but not in the Oxford/Cambridge category. His academic record was excellent, and he came to INSEAD in Fontainebleau from a prestigious position with a major accounting firm, but he lacked the most desirable family background. No British executive of the "correct" class that I ever interviewed admitted that such a thing could have any bearing on a candidate's desirability—in fact, they went out of their way to deny it—while they simultaneously told tales of "knife-and-fork" tests where dinner conversation, appearance, and table manners came under scrutiny at certain points in the hiring or advancement process.

George, on the other hand, was frank about the importance of class and family connections. "I feel constrained by my social background in a class-conscious society like the U.K., and I don't feel readily accepted or have the access to funds that goes with being a member of a tightly knit social group." Aware of these disadvantages and determined to change his class position, he had a strong commitment to earning enough money and acquiring the kinds of responsible positions that would enable him to mentor other capable young people from his same background. His heroes are Dick Whittington (thrice lord mayor of

London) and his clan, the plucky urchins who rose to respectability and fortune by their wits and diligence, and Disraeli, a
Jew who became England's prime minister. ("He climbed to the
top of a greasy pole," George says admiringly.) He also sub-
scribes to a reinforcing series of beliefs: "The more you learn,
the more you earn. Hard work is the key to success. It is better
to be poor and honest than rich and dishonest. Money doesn't
bring happiness, but it sure helps. The world is basically hostile,
so learn to rely on yourself." Although he is now single, his
plan calls for marriage in his late thirties to a noncareerist wife
who will devote herself to the children, with whom he plans to
spend a great deal of affectionate time as well. Getting them
launched at a higher level than he began at is the chief task that
he sets for himself as a future father.

George cannot control his social class, but his choice of
university training followed by earning his prestigious master's
degree from INSEAD is a correct reading of what is valued by
the big British multinational firms. He is a witty and easy conversationalist who can discourse knowledgeably on almost any
subject. He dresses expensively and conservatively, grooms carefully, looks distinguished, and knows how to project himself as
a member of the executive club. He looks very much like a
getting-ahead candidate. However, in taking the career success
orientation test and the career assessment interview, George
shows himself as deeply conflicted. He wants the rewards of
money, status, and class. He does not want to put up with the
foolishness of organizational life. Although his getting-ahead
score was 10 (the top of the scale), getting free and getting high
both ranked 9. This conflict is serious, even for someone early
in his career. His solution is to become an entrepreneur, and he
is launched right now on a search for the right idea. His energy,
ideas, and scrappy determination to make it predict a successful future for him, but he does not have the necessary connections or the capital. He plans to go back into his accounting
firm as a consultant, looking very much like a getting-ahead
executive, but with the private agenda of finding investors, partners, and a product from which he can springboard into his own
business. In ten years, he plans to own a number of shipping

and retailing firms with his brother and brother-in-law. Ultimately, he wants to own his own banking and financial services
group. He dreams of owning a townhouse in Georgia and a
country house in East Kent, attending the Royal Opera House,
fishing at Rye, reading the works of Jung, studying alternative
medicine, endowing a nursing school in India, and mentoring
disadvantaged but ambitious youngsters. The diversity and mix
sound very much like those of successful entrepreneurs looking
back on their lives at the age of sixty-five. It will be interesting
to see whether George can actually pull it off.

A third type of getting-high person is the artist familiar to
us all from movies and plays, the painter who starves willingly
in his Left Bank attic, oblivious to the world, his body's needs,
or the marketability of the vision behind his eyelids that he un-
ceasingly tries to transfer to canvas. Although the technical aspect of the art—performing, plastic, or expressive—is important,
much more important is the feeling. In fact, artists, like entrepreneurs, lose interest in their product quite rapidly. If a poem
is on everyone's lips, that is fine; but the reward was writing the
poem, not its popularity.

A fourth type of getting-high person is the idealogues, the
men and women driven by an ideal of service or a vision of social betterment that mobilizes their talents, sensitizes them to a
range of issues only dimly apparent to others, and rewards them
with a satisfaction for their acts of helping and improving that
sometimes drives a permanent wedge between them and those
who turn on to money and status.

For instance, Gavin, a brilliant corporation lawyer with
whom I did some career counseling, had grown up in a home
where Christian service was not simply an ideal but a way of
life. "More nights than not," he recalls, "I shared my brother's
bed because Dad or Mom had found someone who needed a
place to stay for the night. I was probably ten or eleven before
I realized that not everybody automatically invited friends,
strangers—anybody—home to dinner if it was getting close to
mealtime."

He saw his own law degree from a prestigious eastern university as a complex and specialized tool he had been entrusted with. Possessing it made him, in his view, responsible to work for the same kinds of changes for social betterment that his parents had consistently made on an individual level all their lives. A stint in Washington, D.C., with an international law firm broadened his sensitivities and deepened his commitment; but his wife, who had put up with the years of sacrifice and postponement typical of student marriages, felt a real longing to return to her home city, where she could settle into her place in a network of professional relatives and friends who were also raising children and who were starting to reap the rewards of vacation condominiums, air-conditioned cars, and dance lessons for the children. Gavin could not call Lisa's desire unreasonable; and his high-priced talents meant they could start out with the dream home Lisa had mentally furnished from the ground up to comfort herself while he was in law school.

Five years later, they had the house, the condo, the network, and two more children. Lisa was happier than she had ever been, and Gavin was more miserable. "All I do is make money!" he exclaimed, pounding one fist into the other. "Sometimes I have this dream that somebody I know—I can't see the face but I know that I know the person—is drowning, reaching out a hand. I'm reaching back, but my feet won't move. I look down, and there's this kind of glue around them. I can see corners of dollar bills sticking up out of the mess. And then it's creeping up, and I know that I'm the one who's drowning."

Gavin respects money and what it can do, and the list of community projects and committees he is involved in would hardly support a charge of "unfeeling money grubber," but, obviously, it is not enough. The solution came, appropriately enough, through their church, which had an overseas legal office in Spain. Lisa, also a devoted Christian, interpreted the opportunity, as did Gavin, as a religious duty. They left, however, with very different agendas. At the end of the three-year contract, Lisa assumes that they will return. Gavin, however, is already planning spin-off opportunities in international service organizations or in international law.

How to Get High

The objective of the game is getting challenging and exciting work, staying at the cutting edge, maintaining a grade-A reputation among colleagues and clients, having powerful senior sponsors, being perceived as a master craftsperson, and being willing to seize exciting new opportunities.

Be Prepared and Pay Your Dues. What you are buying is exciting work. What you are buying it with is not your loyalty or willingness to work hard—although those are also factors—but the sheer quality of your technique and your ability to deliver brilliantly. That means that you must have something to offer. You must get the education and training needed to make yourself marketable, and you must find the company that will provide you with exciting opportunities in return for your unquestioned competence.

A classic example of the search for the perfect setting was the dilemma of Nelson, a physician. He was three years into a very lucrative practice in Colorado, with every prospect of making unlimited money. His residency had been in rheumatics and arthritis, two widespread conditions upon which little is known, and he had consequently spent much of his time in the laboratory. His eyes lit up as he described some of the experiments he had generated and possibilities that had become realities under his direction. His practice, though, had become a nightmare of boredom. Because cures for arthritis are not yet possible, he was on a treadmill of prescribing one pain-relieving drug after another for patients, most of whom were gerontology cases from a nearby retirement community.

It became quite clear that working with patients was painful for Nelson. Although he was a compassionate person and seemed to be a loving and creative father to his five children, he expected a different set of rewards from his work. What he really wanted to do was go back for his second residency. I explored another range of options with him and assured him that many physicians found actual practice a real letdown after the intensity and absorption of medical school and internship, no matter how unpleasant the actual experience might have been. A process that worked for many of them was to set up their practices to be lucrative and professionally satisfactory but to invest their real talent and energy in a parallel career or avocation that was satisfying to them emotionally: golf, a community cause, church service, or an active investments program. Nelson became visibly agitated. "I know guys like that," he exclaimed. "They're . . ."—he paused, his lip curling. He was obviously trying to find a polite synonym for *disgusting*.

Nelson is now in his second year of residency at a top-flight Seattle hospital, specializing in radiology. When I checked with him recently, he was a changed man—energized, vibrant, overflowing with ideas, obviously running full blast. He loved the computer and nuclear components of his job. I could also tell that this specialty, which acts as a reference service to other physicians, was going to continue satisfying his need to specialize in his craft.

Seek Out Stimulating Tasks. To some extent, Nelson had not thought through his career when he embarked on his specialty in rheumatics and arthritis. He had been seduced by the intriguing problems of his early training, but he had not envisioned clearly what lay beyond. A getting-high worker who is not able to get at least a partial diet of stimulating work is going to starve to death emotionally. This technique is easier said than done, of course, since any job has its mundane aspects and will require certain stretches when you "just have to put your head down and plod," as one person said.

Paying professional dues can sometimes be oppressive, but the long-term benefits are vital. One script writer I know has never done it. She is nothing short of brilliant at adapting an existing novel or developing an idea into a vital, exciting script. Her ability to generate her own ideas and come up with story lines that make producers grope for the phone while they are still reading is almost legendary. But she has a bad reputation in the field, and many of her scripts end up purchased but not filmed because she is so difficult to get along with. She has never taken the classes, apprenticed with the major studio, or been willing to put up with the politics that would let her build a reputation as a writer who will stick with a project. Her bitterness at the film industry may cancel out her talent and her competence.

Two strategies can help you avoid this pitfall. One is reading your organization accurately so you know where the action is and then stay there. Several of the navy officers I studied had developed great astuteness at "walking the margin." That meant being top-rate, first-class fighter pilots so that they were automatic candidates to test new aircraft, fly experimental missions, or perform unusual flying assignments. However, they had to be crack pilots *and* avoid being promoted to desk commands. For most of them, the strategy included "screwing up" every so often—something serious enough to earn a reprimand and remove them from the promotions list as long as possible but not enough to get them grounded.

The second strategy is to have a long-term career plan with several options so that, if one possibility fails, it can be easily replaced with another. Someone whom I would consider to be a model of how to manage a long-term career for maximum variety is Glade M., a getting-high person with a strong technical orientation. He burned up his classes in mechanical engineering at a topflight midwestern school, got a bachelor's degree, and then hired on with a fast-growing electronics firm that has a parallel track for its engineers. This was an appealing feature for Glade, since the technical problems involved in computer work really turned him on. That a person could switch back and forth between the two tracks was another appealing feature.

He made good progress and got good assignments for the first two years but in that length of time could easily see that it made a difference which department you were in. When a new plant opened in the Midwest, Glade asked to be stationed there, because it would be dealing with some exciting projects. His manager refused and offered him an assignment in another department, which, to Glade's eyes, would "just repeat what I'd already learned. If it's not a growth experience," he declared, "I don't want it." He took an unusual option at that point: he applied for leave without pay and went back for a master's degree in computer technology. He whizzed through it in a year with spectacular results, then called his company again and negotiated to rejoin his Midwest operation as quality-control engineer with a jump in status to third level on the technical track.

He had a great experience with quality control. "The managers who'd been doing it before used to take the government specs and paste them on little cards and give them to the foreman, and that was quality control," he snorted. His technique was to "bash things out with the foreman," explaining the problem and getting high-quality input about the technical requirements. "It's great for morale and great for production. It didn't bother me that they were getting 75 percent of the credit," he insists. "We were all looking good." However, he ran afoul of the hierarchy in his company when a particular design-development problem emerged. He tried his usual conference approach and ran into "an arrogant son of a bitch," as he said, whose response to collaboration was, "Look, I'm Dr. Schultze, and I have my Ph.D. from Cornell, and you just do your job and don't try to tell me how to do mine."

Glade's first (fortunately unspoken) reaction was, "I'm going to get my doctorate and stuff it down your throat." Although this was not his only reason for getting a doctorate—he had been planning on it since he had finished his master's degree —it was probably crucial in precipitating the timing. He got a grant from his company that paid three-fourths of his salary and tuition for the three years he spent back in school. He had a wonderful time. He was also working part time, building a house, and serving as a lay leader in his religious congregation. He was rehired at level four and launched into a new stage of engineering activities. He coordinated seven groups of design-development projects. "They gave us project control." He registered several patents and technical disclosures and traveled around the world to professional conferences.

Once again, politics intervened when the promotion that he wanted and deserved went to a member of the company's minimafia, in effect promoting an insider over him. It was not a comfortable relationship, and when a forced move to Dallas started showing up on the horizon, he immediately resigned and organized his own hardware company in California. Within three years, it was making a million dollars a year and employing about 500 people. Glade, at forty-five, has had a wonderful time "being in charge of the entire technical integration" but can tell "I'm about two years away from losing interest in it. I'm looking around for the next thing to do."

Learn the Skills of Persuasion. This third step is difficult but important. In Glade's case, he solved his problems with authority by sidestepping and eventually by getting out. Not everyone has that option. Salt Lake City automobile dealer Kendall Day Garff, one of that city's outstanding entrepreneurs, is a classic example of being able to come up with a good idea and then sell a financial organization on it (Derr, 1984). In the summer of Depression-ridden 1930, he and another man were hired by Cache Valley Knitting Works to peddle its fine woolen clothes in a sales territory running from Montana to North Dakota. Persistence and long hours simply did not pay off, but Ken's idea did. He would get information about a family, such as the ages of the children, the parents' occupations, and other relevant details, from a neighbor, and then he would select only items that would fit the members of the family. It was easy to swap a red dress for a blue or a sweater for a jacket once the initial contact was made and the woman of the house was envisioning her daughter in the tasteful skirt Ken was holding up. He was so successful that the company offered him a position as division manager and let him move out its back merchandise for twenty cents on the dollar. He made a thousand dollars in one week of a wild warehouse sale.

Stock was his next venture. With the strength of a security-analysis class at the University of Utah behind him, he bought the then-undervalued United Bond and Finance Company (UB&F) common stock for ten cents on the dollar. The company president owned some new apartments in the city, and Garff persuaded him to let him pay his rent in United Bond stock. As a result, the family lived in a $75.00 apartment for $7.50 a month. The president refused Garff's next offer—stock as down payment on a house—but agreed to accept UB&F bonds. Garff approached bankers in the small Montana towns where many of the investors lived, persuading them that since the bonds had never paid a dividend, one share of Montana Power stock, then selling at $40 per share, was equivalent to one $100 UB&F bond. He then bought $2,100 worth of Montana Power stock and, using the bankers as references, approached the bondholders and offered to trade his stocks for their bonds. He thus acquired $5,250 worth of UB&F bonds for an investment of forty cents on the dollar. Back in Salt Lake City, he triumphantly used the bonds to make the down payment on the house he had had his eye on.

Garff had predicted since college days that there was a fortune to be made in automobiles—then a rich man's fancy. Just before World War II, he borrowed $3,000 on his house to buy an infant used-car business. After the war, he raised every cent of capital he could and persuaded John Wallace, president of Salt Lake City's Walker Bank, to loan him $30,000 on the strength of his reputation and his well-worked-out business plan. With that money, Garff bought the local Oldsmobile dealership, and, for the next few years, he sold every car he could get at full list price. "Making the money, having happy customers, and getting a good reputation in town was a thrill," he says.

By 1951, he was solidly established as one of the biggest businesspeople in town. He had expanded into ranching and into the mobile home business in a big way. By the mid fifties, he and his partners could sell mobile homes, space in mobile home parks, insurance for the units, and Norge appliances for the units. They could also finance the loans for the transactions. He also took on the Mercedes-Benz franchise in 1958, when the car had little reputation in the United States, the Honda franchise in 1973, when the Honda was little more than "a three-wheel motorcycle with a shell around it," and the Saab franchise in 1977. All of them have been spectacular money makers.

Lest it look easy, Garff concedes a string of less-than-profitable speculations: an open-pit mine in Nevada, a Jaguar franchise, a uranium mine, a turkey farm, a cold-storage business, a dry-cleaning business, and a chinchilla farm. His son, currently a partner in his business, attributes much of his father's success to his personal charisma and ability to generate venture financing. "Your relationship with your banker is important," he said. His father would entertain prospective investors and bankers at his ranch, personally preparing their breakfasts, locating them in shooting blinds, flushing the game, and then being the first to "clean the pheasants, making up a bag to give to the guests. It was the kind of service you couldn't hire, and he loved doing it for them." When it came to talking business, the same assiduous attention to detail and the same enthusiasm proved to be a winning combination.

Other getting-high careerists discover that they must apply a great deal of creativity to convincing their superiors that a "crazy idea" is really viable. "A good track record speaks for itself, though," observed one, "and even a failure isn't fatal as long as the top brass can understand what happened. But being a lonely genius doesn't do it." Developing good communication skills is one of the prices that must be paid to ensure the most desirable kind of work.

Develop Patience and Political Skills. Even in the best possible scenarios, such as Glade's career, there are still seasons that are less than stimulating. Each getting-high careerist must decide whether the proportion of challenging work is worth the amount of unstimulating work that has to be chewed through to get at it. And some people simply have lower boredom thresholds than others. For instance, I came home the other day to find Dan in our living room. He was hardly a stranger. He had spent twelve weeks building in bookshelves, wrapping a crown molding against the ceiling, refashioning our fireplace to make it look like the architect's drawing, and painstakingly applying the decorator colors. Our living room is a small space, oddly shaped and difficult to change. It was precisely these challenges that Dan had stewed, scowled, and muttered over, until he finally pronounced the magic words, "I'll do it." The final result was, to our view, completely successful: intimate, warm, and sophisticated. Dan was sitting on the couch looking blissful. "Just wanted to come look at it again," he muttered sheepishly.

Dan has a long waiting list, but he has no scruples in rejecting a job, even if it would be "easy money," if it is "just the same old thing." His prices are high, but he does not make much money. He is so meticulous that his projects are very labor intensive. Also, he cannot bear to turn any part of a job over to an assistant. There is not a contractor in the valley who does not know his work and accord him the highest accolades, but there probably are few who would willingly offer him a job. When a money crisis has forced him to work as a finish carpenter on another person's project, it has been agony for everyone concerned. Dan is totally lacking in patience with clients who do not instantly agree that his way is best, and he cannot get along with anyone who tries, however tactfully, to tell him what to do or how to do it.

In some ways, Dan is like Gaye, the sufi-dancing intelligence director. Like all getting-high people, they need to develop enough patience, tolerance, and minimal political skill to fit into ongoing organizational life. It is also helpful if they can sense and accept the cycles of their work so that when a down time comes—right after a stimulating assignment or during budget season—they can concentrate on relationships and leisure-time activities.

A ruthless concentration on feeding yourself a steady diet of thrills can work against your ability to get it in the long run—sometimes the only lesson learned by the self-indulgent. From my outside perspective, Gaye may have had either the world's most appealing resumé or the most terrifying, depending on the manager who was reviewing her file. Obviously, she has not one but two or three parallel careers going simultaneously. What job would not bore her within a few months? And, although her experience for the first ten years clusters within a group of related government agencies, it may look spotty and erratic if she keeps up the same pattern for another fifteen.

The political skills are also important. Psychological research warns that many of these careerists are not good at dealing with people. Still, it is important to have enough understanding of the culture to know where the norms are. If you are not tied into the right networks, you will not learn about the exciting job opportunities. If you do not conform to certain minimal company norms, you will not be trusted with good assignments. If you cannot attract and keep the sponsorship of powerful mentors, you will not have anyone to argue for you ("bizarre but she'll come through") on an assignment you would kill to get.

Be Ready to Jump with the Opportunities. We have already talked about Gaye's resumé. It is fairly typical of those of getting-high people, who frequently have discontinuous career patterns or who even career hop. Michael Driver's (1979, 1982) research shows that transient careerists, who include many getting-free people, tend to view their careers in chunks. They have a real need to change from one thing to another every three to seven years. A variation is to plan ahead to spiral into a related field, something that lessens the risks of failing but provides the challenge of something new. Garff's expansion from automobiles into mobile homes is this kind of move. So is the jump of a navy pilot into being an astronaut.

This strategy is not risk free. Although a real getting-high person will put an exciting challenge at the absolute top of his or her priority list, it may be just baffling, frustrating, or confusing to a spouse or colleague who says, "Hey, wait a minute. We had an arrangement. How come you're changing the rules again?" In a strictly practical sense, personal relationships and binding institutional affiliations become baggage that makes it hard to jump. One father of four who has a flair for putting together new ventures confided, "My family is tops on my priority, because I know what I'll want to look back on at the end of my life. But it's a hard decision day to day. I love having a bunch of balls in the air. And I can manage it when one or two come down. But when five or six come down at the same time, I just can't manage everything and still keep up my commitments at home. And it's incredibly painful"—he half laughed—"not to be free to work around the clock. I want it all."

Companies that have parallel tracks, a record of lateral moves, a heavy investment in employee training programs, and even a pattern of regular moves from city to city may be good ones for you to investigate. As a general rule, you should always have a back-up plan in mind in case your current job or assignment goes sour. Could you move into another branch? Could you move up? Could you switch companies? Some companies or professions have close ties with universities and other academic settings so that cycling from the classroom or laboratory back to the office can be an accepted pattern. Another useful strategy is to keep a parallel career or avocation developed well enough that, sooner or later—sooner, if necessary—it could actually become a new profession.

Choose the Right Organization. Although most of the getting-high people we have talked about either have been in business for themselves or have had an exciting role in a larger organization, there is usually at least a peer group to whom the careerist must relate. Your organization, if you are affiliated with a company, needs to be one that will reward you with money, the necessary time and attractive prerequisites for your ongoing activities, and opportunities to apply and test out your skills but that will also share you with the greater professional world.

You should compete in the professional world, appearing often in carefully selected places that other professionals will respect, producing excellent products and taking credit for them, serving on important professional committees that enhance your craft, and learning to articulate rigorous positions that appeal to your professional culture. In other words, not only should your company respect your contribution, but your colleagues should, too. If you acquire and keep the image of a "professional's professional," it will be a strong bargaining point for you with your own company. Furthermore, as any getting-high person knows, there are some matters of techniques that only another professional can understand and appreciate. You need to keep in touch with your peers.

If you have a cosmopolitan manager who perceives that having an employee who is an officer in a national association is advantageous to the company, try to involve him or her in its activities, bring back reports to the company, and see that the company gets appropriate publicity and recognition in your professional group. Be canny in using your professional associations and colleague groups if you have a manager who feels that any affiliation outside the company is disloyal. Continue educational activities in a nonaggressive, nonthreatening way and downplay a visible "getting together to compare notes" with professional colleagues.

It is also important that you have ongoing developmental activities that will keep your skills sharp and foster new ones. An example of an organization where such activities are available is the World Bank. Although it has the outward appearance of many conservative financial organizations, with layers of management and a reputation for caution, it has attracted a surprising number of careerists who have classic getting-high profiles, largely, I'm convinced, because it offers a great deal of autonomy, a rich menu of opportunities for self-development, and occasional—but apparently enough—chances at stimulating turn-the-economy-around types of assignments.

If you are considering a career switch, either within your company or to a new job where you can maximize your orientation toward getting high, look for one that honors and respects craftsmanship. One chemical company has a legend about its founder, who hand calibrated an instrument and drew in all the settings himself with India ink. Other important signs of your kind of culture are that norms of dress code, appearance, and work hours are less important than results and that words such as *complete, thorough,* and *precise* are terms of praise. Adventurers and artists will look for cultures in which a little "craziness" is respected and even admired and where competence is assumed but scrutinized closely.

Benefits and Costs

Benefits. As with any career perspective, the chief person to benefit from getting high is the worker. A getting-high person with a good career fit is someone who can talk eloquently and passionately about the benefits of his or her craft, who works at high and happy speeds, and who routinely racks up a record of productivity that makes less motivated and skilled people shake their heads in amazement. Colleagues will say, "You can learn everything there is to learn from Helen—if you can keep up with her." By personal example and articulate statement, these individuals are able to communicate their own skills, their knowledge, and the culture and standards of the profession in lasting ways. People who have this orientation themselves can usually identify a mentor or role model somewhere in their past who gave them a burning vision of "what it meant to do the job right."

The spouse and children of such people almost always respect their skills and integrity, are excited by their enthusiasms, and are energized by their own energies. Most of them recognize that "work will always come first," but they also recognize that the interest and vitality of even comparatively infrequent moments together are a great compensation.

Costs. The down side of this particular career success orientation, however, is potentially disruptive. Although an apprentice learning from a master craftsperson has an unparalleled opportunity to absorb skills and philosophy, the relationship is always a temporary one. The "master's" standards may seem unreasonably high, and his or her insistence on doing everything one way can create difficulties, especially since the best apprentices will not merely be clones but will have their own ideas about how to do things.

By the same token, these people are difficult for organizations to manage. They like being loners and resist situations requiring interdependence even when the consequences are social embarrassment, financial ruin, personal devastation, and even the danger of death. H. Levinson (1978) reported on a certain David Sandstrom, who had uncanny ability for taking charge of a "tough problem, like a failing division" and "bulldozing his way through corporate red tape" to turn it around. No one questioned his brightness, his competence, or his dazzling performance record. But no one wanted to work with him either. In staff meetings, his incisive ability to get to the heart of the problem made him ruthless with those who thought and talked their way to a solution more slowly. He terrorized his subordinates, antagonized his peers, and insulted his superiors. He was "an intellectual bully with little regard for those . . . who could not keep up with him." He hated to delegate anything, even a $25 decision. He had no sense of humor, and his two recreations—golf and tennis—were just new arenas for competition. "He did not know what a *game* was," said one colleague (H. Levinson, 1978, pp. 86, 88).

Quite frequently, the real cost for a getting-high executive comes in terms of family relationships. Nelson and Glade were both fortunate in that they had wives who were willing to do most of the parenting and who could survive emotionally with infrequent but intense periods of concentration on their relationship. Gaye had several temporary relationships, sometimes simultaneously, but did not feel the need for anything permanent. In an unusual case, Anita, a partner in one of California's highest-rated modern dance troupes, became obsessed with dance when she attended a summer workshop in Mexico as a teenager. Her instructor was from the University of Wisconsin, then the nation's leader in modern dance, and Anita's later study there connected her with the national network. She retained these contacts after returning to her hometown, taught some of the earliest modern dance classes offered at the local university, and formed a number of companies before the one she now runs. She married and had three children but never lost her obsession with the excitement of dance, the thrill of new learning experiences, the rush of choreographing her way through a difficult dance problem. Her husband, a high school principal in a small rural town thirty minutes away, was willing to work out a marriage that was very unconventional for the times. Anita maintains an apartment in San Francisco and, during an intensive project, would simply hole up there, eating, breathing, and sleeping dance. When the recital or tour was over, she would swoop back home for a season of equally intensive involvement with her family. Her husband's stability provided a counterbalance to Anita's comings and goings, and all of them seem to have enjoyed the rhythm of her career.

In contrast, most getting-high careerists report a certain amount of seasonal strain related to their "intense" periods. One friend complained to me that her husband, an artist, "is off in his own world again." His studio is in the house, but he is so absorbed in his work that even when Linda or the children come in and discuss something with him or try to engage him in solving a problem, he genuinely does not remember talking with them. He misses meals, goes for long walks right before a party is due to begin, or starts hammering and welding at 3 in the morning. When Linda had an appointment and arranged for Arn to pick up their son from his preschool at noon, she arrived home at 8 P.M. to discover that Arn was oblivious to the world in his study and Jonathon was at his teacher's home. Arn claimed that he had not even heard the steadily ringing phone.

Situations like this would impose a heavy strain on any relationship, but money problems were almost the final straw for Linda. Not only did income drop, but Arn was literally incapable of helping Linda solve the problem of making the house payments, buying groceries, and getting new tires for the car. Such a pattern frequently creates near-intolerable tension around the beginning of new ventures.

Managing Getting-High People

Getting-high careerists sometimes end up as managers. Lottie Bailyn (1982) found that several of the technical careerists in her study of engineers occupied high-level managerial positions, because they had astutely seen that these positions would give them the power to screen incoming assignments and grab the best ones for themselves. They do not, however, necessarily make good managers. Bailyn's research showed that, while these getting-high people were off having a wonderful time with the choice assignments that they had captured, their managerial responsibilities frequently soured in the basket. In short, as soon as top management figured out what was going on, those managers were moved into other positions. Furthermore, as high-level managers, they often want to raise global issues and philosophical questions that require incredible time and energy to incorporate, taking hard "right-wrong" stances that make compromise impossible.

Thus, getting-high careerists in an organization are often going to have to work through other people, a near-intolerable situation to begin with. And there is probably more built-in conflict between a getting-high employee and a manager—any kind of manager—than with any other type of career success orientation except for the getting-free person. Managers complain that their technological geniuses are a pain to have around. They work too slowly, fiddling endlessly over details that no one will see. They overdo quality control until it is ridiculous. And they do not understand the big picture—always thinking that their projects are the center of the universe.

Organizations in our new technological and information economy desperately need new ideas and cutting-edge expertise. These technical-professional employees can, however, get off in their own orbit and contribute little to the company. They can become more productive in an organization or occupation when a manager can support and direct them in a certain way, but how to both stimulate and control them is the critical issue.

Generally, getting-high people keenly want and need interesting and challenging opportunities to apply themselves; clear parameters or limits—time requirements, financial ceilings, rules to be observed; and, within those limits, support in the form of equipment, training, staff, application time, and encouragement. The manager who feels suspicious and bothered by what is going on behind that closed door probably is going to have a harder time working with getting-high people, unable to understand why they are working so hard for such unorthodox rewards. The manager who can build in enough checkpoints to satisfy managerial needs but not so many that they block the getting-high person has found the right formula.

Getting-high people usually do not like superficial short-term assignments. They are talented, and they feel the need to test their talents. Trying to herd them into a "safe" but boring series of tasks usually means some kind of sabotage further down the line, since such careerists tend to redefine the task to make it more interesting. Some extreme getting-high people do not mind short-term assignments as long as the risk and danger are high. They are troubleshooters, the heroes of the moment, the chance takers. They get high on the challenge of the assignment and pull it off in a surprising number of cases. They seldom want to stay around and pick up the pieces, however, so it is wise to have someone in reserve who can step in, systematize, and tidy up the project to minimize the unintended consequences.

Some organizations have found it best to use part-time and consultancy options to manage these getting-high people, since a bored getting-high person will sometimes manufacture action, much of it counterproductive, resort to drinking, or take up a dangerous sport, such as skydiving or stock-car racing, to use up surplus energy. Other organizations have the internal resources to turn these people into "intrapreneurs," offering them a support system and a significant ownership bonus to work out the challenges of setting up what amounts to a small company within a larger one.

Getting-high people cut across the profile of American workers to include artists, entrepreneurs, adventurers, and those ideologues consumed by a great vision. They provide an aggressive creativity and technical proficiency that can be vital to a company that depends on state-of-the-art work or on craftsmanship and quality as its key to success. It is probably safe to say that this group has produced more of our new ideas, our new products, our new art, and our new ways of viewing ourselves than any comparable group. But it is also fair to say that relatively few of them can manage without translators and sponsors unless they are willing to develop the political skills and networks that make their abilities comprehensible and usable to the rest of the working world.

Not every organization can afford getting-high people. But those that depend on cutting-edge technology or innovative marketing to keep the jump on their competitors cannot afford to be without them. Money can seldom buy the quality and quantity of work and ideas they produce, nor can money hold them if the challenge beckons from the other side of the fence.

 NINE

Getting Balanced

Career, self-development, and relationships with others—these are the three oranges that a getting-balanced careerist juggles all the time. If the juggling act is working perfectly, each orange has the same value and gets an equivalent amount of time. Work is important, but it does not take precedence over important relationships with friends, lovers, and family members. And no one person or project gets to occupy so much time that there is none left over for oneself.

For instance, Soren and Marsha are almost too perfectly Californian in their life-style. They have lived together in a stable relationship for four and a half years in a commune apartment complex with five other couples, two of whom have children (Soren and Marsha do not). She is a management training consultant, high priced, good at her work, and in demand. He is a jazz musician, also in demand and probably with national appeal. But neither one is willing to "go for the big time." "Sure, we get tempted," said Marsha. "I'm with people every week who can snap their fingers and make miracles happen because they've got money. I'd like to do that, too. But then I look at the tight lines around their mouths and see them drinking Alka-Seltzer with every meal, and I go home to warmth and peace and love. It doesn't look so tempting from there."

In addition to their natural talents, both of them are very good at what they do because of the sensitivity they have developed to people and groups and their willingness to put a significant number of hours into their relationships—and not only with each other. They belong to one group of couples, and Marsha belongs to three women's groups. Every morning, both jog and meditate for an hour, including a form of prayer. Both have weekly acupuncture sessions and regular massage. They frequently go on weekend retreats, not only with their own groups but with ad hoc groups organized around the visit of a traveling yogi or guru. They have recently joined a home computer group, a typical learning style for them to find out about something new, and are very active in the nuclear freeze movement. Although they have no children, they are working at life just as intensely as the more conventional balancers who are trying to juggle children, careers, and a long-term marital relationship. Getting-balanced people are not juggling just because something will fall on their heads if they do not. They are not spending quality time on relationships just because they do not want their work slowed down by counseling or a divorce or because they are absorbed in a love affair. Their work is very important, but they will not sacrifice it for a relationship. Nor will they sacrifice a relationship for work. And they insist on the wisdom of the eighties that there has to be "room for me, too."

Getting balanced is a relatively new phenomenon in the work force, especially in conspicuous numbers, but it is hard to define. We all have times when we feel out of balance and shake up our schedules for more time with an important person, for cleaning out our mental closets, or for digging into a major project at work. But we may still differ in important respects from getting-balanced careerists. Getting balanced is not the same thing as getting ahead, even though getting-balanced people pay their dues at the beginning of a career in the traditional fashion, grind away at research projects, and jet around the country with the best of them. In a parallel fashion, getting balanced does not describe the red-hot careerist who burns out early, gets fatigued with a stressful schedule, or gets bored by a mastered task and then checks in again with the family to recharge his or her batteries. This career pattern also excludes those who are not work oriented but who simply work to finance the rest of their lives, as well as those who believe in letting luck and circumstances dictate their career decisions and who do not have clear preferences about pleasurable types (as well as amounts) of work. Instead, getting balanced is a pattern that emerges over the long haul. It includes definite career goals and a high priority on work. But the career has to remain in balance with self-development and relationships. It also has to stay in balance with itself so that it remains meaningful and engaging.

Getting balanced is unlike the other four career anchors in that it includes people who have chosen it as a conscious and long-term yet temporary alternative to what they would consider their real career success map. One roommate from college days clearly defines himself as in a balancing mode at this stage of his career. Things are well under way for him, but if all options were absolutely open, he would probably be a prime getting-high example. He likes the fast-paced action that is centered on solving a particular problem, getting a particular project moving, assembling resources and people to confront and solve a given task, and then moving on to the next project.

"Ideally," he says, "I'd live close to my work and figure out some way to handle the periods of burnout. Realistically, though, I'm not willing to pay the costs. I'm not only committed to having a good marriage and nourishing the love between us, but I'm also committed to Pamela's happiness. Her professional life is important to her, so it has to be important to me. We have three sons, ages nine to sixteen. They need our daily attention for their household chores, the paper routes, their schoolwork, their emotional well-being, and their own explorations of themselves. I want to be in on that. When I leave for a two-week consultancy, Pamela has to cover all of those bases herself—plus meet our obligations with our extended families and in our community—while her research and writing suffer. I can't make those kinds of demands without being available for intensive reciprocal 'on-call' time. Somehow, we do it. We both juggle, postpone, and do 'crisis' work oftener than we'd like. I fret about tempting plums I have to pass up— so does Pamela—but I have no compunctions about the overall trade-offs. I simply would not buy more career success with the stability of my family life. But when the children go on, I know I'll be ready for a second career."

When I do workshops, one of the early exercises, after

some preliminary discussions and descriptions of career success maps, is to divide up into groups according to self-diagnosed maps. The getting-balanced group is always the largest. I usually have this group divide itself again into those who are there because they have chosen this orientation and those who are there because circumstances or perceived constraints have nudged them in that direction. In short, the very flexibility of this career success map—which is one of its greatest advantages—is also one of the factors that makes it amorphous and hard to pin down. Many men who choose it are in long-term relationships with women who supported the change or even actively encouraged—sometimes demanded—it. Nicola, a human relationship specialist in a large Minneapolis firm, says, "Frank and I lucked into it." A senior copilot with a major airline, he was in line for promotion to pilot when he discovered that he did not really want it. A midlife crisis was in full bloom. "I wanted to bring my nurturing self more into line with my achieving self," he said, "and it coincided with Nicola's need to do something for her achieving side. These same needs on a different schedule could have broken up our marriage."

He negotiated complex working arrangements with his supervisors to allow him large chunks of daytime hours with their two elementary school–age children. He had complex feelings about scaling down his own career aspirations. "For all practical purposes," he said, "I found myself taking my name off the list. At first I panicked—felt angry at Nicola because she needed me to do this and that for her schooling, felt angry at myself for 'sabotaging' all of my ambitions. Then I got some counseling and started listening to the messages I was giving myself. I need to do what I am doing. It's been great. With both of us putting the children first, neither one of us has to put our work last. But neither one of us gets to put it first either, for longer than a couple of weeks." When I met Frank, he was in Washington, D.C., working on a commuter master's degree. He and Nicola have a long-range goal that both will retire and set up a consulting practice in which they are interchangeable parts and can trade off child care and work as they need to.

Here are some guiding questions to help you decide on

the getting-balanced potential of a job, the proper strategies to employ, and your potential for assuming this career success map.

1. Can I find a job that is stimulating without being too demanding?
2. Can I find an organization that is willing to allow my values system?
3. If I try to renegotiate an unbalanced "contract" to give me more balance, will I just be asking to get fired or plateaued?
4. How long does it take to build up enough credits to negotiate from a strong position—and do I have that much time?
5. Am I looking in the wrong place for an answer? Should I change to part-time work? Consulting? Would job sharing, flextime, or cottage industry provide a solution to this problem?
6. If I had to postpone some personal and relationship issues, would the relationship survive?
7. Part of any getting-balanced pattern is that it changes constantly. How disruptive will these seasonal maladjustments be for us?
8. Will my partner, children, and friends give me the support I need to be balanced?
9. Is my health good enough that I can be a superperson and do it all?
10. Do I have the will power to do the kind of planning and follow-through that this will take?
11. Getting balanced nearly always means increased costs for child care, transportation, housekeeping, entertainment, and other factors. Will the benefits outweigh the financial costs?

How to Get Balanced

Look For the Right Company. Getting-balanced people can walk you through an incredible search for the "perfect company" that usually begins back in college. In fact, many of these people were getting-balanced students who did not merely give lip service to meeting their own needs and maintaining high-quality relationships but scheduled their time so that they could follow through. They seemed to learn early that they were not really for sale and developed an ability to read the needs and wants of organizations, to ask the well-placed question, and to find the right kind of organizational milieu or culture, one that might be called androgynous, in contrast to the high-pressure, twenty-hour-day "macho" organizations.

Stan, a pediatrician with a four-star practice in California, says, "I picked my clinic carefully when I was going into practice. Laura and I had three children then and were planning on at least one more. She was just setting up her accounting firm at the time. I knew that a solo practice or a partnership couldn't work unless I was on call round the clock, and that didn't fit with my own need to keep in touch with Laura and the children. In my clinic, there are enough of us—seven—that we can cover for each other without major stress. There's a lot of talk about 'put children first,' and the clinic has close ties to a religiously run hospital. I negotiated two-thirds time plus half-Saturdays twice a month so that I could spend more daytime hours with the children while Laura was dealing with her own business and another pregnancy. I think my partners would have really preferred somebody who was there for forty hours a week plus, just as they were, but within the context that already existed, I was only pushing things a little, not breaking them."

Here are some questions that will give you insight into a company's culture as it favors or punishes the getting-balanced careerist:

1. What kind of travel is required?
2. What kind of experience or background might short-cut some of the "apprenticeship" time to move you ahead faster?
3. Does this company have benefits for child care? Paternity leave? Day-care centers on site?
4. Does it show itself generally sensitive to the needs of dual-

career couples by offering employment-search services for the spouses of employees who are moved?

5. Does it offer such on-the-job options as flexible scheduling, at-home work stations, or part-time work?

6. Does there seem to be a general willingness to allow employees considerable say in how they use their time to get the desired outcomes?

Another example of luck is Marilyn, who works for a large energy company in the East. Her husband, chairperson of the economics department in a prestigious university, fell in love with a student and walked out without warning after thirteen years of marriage. "I was determined to survive," she says. "I spent the next twelve months like a zombie, pouring every ounce of energy I had into taking care of my boys"—her two sons are now fifteen and thirteen—"and finishing a management course. I was fortunate enough to get some very good career counseling that led me to a stable, high-paying job where being a woman was an asset. It wouldn't have really mattered what it was at that point—I would have done anything—but I'm doubly fortunate in that it's work I like and am very good at. I consider it a long-term career." It does not involve much travel or emergency assignments—another advantage—because she still spends prime time with her sons, supports their school and sports activities, and plans at least one weekend a month with them as a "semimajor field trip."

Marilyn sold the house in which she had spent all of her married life because "I wanted to say goodbye to that part of my life and get on with the new," but she made sure that their new apartment was in the same neighborhood so that the boys could keep going to the same school. She became more involved in their local synagogue and was in charge of bar mitzvahs for both. A challenging job offer came from San Francisco, "but I refused it. Moving now just wouldn't be good for the family, even though it might be good for me."

The number of androgynous companies is growing, but they are still relatively rare. Only 200 or so American businesses were providing day care and only a few more offered financial aid for parents with day-care needs in 1984 (Walsh, 1984). Fewer than one firm in ten provides any form of paternity leave (Langway and others, 1981).

At a recent seminar I ran at Radcliffe for women executives between twenty and thirty, the most commonly voiced source of dissatisfaction was the lack of "esthetics" in the male corporate/technical world. "I'm not just talking about plants on the desks," insisted Penny, a dark-haired advertising executive. "It's a feeling. I don't know that I want to get married right away, but I'd like to feel that my work choice doesn't exclude that option. I'm not sure that I want to have children of my own, but I'd like time to spend with the children of friends and with my own nieces and nephews regularly enough that a relationship can develop."

Stark, hard, and *macho* were descriptive adjectives supplied by other women at the seminar—and they were not compliments. "I've given up on the corporate culture," says Lilly, a strategic planner for a government agency whose brilliance at synthesis and persuasiveness has given her a fat salary and a place on the fast track. "I don't want to stop being a woman to make it in the world. No options exist for how those men relate to their world. They're completely absorbed in getting ahead." For some, an "offbeat" company such as a brand-new high-tech outfit, a cooperative, or a woman-owned business is the answer. For others, it is going into business for themselves.

Pay Your Dues. Whether you are in an organization that can accommodate getting-balanced people or you have set up your own company, you have to establish your technical and personal expertise by acquiring the skills necessary before you can achieve the kind of balance that you probably find most desirable. Some people decide while they are still in college to go into business for themselves, not for the entrepreneurial excitement but for the balance it can give them. It is a wise strategy to get as much education and expertise as possible before making this plunge. Lawrence, very much a getting-balanced type, warns the envious, "What you don't see is the three years it took to get the company off the ground when I worked eighteen hours a day." For a getting-balanced person, these kinds of sacrifices are worth it because they are temporary.

In most companies, it is almost an axiom that you have

to have a certain amount of seniority, respectability, credibility, and status to get enough leverage to move the rules a little further apart. If the company of your choice gives executives on a certain level the kind of freedom you are after, be willing to meet its standards to get a job on that level.

Keep the Rules. Most of the literature seems to show that getting-balanced careerists who find companies that they think are good matches are energetic, productive, and very loyal. In fact, their appreciation for the accommodation and trust shown in them by their companies really pays off for the companies in terms of increased productivity. Not only are they showing gratitude for their own situation; they are unwilling to make things difficult for anyone else, either, including supervisors. If it is important to the company to have people in place at 7:30 on Monday morning, getting-balanced careerists make the necessary adjustments to their nonwork lives to meet that commitment. If they have to do an all-nighter every fourth week to get out a magazine, they do it. If the company picnic is a significant event in the culture, they go and take the family even if it means the children will miss swimming lessons and the spouse has to juggle schedules.

Most getting-balanced careerists are model citizens of their companies. Not only do they try to fit in because they want to stay; they also find themselves sharing such a high percentage of the corporation's values that they become spokespersons for those values.

Keep Your Career Strategy to Yourself. It sounds as though the only problem were finding this wonderful company waiting to shower you with flexible scheduling and part-time options. The fact is that the wave of the future is not the wave of the personnel office or many managers. Most managers, acting in the approved getting-ahead style, would probably get rid of any getting-balanced careerists they could identify early in the career. The economics are simple: even though getting-balanced careerists are creative, energetic, and productive workers, very few of them can put out in forty hours as much as a classical getting-ahead careerist will put out in seventy. Frank admits that dropping back to part-time work was "probably the only way I could really stick to my other commitments. No matter what I'd wanted, if my status had remained the same, I would have been under immense pressures. I fit in a different niche now.''

A German student at INSEAD whom I will call Werner had arrived with a doctorate in physics that he had collected from the University of Heidelberg with exemplary promptness. Germany, unlike England, the United States, or France, does not have elite schools—only elite degrees. His doctorate is thus, to some extent, an open sesame to his future. After two years of experience with a leading American computer company, he decided to pursue his INSEAD M.B.A. degree while his wife stayed in Germany to finish her own medical education.

In many respects, his story is a typically German one. An only child, he received a great deal of attention and concern from his parents, who both worked very hard to give him the elements of a successful life. In the process, they gave him the one-sided workaholic approach to life that is now conflicting with new questions about a meaningful life. The student revolts of the 1960s challenged his parents' values and made him appraise uneasily what constitutes happiness. He knows already that he has a hidden agenda. Both he and Anna-Lise have a favorite section of Germany where they want to settle down and are serious about having a dual-career marriage that will allow both of them some relief from unremitting work. Naturally, no company would be interested in a manager who has no intention of moving around after five years, so Werner is aware of the need to conceal this private agenda.

Anna-Lise has five critical years left before she can finish her residency and establish a practice that is sufficiently stable to allow part-time practice, if necessary. Both of them realize that they must establish themselves in their careers now. Werner's private agenda is to achieve the kind of professional security within those five years that will let him pull back and get involved in the children they plan to have. He also has a serious commitment to tennis and gardening as hobbies but never mentions them except lightly, as ''relaxing'' activities that are socially acceptable for a young executive. He does not play with colleagues, participate in tournaments that might get his name in the paper, or bring flowers or fruit to work. His long-term agenda is getting balanced, but his secondary map is getting ahead—and it is this secondary image that he wishes to portray. His double agenda is a great handicap in moving toward his future career, but his consciousness of what he wants, even though such self-awareness is unusual so early in the career, is a great strength.

From talking with people, reading the literature, and sampling my own subjects for counseling, I can tell you that there is very clear handwriting on a very tall wall: if an employer feels that you are not available for an important project or that you are not going to deliver on critical work, you lessen your value and cut yourself off from future opportunities. You have to be able to read the culture to know which things are important. You can be clear about not being available for some optional activities; nevertheless, you need to be equally clear about being competent, valuable, and able to manage your nonwork life.

Here are three strategies for fitting in with your culture and easing the inevitable strains: (1) Communicate clearly your commitment to the job. When you must refuse or postpone a work demand, do it in terms of the work rather than in terms of your other commitments—if you can do it honestly. For instance, say, "I don't think I can give you a good response off the top of my head. Let me study these figures overnight and get back to you first thing in the morning" rather than "I've got to leave in ten minutes to car pool the kids to soccer lessons." (2) If your manager is the kind who likes to specify not only the job but the conditions of doing it, see if you can negotiate for more space. "Let me see if I understand the dimensions of this project—the deadline, the budget, and what the outcome should be. All right. Why don't I check with you at two points: first draft and just before final draft?" (3) Communicate clearly the kinds of conditions you need to work best. "Listen, Bill, when there's an emergency, I'm right there with everyone else, but this same emergency has happened at the end of every quarter for the last three quarters. I really don't do my best work under this kind of pressure. Could we look ahead to next quarter and set some preliminary deadlines so it won't sneak up on us so fast?"

Get a Sponsor. It is important to have a sponsor to tell you the best places to invest your limited energies, identify taboos you should not violate, and give you some warnings or encouragements at important points. It is also invaluable for you to deliver for that sponsor—to "collect credits"—so that when an emergency flares up, you can go in and say, "Things are really coming unglued this summer. I can deliver Project *X*, but I'll need two more months on Project *Y*," or "I need to go part time for the next three weeks, but I can make it up after that." You need to keep your fences mended with sponsors so that you have someone who will argue for you and run interference for you when you need it. Even though these sponsor relationships are costly in terms of time and energy during the early career, when time and energy are both scarce, they will pay off in a long-term reciprocal arrangement.

The flip side of bargaining like this is that you have to be prepared to come through in a crunch. Timing is crucial. From time to time, you will simply have to put forth bursts of energy and do something very productive to maintain your status. Use your sponsors and your reading of the company's culture to engage in important tasks and establish your expertise—working smart rather than just hard. It is much more important, for instance, to have a relatively rare skill such as computer technology than simply to be a faithful employee in the mailroom. Take and make opportunities to communicate how important work is. Communicate the message "I may sometimes have limited availability, but I don't have limited commitment."

Resist Temptations. One of the constant seductions for getting-balanced people is the tempting offer that can hardly be refused. Marsha's partner in their consulting firm is a getting-ahead person who is constantly baffled by her ability to say no. "Look," he argues, "she's got this incredible amount of potential to really make it big. I've got more business than I can handle and lots of really glamorous contracts she could have on a silver platter. I'd really like to help her, but somehow she just doesn't see it. I can't stand watching all that talent going to waste." From Marsha's perception, of course, she is making a choice, not indulging herself in willful blindness. Like most successful getting-balanced people, she perceives the opportunities and the possibilities but also perceives the costs as being too high. It is not a matter of failing to see the big picture or being unwilling to pay the cost of being successful. Getting-balanced people simply have a different definition of success.

Nicola agrees that it takes "a strong sense of self and my own ethics" to say no when it would be very easy to say yes. "I've learned a few techniques for sidestepping without losing credibility, because I want to keep the options of those interesting work opportunities. But it's hard to walk that fine line. Sometimes I can't sleep at night because I think I've let something go that I should have grabbed. Probably one of these times I'll make a real mistake. But when it happens, I'll just have to live with it."

The careerist operating in this system may refuse a promotion that would take him from Aspen, Colorado, to Los Angeles because his daughter is on the ski team in her senior year of high school. The husband in a dual-career couple may get himself shifted from sales to public relations so that out-of-town travel diminishes almost to the vanishing point because they plan to have a baby. Still another couple, seriously concerned about the area schools, will analyze their interests, ability, and career commitments to decide which of them should run for PTA president rather than focusing on work-related goals. Be prepared to grieve for lost opportunities. Any choice is a loss. But be sure you know how to celebrate what you are getting, too.

Watch Your Timing. Timing is perhaps the most difficult skill of all to develop. Obviously, a beginning careerist cannot start out in a getting-balanced mode. Organizations have legitimate needs for workers who are accessible, who will put in long hours when needed, and who will travel when it is required. If the options are being fired and being shunted into being an executive assistant rather than being the executive, you want to have a choice about those options. Even if you quit to start your own business, you usually have to go through another apprenticeship period. People who discover their career success maps late may not have the option of having a whole new career. What kinds of opportunities and trade-offs exist in the external career? Can you go into a holding pattern to recharge your batteries and then back into the rhythm of the work cycle? Is a parallel career a possibility?

Benefits and Costs

Benefits. The most obvious benefit from a getting-balanced orientation is a supreme sense of happiness and energy when the balancing act is working. Of course, every other type of careerist also experiences the same jubilation and well-being at times, but getting-balanced careerists tend to report that their contentment seems deeper and more satisfying, "because I don't have to compartmentalize," as Nicola puts it. "I regularly go to lunch with three or four women who are bouncy and enthusiastic when they're talking about their jobs, but they start jabbing their forks into the lettuce and mumbling when you ask about the kids or how the rest of their lives are going. I don't want that."

Helena, a single woman who works in the Washington, D.C., headquarters of a large government office, deliberately decided to get balanced. In her mid forties and never married, she feels calm about the prospect of being single for the rest of her life—"and I want to choose what that life is like." A bright and skillful manager, she spent a decade getting promotion after promotion, making very good money, and being groomed for top positions. "But I also felt incredibly hassled and unfulfilled. Things kind of clicked for me when I saw the fall schedule and realized that in a three-month period I would have gone to Singapore, Toronto, Tallahassee, and Phoenix, twice to Los Angeles, and five times to Boston. I locked my office door and cried. Then I walked out, said I was taking the rest of the day off, and went to the Arlington National Cemetery. I spent the rest of the day thinking and making lists. When I came back the next day, I had an action plan that moved me to a different career track."

Now a senior professional staff member, she finds her work "exciting and manageable." She belongs to several groups, both mixed and women's groups, regularly spends time with her nieces and nephews, and is working on an advanced college degree, something she always felt that she had to postpone. There were no external constraints nudging her toward a getting-balanced career style, but she had strong internal constraints, "which, fortunately, I recognized before I had a heart attack." And she has no regrets about the change.

More and more men are also willing to buck the cultural current trying to sweep them into getting-ahead orientations to say, "No, what I really want is more time with my kids" (or "with my tuba" or "to see Japan"). If getting ahead pays off in cash, getting balanced pays off in wholeness. An additional benefit is that this orientation works for dual-career couples in ways that let them achieve satisfaction in all their major life areas without having to be superpeople. In some ways, it is the career success map of choice for women entering the work force and the strongest fallback position for men. A recent survey indicates that 50 percent of the men with working wives (about two of every five U.S. mothers with children under six work out of the home) are willing to share household responsibilities and daily child care, while a million children in the United States were being raised by single fathers in 1981, a 65 percent increase from 1970 (Langway and others, 1981, p. 93). An estimated 50 percent of married American men can rely on two paychecks to fight off financial woes (Bralove, 1981a). These family shifts are, for the most part, occurring among the younger, more highly educated and affluent males who will be first the trendsetters, then the mainstream. However, these trends are still in the early stages. Of 1,460 working women with children in a recent study, many of whom were married or partnered, 70 percent said they did all of the housework. In a parallel study, fewer than 60 percent of the husbands reported helping around the house—and then only for about eleven hours a week, compared to the wife's twenty-six to fifty-two. Since only 30 percent of the working women in their twenties in this survey expected to remain childless, an orientation that permits a more equitable distribution of tasks seems like an advantage to all concerned (Nickles, 1981, p. 165). *Ms., Savvy, Working Woman,* and other publications for professional women now include stories on the importance of love, the dangers of overworking, the necessities of setting priorities, and the commitment to children. Further, the number of women who gave birth to their first child after age thirty was 1,312,205 in 1980 —up 94 percent over 1975 (Berg, 1984, p. 68).

Between 1980 and 1990 in the United States, the number of people in prime midcareer, workers between the ages of thirty-five and forty-four, will increase by 42 percent, but the increase in the number of jobs available will trail at an estimated 20 percent. Slow economic growth and the resulting lack of new jobs, the baby-boom oversupply of workers, the easing of retirement laws, the increased work spans of senior citizens, and the dramatic entry of women into the work force have all combined to create a midcareer "glut." One-reward organizations may find themselves unable to hold their most productive managers, especially if they can no longer offer the same rewards. It is to business's advantage, argues Bailyn (1980), to decrease competition for the executive suite and encourage a rhythm of intensive and less intensive work.

Another reward is a strong sense of purpose. Bailyn's (1978) research on male careerists identified a group of "accommodators," who placed the family's needs ahead of work in their own hierarchy of values, a pattern that she attributed partly to their own attitudes and partly to external circumstances. Accommodators, according to her research, did not often make it to top management positions and were penalized in terms of promotions and assignments, but they also benefited. By rejecting the cultural value of getting ahead, they chose to reward themselves in other ways. They experienced feelings of integrity and social purpose. They got great pleasure and rewards from their family life. They were more socially conscious and more tolerant than nonaccommodators. Their wives were more likely to have careers, and these women rated themselves as more satisfied with their lives than did the spouses of nonaccommodators.

For thoughtful, sensitive people, new circumstances mean thinking through priorities again. Sophia, a student of mine, had acquired prestigious degrees at Wellesley and had gone on to Purdue to complete a master's degree in business administration while her husband, Charles, recruited to Utah's high-tech community to teach engineering, had moved to Salt Lake City. Sophia was bright and committed to her career. She had enjoyed her several years of working in Boston at a fast-paced computer company. She was thirty-six, though, and her later move to Utah coincided with their decision to have a child. She entered a Ph.D. program in management, something she could pursue part time. Career development clicked as a field of study, and she has a plan for specializing in counseling entrepreneurial women in a few years. She was back in class four days after the baby was born and did not lessen her drive for academic excellence, but the class itself gave her some skills for analyzing how she was feeling in her new situation. By the end of the first summer, she and Charles had decided to shift gears again, have another child, and let Sophia focus for this season on personal concerns, with a minimal but continuing involvement in her career. "Work is very, very important," she insists, "but I'm not willing to trade irreversible things for it. I'm really enjoying our daughter. Charles and I want children. We can choose them now. In a few years, we won't be able to."

Costs. A getting-balanced career success map may look horrifyingly unfocused and undisciplined to a getting-ahead person. It can also look self-indulgently simple. The reality, according to those working with such a plan, is that balancing is hard work. "We have to negotiate *everything*," sighs Nicola. "Not once but about every two or three months: child care, household duties, who needs which block of time for which project. I get really exhausted sometimes and long for the simplicity of just trying to do one thing at a time."

Others agree that it takes not only a real commitment to the shared value of negotiating but also some highly developed skills. "How do we work it out when I'm feeling a need for space at the same time Marsha is feeling a need for closeness because she has just put in three weeks on a project?" asks Soren.

"She's wondering why I didn't get my space during those three weeks. I'm wondering why she wants to do heavy-duty relationship work when she just got back from a draining experience." A son whose grades are slipping may need a lot of concentrated attention from one or both parents. Who can cut back on weekend and evening work for several weeks to rebuild that relationship and, hopefully, maintain it?

It may be difficult to find the perfect company. From most of my evidence, male careerists who refuse moves, time-consuming projects, or extensive out-of-town travel for family reasons are viewed with the same suspicion as women executives who have children and then cut back on career commitments. "Not productive" is a label that removes them permanently from the fast track.

Careerists in the early stages have to pay their dues or they do not become valued members of the organization. Younger workers who "want it all" and re-entry workers simply may be unwilling to go through the apprenticeship phase, with its long and unusual hours, its need to be available to the company, its acquisition of technical competence, its realities of politics. Companies legitimately need people who will travel or move. Personal schedules cannot always correspond to requirements of the task. Sometimes imbalance in the early stages of the career is necessary to acquire the prestige, job security, and negotiating chips to buy balance in the later career; but how do you know ahead of time whether the dues paying will actually pay off or whether the long-run benefits will justify the short-term costs?

A related dilemma is that working relationships may suffer because a getting-balanced careerist on a tight schedule does not have time for the leisurely two-hour lunch that develops peer relationships, the weekend entertaining that cements a sponsorship relationship, or the extra thinking hours that would make him or her the most valued member of a project work force on the job. "I swim on my lunch hour," says Marilyn. "That's my choice because I feel I really need it. But the rest of the supervisors are playing computer games. I know that sooner or later I'm going to have to catch up—not because

I want to be the video-game queen of the office, but because I need that kind of technical expertise to make the kinds of decisions that go with my position. I've been able to keep up in a secondhand way by reading and picking brains. But I've got to find the time for some hands-on experiences as well."

If something gives way, it is nearly always self-development. Frank observes, "I went away for a weekend retreat last month. I needed it. I could tell I needed it. I had run out of the energy to put top-quality time into relationships or into work, and I was just maintaining on a lot of fronts. I came back with that energy. But—this is the crazy part—even though I knew I needed that renewal, knew how to get it, and Nicola wanted me to go, I had a hard time leaving. It seemed like such a selfish thing to do—to just do something for myself."

Nicola pinpointed another problem of getting balanced. "How do you tell if you're succeeding?" she asked. "It's easy to say, 'Yes, I'm giving myself some time and space; I'm giving my work good attention; I've got the time to focus on Frank and the girls.' But are they all just getting crumbs? Is any of it enough? Sometimes I find myself evaluating my success by the schedule. I think I must be succeeding because I'm going in to work early so we can have a trip to the park in the afternoon and I'll get time to write this Saturday between 5:30 and 7:30 A.M. But how do I *feel* about all of this? Is it making *me* feel good, or does it just look good on paper?"

Getting-ahead, getting-free, and getting-high careerists who feel the pressure of external circumstances to alter their basic orientations, if only temporarily, have to deal with another kind of question: If I make this kind of compromise, can I live with myself? How will I feel if I have to pass up this once-in-a-lifetime opportunity? Can I accept the trade-offs without passing on some resentment that would damage the very relationships I am trying to preserve?

Careerists who have selected a getting-balanced fallback position also have to deal with the fear—firmly based in reality —that they may not be able to change back. On the positive side, they may decide that they like getting balanced. On the negative side, the options could narrow. "How long can dropouts stay current?" asks one. "Am I taking myself out of the

mainstream? What are the limits to starting over? Who will
want me in ten years?"

Managing Getting-Balanced People

Although organizations have been largely cast in the role
of the roadblock to be scrambled over or around for the aspiring getting-balanced careerists, the news is not all bad. Getting-
balanced careerists almost always, within certain limits of time
and energy, provide high-quality, creative, dependable work.
The manager's task is to get a clear reading on what those limits
are, be sure that they are compatible with the company's goals,
and be open to negotiation and flexible arrangements when
needs change—either the company's or the careerist's. Possibly
the hardest part is getting the reading. Because organizations
seem to value and reward the getting-ahead types, getting-balanced careerists learn early to camouflage. Candor is not always
rewarded, so why should a getting-balanced type be open about
his or her real career objectives? As a manager, you need to figure out where you stand on the issue, since your reaction is, for
better or worse, the company's position to this careerist.

Some managers, like Marsha's partner, are frustrated because the traditional rewards do not work. They see getting-
balanced careerists as unmotivated and disloyal, unwilling to
pay the price, to be good team members. They respond with
anger to this "deviant" behavior and try to punish it. For some
managers, there is also a moral issue at stake. An employee who
asserts a different set of values can be threatening. If the manager puts work first and an employee refuses to do so, there is
an implied criticism of the manager's choice. The situation can
become explosive if the employee continues to get promotions
and rewards ("this deviant behavior is being rewarded; that jerk
should be out on his ear") or if the employee is succeeding in
areas that the manager values but is failing at (having a happy
marriage, for instance, while the manager is having a divorce).

As a manager, can you accept getting balanced as a valid
and legitimate career orientation? If you can, then careerists
will almost certainly be willing to open up their commitments
and limitations. They will be willing to negotiate and, within

the terms of this agreement, will usually be very competent and energetic employees. Getting-balanced careerists are not stupid. If the company is willing to accommodate their needs and give them enough lead time to arrange other aspects of their lives in changing situations, they will be loyal employees, usually willing to meet a crisis or contribute extra hours in an emergency. Most often, they have a strong sense of fairness and do not take advantage of a company willing to give them extra consideration when emergencies develop in the other areas of their lives.

Since getting-balanced careerists have a genuine commitment to their work and are not just trying to extract money from the company to run their lives, managers can only benefit from involving getting-balanced types with career options. If an employee has the chance for input into an assignment or consultation on changes that will affect him or her, the results—even if the decision is not what the careerist would have personally chosen—usually involve hard and productive work. An organization that values getting-balanced careerists might consider some programs and benefits—if it does not already have them—especially attractive to these careerists, such as job sharing, flextime, home work stations, on-site day care, negotiable use of sick leave and other leave time, and a project-management orientation.

Getting balanced is a challenging, exciting, deeply satisfying, and highly problematical career success map. There are clear hints, however, that it may be the life-style of the future for a generation that views the "organization-man" era of the fifties and the "drop out, tune in, turn on" orientation that succeeded it with the same shudder accorded to the withdrawn passivity of the seventies. These are people who want it all, need it all, and are willing to work very hard to have it all. There is no evidence that modern women or men expect to avoid careers. What is more likely is that many of these new individuals, new couples, or couples who can successfully renegotiate their marriages will select the getting-balanced career success map. Even though it remains the orientation for a minority at present, there is a clear trend, and the direction is up.

 TEN

Identifying
and Managing
Career Transitions

Before the concept of a career—as opposed to a job—developed, no one questioned whether it was possible to change orientations. In fact, a fuzzy rule of thumb was that if your company wanted a production person, you became a production person. If it wanted a salesperson, that is what you turned into. What does the new research say about the possibilities of being able to change a career success orientation that seems to be so intensely personal, so internal, so intimate a part of oneself? Is it possible to make a genuine shift in career success orientation? Where is the line between changing jobs and changing careers? What kinds of career success maps seem to be logically related as backups to each other? And what are the implications for managers?

Changing Career Orientations

Schein (1978) maintains that the discovery of the career anchor is the discovery of an essential part of oneself, there forever, stabilizing and constraining by its very existence. In fact, he used the image of the anchor because it connoted holding and binding in a certain way. This position receives some support from cognitive psychologists, who argue that, after a certain developmental period, personality traits do not alter in any

165

significant way. Countering this position is that of the developmental psychologists, who assert that people can change at any time in their lives—in fact, that people are constantly in the process of change and that many events or combinations of events can trigger immediate and drastic life changes.

My personal experience with career counseling and career research supports flexibility. Career-oriented people can change their internal careers and redefine career success two or three times in a lifetime. This does not mean that change occurs lightly or easily. Most careerists have a serious commitment to their career success maps. Change is thought of in five- or ten-year segments. Sometimes a change is permanent. Sometimes an apparent change is really a sabbatical to fill in a missing piece of a person's career life followed by a return to the main career anchor. Sometimes an appropriate change is just an experiment that confirms the solidity of the original orientation.

These experiments are fairly common among younger workers. My experience in workshops frequently includes people in their middle to late twenties who are serious about their careers and who come to grips with the material on career success maps but who are confused because the results are inconclusive. My observation is that they simply have not had enough time, experience, and feedback from work for a career success map to take shape. As we have discussed in our description of work and life stages, an important part of one's identity takes shape around ages twenty-seven to thirty-four. Many people report, after a period of questioning, "locking in" on an identity in a way that "seems settled" and releases energy for solid productiveness. This stage usually coincides with the emergence of the career success map as well. For the majority of careerists, the discovery *is* a permanent one, and so is the career commitment. Byrne (1975) recorded that only 6 percent of the professional, technical, and managerial male employees he studied actually changed careers, although many of them changed jobs, and some of them changed rather frequently. Scism (1974) examined a large sample of government employees. Over two-thirds of them never changed jobs or geographical locations. Still, one-third is a considerable number.

Many people are pleased with their initial discovery of a

career direction. Then, a major life event triggers major changes, including a shift from a first to a second career. And, for most, career changes stop there. But others become what Michael Driver (1979) called "transitory careerists," people who shift very frequently from job to job and from occupation to occupation. Clearly, from a career perspective, it seems unlikely that these individuals have a strong career orientation. Another type Driver uncovered was the entrepreneur activist, who keeps innovating and moving from venture to venture. In the case of entrepreneurs, I would argue that such individuals are shaping their external careers to accommodate the demands of their internal careers. Tarnowieski (1973) found that 49 percent of the supposedly satisfied top-level managers and professionals in his sample were contemplating major changes. The pattern for the past decade, and presumably for the next, is that women who have spent full time in mothering activities or who have been socialized into such typically female professions as education, nursing, and social work are making major switches in their work patterns. In many cases, they are coming late to a discovery of their internal careers.

In at least four cases, what appears to be a major change in the internal career actually is not. The first case is the experimentation of the young careerist. Since it seems necessary for a certain amount of time to pass before the career success map emerges, changes during this period are part of collecting information to find a direction, not changes in the direction itself. The second case is that of people who are noncareerists, a situation unrelated to age. Either their career success map will form very late or they will not have one. Their lives are not work centered. One of my former students was a woman in her early fifties who had been a skilled and highly valued executive secretary in a large public firm. At the time she registered in my course, she had completed a bachelor's degree and a master's degree and was looking into an M.B.A. program. Someone so motivated and committed to education should have some sense of future work. We are used to thinking of education as preparation for major changes. However, as I did career counseling with her, a different pattern emerged. Unmarried and living with her parents, who will require increasing care, she expressed two strong needs: for structure and for service. The orderly progression of courses toward degrees satisfied her need for structure. Active in volunteer work in her church and community, she saw herself as using her considerable education and talents to help young women establish themselves. She enjoyed her work and her mastery over it. She felt no need for new on-the-job challenges or for a sense of internal direction; the rest of her life was meeting them in a very satisfying way.

A third form of apparent transition is the temporary refocusing that results from an external crisis. Commonly, someone going through a divorce will also experience feelings of anxiety and insecurity about work. Suddenly, this individual will begin to manifest behavior typical of a getting-secure orientation. However, security is not the real career success map; the preoccupation with security is the halo effect caused by the crisis in the private life. A heart attack or other serious illness can have the same effect.

One of the career women I did some counseling with at an eastern workshop consulted me on a strategy for withdrawing temporarily from a very high-powered program. In her late thirties, she had just had her first baby and had demonstrated the kind of new female "machisma" expected of some women executives. She had worked steadily through her pregnancy and went directly to the hospital from her office after several hours of labor. A week later, she started coming in half days, despite her obstetrician's concern. However, she found herself in love with her baby. How could she put her program on hold temporarily while she savored this new experience without hurting her career? Furthermore, if she and her husband wanted another child, they needed to make immediate plans, since, biologically, time was running out. From a manager's perspective, she may have been backing out of a psychological contract and making a major shift to a getting-balanced orientation. It is far more likely, however, that she was making a temporary adjustment to accommodate this major life change. A wise company, recognizing her skills and commitment, would expect her loyalty to increase if it responded to her need with flexible hours or part-time options.

In the fourth case, several of the people I have counseled

with have clear career success maps, but they are ineffective by comparison with those of others with the same map. They have a goal but no clear strategy for reaching it. As a general rule, these people are unhappy workers. They complain eloquently and are always on the brink of leaving or taking some decisive action but never do. If they are given the promotions they want, they usually perform competently, but their immediate satisfaction gives way sooner or later to a repetition of the earlier negative pattern. They seem to lack the energy and motivation of the typically career centered, even though they have somewhat matching profiles. They are caught in the middle and seem to be sinking in a quagmire of internal conflict and ambiguity, neither clearly job oriented nor career oriented. Obviously, they pose special motivation problems for managers.

Lots of people change jobs. In fact, a high level of mobility is usually possible within most occupations. Teachers burn out on junior high and find real pleasure in fifth grade for a few years. Bankers decide to leave the little local firm to aim for a branch of Bank of America. Accountants and engineers rotate in and out of firms. If you are using the same skills, motives, values, and talent profile in a different setting, you have changed jobs, but the career orientation is the same. The question was critical for navy officers I studied, since they could retire after twenty years with half of their base pay. Many who had been administrators were putting out feelers to large corporations where they would continue to manage big projects or operations. Nuclear submarine engineers had a well-beaten path into the nuclear power industry. A small percentage of naval officers were, however, contemplating a major career switch: elementary school teaching, auto mechanics, or ski school. Several were planning to go back to college for a degree. This program would allow them three or four years of transition into something different, building on the talents or motives they would discover during that process.

Identifying Transition Points

Internal career transitions are triggered in two ways: when something in our personal life requires a change in our

work life or when our external career shifts in a way that demands a corresponding internal shift.

Changes in Personal Life. The realities of our home and
family situations or a shifting constellation of personal relationships can create major incongruities that have an impact on
work. Some people are so committed to their careers that they
will work hard to modify the personal constraints: hire more
help, commute long distances, or even get a divorce. Making major alterations in their personal situations is more important to
them than modifying their internal career aspirations. This decision is largely a matter of where you perceive the "real you"
to be.

A getting-high woman I worked with in management consulting had always had a commitment to her career but had
maintained a getting-balanced stance for several years until her
two children were in elementary school. Then, as project manager in a large high-tech company, she found herself going for
the excitement and the opportunities. She loved the thrill of
putting together a project and working round the clock to make
it come off. "I want more," she said. "I don't think I'll ever get
enough." Although her family was still important to her, it
could not meet this basic need. She and her husband divorced,
and she allowed him uncontested custody of the children.

For many, however, the costs are too high, and the trade-
offs are not adequate. They are willing to modify their internal
career aspirations to accommodate their situations. A person
who identifies herself as getting ahead, getting free, or getting
high may shift to a getting-balanced or getting-secure orientation to accommodate the needs of a husband, children, or parents. These changes can be considered fallback strategies, voluntarily chosen, and probably temporary, even though it may take
between eight and fifteen years to work through the commitment.

Sometimes this change is triggered by a rather slow awak-
ening to some inner needs that are not being met. One workshop participant, a getting-ahead executive in a rather conservative and slow-moving company, was drunk by 2 P.M. every day
of the seminar and once was drunk for an entire twenty-four-

hour period. He maintained that his drinking was social, and he typically tried to lure someone else in the workshop into "stepping out for a couple of snorts" at about 10 in the morning. Some serious confrontations occurred, triggered by this behavior, and Allen seemed to realize that he was using alcohol as a means of feeling the power denied him by the career plateau he was then experiencing. He made a commitment to some serious life changes and later entered an alcohol rehabilitation program. As a result, he gave up his unexamined ambitions for power and redefined his career success goals as those of a getting-secure person. He is now a more loyal, relaxed, and mellow worker, according to his own evaluation. The cost was that he also gave up the aggressiveness that kept him in the running for top-level jobs. Since he was free of his alcoholism and the kind of ill will he steadily generated by his inappropriate behavior, however, he did not regard the cost as unduly high. It is not completely clear in my mind whether he was able to move from getting ahead to getting secure on the basis of sheer willpower, once he recognized how inappropriate his behavior was, or whether getting secure was really his career success map, buried under unexamined youthful assumptions that "only the top" was good enough for him.

In a less dramatic example, a student in one of my Washington seminars had been on a fast track with a large medical supply company. Then she realized that she simply was not willing to turn her entire life over to the company to get ahead. There were no externally imposed crises, but she just knew she wanted to do something else. She requested a transfer from the West Coast plant to the East Coast office to make a break with the environment in which people had certain expectations of her. She accepted a different type of position, one that lessened the competitiveness of her situation, allowed her to be loyal, responsible, and efficient, yet still left some time for herself.

More typically, the trigger is not this gradual realization of internal values but an external crisis that prompts a re-examination of inner needs. Clopton (1973) links many major life changes to a realization that time is running out. One of the women I counseled with in the Midwest, Patricia S., had been very close to her sister, who was active in New York theater society. Patricia, a gifted arts manager, had collaborated with her on organizing a very successful world conference on African theater arts. Then her sister died suddenly of a rare virus. On her own, without that sustaining partnership, Patricia felt disoriented, betrayed, lost. Was she really the managerial type? Did she want to continue her professional activities or pursue a different orientation? How much of herself had been shaped by her sister? How much time did she have left?

Another counseling case was a southern woman who had grown up in a poor family. Security was an overwhelming preoccupation for her, she thought, and she spent the first twelve years of her marriage throwing every effort into helping her husband build a secure economic base, which she translated into family security. But once it became apparent that they "had it made," even by the most conservative estimates, her insecurities left her. She was ready to test her wings but was a little frightened of the strength of her own desire to fly. "I keep thinking I could do anything," she told me. "I watch a TV show and think—med school. Why not? Law? Government? Business? I feel as if I could do anything. I know that's crazy. Isn't it?" She was relieved to find out that mentally trying on lots of roles or even doing short-term experiments to test a situation is highly appropriate during a search phase. We will not know the outcome until she actually experiments and decides whether her career success map is still getting secure or whether a more absorbing orientation—such as getting ahead or getting high—is really what she wants.

Changes in the External Career. The economy changes. Companies change. A product becomes obsolete. Offices open overseas. The implied contract between you and the company changes. What do you do? If the economy is fluid enough and jobs are plentiful enough, an easy strategy is to simply change jobs so that you maintain your career direction in a different setting. Sometimes this is not an option. Your investment in the company is too great. Your chances of finding another job are too limited. The economy no longer wants the particular skills you have, and you are not sure that you can set up a company of your own. Some people stay on the job but essentially stop working. They moan, they complain, they drag their feet. They have been there too long to get fired, but they perceive themselves as being dead-ended by the company's changes. That perception may reflect reality, or it may not. One thing is certain: that kind of passive-aggressive behavior creates its own self-fulfilling prophecy, and they *will* become dead-ended.

Another real option is to change internal directions to match the realities of the external situation. Some people will argue that this is dishonest, that it betrays their inner self, and that it shows a lack of integrity. Obviously, people who feel this way should not make that kind of personal decision in their own careers. But the reality is that human beings are highly adaptive to demands from the external environment. After the initial shock of the change has worn off, an honest exploration of this option will be fruitful, even if you decide not to take it. Mihal and others (1984) show that in most careers there are discrepancies between the actual and the ideal; it is only when the individual's tolerance for the discrepancy is surpassed that a search for a new solution is launched.

For instance, a contractor with whom I am acquainted, caught in the throes of the last recession, declared bankruptcy. Originally a getting-high wheeler-dealer who had been a classic entrepreneur, he gave serious thought to the future building market and decided it would be difficult, as a one-man contracting firm, to continue in that style. "It would be logical to get out of contracting and developing," he told me, "but I really like the business and feel that my reputation was made here, my skills are sharp here. I just need to look at the best way to survive in this market." His decision was to stay in contracting but to be very careful, take few risks, be sure that jobs were lined up with solid financing, concentrate on managing his workers, and allow no deviations from payment schedules. In short, he made a transition from a getting-high orientation to a getting-secure mode of operation. Even though external events seemed to motivate this change, it seems to have been a thorough one. As nearly as I can tell from the few follow-up visits we have had, he looks, feels, and acts like a getting-secure individual.

Other external events—without being crises—can precipitate the same kinds of re-examinations and possible reorienta-
tions. When children go to school, a window opens. When a wife
or husband dies, everything has to shift around. At a university,
a professor gets tenure and feels secure enough to launch out in
a whole new direction. At certain times, it seems inevitable to
ask such questions as: Who am I? What do I want to become? I
have invested six years in becoming a professor (an auto dealer,
a computer programmer). What kind of professor (auto dealer,
computer programmer) do I want to be now? Do I even want to
stay in this profession? If I want to change, what are my options? If I make a change now, will I turn into a perpetual student? A career hopper?

Compatible Career Orientation Combinations

If you are going to change, what will you change to? My
experience shows that at times we are wide open to change and
can make very dramatic shifts in our internal career orientation.
But according to cognitive psychologists, internal stability increases over time. With increasing age and experience, their
theory goes, the margins narrow. The answer is probably somewhere in the middle. Although we can change our internal career success maps radically, we are more likely to change them
by degrees.

Career orientations seem to fall along a continuum. Getting free seems to be on one end, clustered with getting high
and getting balanced. Getting balanced occupies more of the
middle position. Clustered at the other end of the continuum
are getting ahead and getting secure. Getting high and getting
free require different payoffs: exciting work for getting-high
people (even it comes wrapped up in a lot of red tape) and autonomy at any price for getting-free people. Still, they are compatible, because they both require some degree of autonomy
and some degree of challenging work. Getting ahead and getting
secure have less in common internally than getting high and
getting free, but putting getting secure at one end of the spectrum makes sense. Getting secure and getting free are polar op-

posites, negatively correlated and mutually exclusive, as DeLong's (1982) factor analysis for M.B.A. alumni indicates. This makes sense if you think of getting free as being the starving artist and getting secure as owing your soul to the company store—or the rugged individualist versus the company man.

Getting ahead shares an intense absorption in work with getting free and getting high. But getting secure and getting ahead are very different in their goals. Getting-ahead people are more self-interested, while getting-secure people put the company's interests first. Interestingly enough, getting-ahead people who decide that they cannot make it often fall back to a getting-secure position. This is less odd than it might seem when you realize that company loyalty, general management skills, the desire for economic and status rewards, and involvement in still-existing work are high values in both orientations. On the other hand, getting-ahead careerists frequently fall back on a getting-balanced mode, especially if their transition takes the pattern of combining work with more attention to self-development. In this case, some of the need to manage may be fulfilled by heading up volunteer service activities. Some sports allow for the use of a variety of emotional, analytical, and interpersonal skills that make developing such a hobby very satisfying. If getting-ahead careerists can overcome the fear of intimacy and close relationships that seems typical in the breed, they can also get balanced in ways that create close and rewarding involvement with their spouses and children.

Getting free and getting high factor closely together. Still, getting secure remains the major fallback position for getting-ahead people who burn out on the way to the top and settle for security instead. Getting balanced, if charted on a sociogram, would represent a middle position, simply because it avoids behavioral extremes on both ends of the spectrum. Still, it requires the ability of a getting-ahead person to perform at work well enough to remain a valuable though limited employee and a high need for autonomy to juggle schedules and priorities enough to make the three spheres work. Getting balanced is a very logical fallback position for getting-high careerists. They often burn out and may need a five- to ten-year change of pace.

Frequently, their support systems cannot stand the "go for broke" intensity of their work life, and they must decide to trade off some of that work orientation for love, health, or the sheer demands for fairness from a partner who is also working. They may not have all they had hoped for in their career by maintaining more limited but still interesting work; still, they are somewhat fulfilled and have preserved other important aspects of their lives.

A common temptation for a getting-free careerist, though, is to write off close personal relationships, even those that extend into volunteer service, team sports, and community action. He or she will also toy with the advantages of dropping out of a career orientation altogether and taking on various interesting jobs to support a life-style rather than integrating the facets of a life in a getting-balanced mode. In fact, getting balanced for such a person may have more to do with work than with individual self-development activities.

If you are considering a career change, getting free and getting high are much more likely to become getting balanced than either getting secure or getting ahead. Getting ahead might back up to either getting secure or getting balanced, but many getting-ahead people also find the excitement of getting high a real attraction. For many careerists on the point of making a change, the real decision is sorting out which aspects of a career constitute a bottom line.

Getting secure is probably the hardest position to abandon, because it involves so many aspects of personality besides work style. Given enough financial and personal security, a getting-secure person might feel he or she has enough slack to make a switch. A company, such as AT&T, that has valued and attracted getting-secure employees for much of its history, precipitates a great deal of emotion-laden introspection when it suddenly changes direction from the top. Fueled by feelings of abandonment and betrayal, many employees have been precipitated into major changes. A frequent fallback position in such cases is a getting-balanced orientation. If getting-secure careerists have working spouses, sometimes they feel enough economic security to work more on aspects of self-development and hobbies that ensure getting more fun out of life. They may also move the emphasis to their major relationship, thus maintaining a career sense of direction.

But how do people make the transition from less to more absorbing directions in changing internal career perspectives? In this case, many who have or have had a getting-balanced career success map have responded to either internal or external stimuli. If money suddenly becomes a prime need, if the children are grown, if an offer comes along that cannot be refused—all of these factors can precipitate a shift into a pattern that invests more in work. In small businesses or in the professions, it is possible to postpone an all-out drive to "the top," whatever that may be, if a getting-balanced careerist shifts to a getting-ahead pattern. A more common route, however, is shifting from getting balanced to getting high—allowing work to have a greater role because it is so satisfying. It is possible, of course, for a getting-balanced person to shift to a getting-secure or a getting-free orientation; but it is unlikely. A getting-balanced person probably does not have the psychological needs that would move him or her permanently into a getting-secure mode unless major health or economic factors changed the whole picture. Also, a getting-free orientation probably would not be appealing, simply because relationships are more important than autonomy for a getting-balanced careerist.

While there are natural conceptual bridges between the getting-ahead and getting-secure career success maps, a getting-secure careerist who aspires to a getting-ahead orientation is an unlikely combination. Some of the basic motives and talents needed for getting ahead seem to be missing from a getting-secure profile. However, I worked with one client whose strong getting-secure orientation was actually an inheritance from a hard-scrabble childhood rather than an internal sense of direction. In the course of career counseling and some therapy, he found new ways of dealing with his needs for security and, with a great deal of confidence, left his original company for a riskier, more entrepreneurial setting, where he has since done very well.

Thus, although there are logical configurations and clusters of career orientations, the internal career must change before a real shift has taken place. It is this internal shift that marks the line between job hopping and the forced choice impelled by the external career.

Managing Employees in Transition

All change is difficult, and, in some ways, career counseling is a form of therapy and support during a change period. As a career counselor, I find myself helping people not by assisting them in making the actual transition but by providing additional information and resources and being a confidential listener as they deal with a major life issue, come to terms with a personal realization, or fine tune a value. Helping individuals uncover their career success maps helps them make decisions about better matching, including the strategies and tactics that are most likely to be successful in getting them where they want to go.

Needless to say, no matter how humane the company or sophisticated the personnel department, there are some built-in problems with taking transition decisions to a manager. It is very risky to tell a supervisor that you do not like the boss, do not like your current job, feel too much stress, wonder whether you are in the right field, or are generally feeling burned out. The chances of such information being used against you are pretty high. If you, as a manager, get such information directly, it is probably because of a close personal relationship—not because you are a brilliant manager. On the other hand, industry places great emphasis these days on managerial career counseling. The purpose of such a focus seems to be for managers to help employees who have getting-ahead or getting-high orientations (in other words, the professional and technical people who want to climb a technical career ladder) to learn about the formal and informal organizational programs and options available to them. In many cases, this kind of career counseling lets the manager sponsor certain employees as help is rendered. Usually, a manager will get a feeling about a person's success by hearing questions about other options, by picking up hints that someone is not entirely happy, or by noticing indicators in performance or attitude that suggest a mismatch. All of us have bad days; none of us is perfectly matched all the time. But when the negative indicators reach a certain level, a sensitive manager will usually know it.

The politics of making a transition can be tricky. Someone who is anticipating making a major change must also anticipate the repercussions in how he or she deals with the organization. Organizations hire an employee to do something, have certain expectations (usually productivity ratios), and expect people to handle personal agendas so that they continue to produce. They are more understanding with physical illness than with mental or emotional malaise, but there are still limits to that understanding. Consequently, it makes sense to hide your intentions except with friends or trusted colleagues. My experience indicates that many people who are making transitions, whether major or minor, seek out transitional programs, such as another degree, workshops, and counseling sessions, where they are with other strangers or with like-minded professionals—people who will not be taking the word back to the boss or alerting the organization about their real intentions. I frequently hear workshop participants say, "I could never say this at work" or "I'd be out on my ear if my boss heard me say this" or "I'm not going to rock any boats for three years, until I have my degree in my hand. Then I'm going to quit cold."

As a manager, you need to be realistic about the politics of this information. Some companies, such as First Chicago Corporation, Arco, Polaroid, 3M, Citibank, and Lawrence Livermore Laboratories, are sincerely interested in managing diversity and have a variety of programs, including multiple career tracks, benefit programs, job postings, and internal career counseling, to match individuals with various career opportunities and assignments. But most do not. "Coddling" workers is a luxury they cannot afford. Their attitude is, "If you don't like it here, you're free to leave." If your company has this attitude, you need to deal with it as a manager. Do you share it? If you disagree with it, how do you maintain company loyalty while working for change? In either case, your employees probably will not be very candid about their real career aspirations. If you are contemplating making a change in your own career under these circumstances, you know you have to manage your transition carefully. Treat the information about your current status carefully. Use your internal career success map as a guide. You will need to collect realistic information about the opportunities in the external career so that you can tell where the matches are. You have to be willing to accept the limits placed on fulfilling your internal career by the realities of your external career. But it is a political issue as well as a personal one. Most careerists that I have counseled have taken fairly elaborate precautions to assure themselves that the information would remain confidential.

The need for confidentiality was underscored for me when I ran a workshop at the annual retreat for a group of grocery-store owners in the Atlanta region. I had people fill out assessment instruments similar to those in Chapter Eleven and then group themselves according to the five major career success orientations. That was a big mistake. While these groupings are a useful exercise for strangers, 100 percent of these grocers defined themselves as getting-high entrepreneurs, getting-free individualists, or getting-ahead executives. There were no self-declared getting-secure or getting-balanced people, because the material would have been politically sensitive, a fact I immediately realized when I saw the enormous getting-high group (a model for small-business entrepreneurs). Afterward, a man of about fifty came up and announced, "I lied in that exercise. I really have a getting-balanced profile, but there's no way on earth I'd let my colleagues know that. The grocers' image is a clear one: work around the clock, be totally in business, run a tight ship, and don't let anybody tell you what to do. I know seven or eight people in this room who lied, too—but we're not about to let our colleagues know that we're different."

What can managers do if they have employees who are troubled by the trauma of moving through a major transition? How can you manage them effectively so that in the long run they will still be an important human resource to your firm? Contrary to the popular wisdom on the subject, it is bad policy to downplay career development and withhold information about career opportunities on the grounds that the new information will increase dissatisfaction with the status quo. Whatever time you buy this way is a short-term gain. Even if the economy cooperates by making the job market a threatening place to be, this condition can only be temporary; dissatisfied workers who see pay cuts or layoffs on the way will simply be more political and more alert to their slender chances to get out. The costly turnover, especially in companies that depend on such scarce talent as engineers and programmers, can cause a potentially fatal talent drain. If people are aware enough of their own dissatisfaction to be searching, then *something* is going to happen.

The best thing you can do as a manager is to help that search, support it, and manage it rather than sweep it under the carpet. You may be able to create a better match between your employee and your organization that will benefit both. The potential consequence of ignoring it is losing the employee, either physically or psychologically. At least, good will and good feelings will remain, even if the person goes elsewhere. Discouragement leads to consequences you may not intend: players become more political and covert. They will feel that they had to change jobs because of pressure to perform in unacceptable ways. Many of them will also feel justified in subterfuge and sabotage ("what choice did I have?") and will no longer feel bound to act ethically if they feel they are being treated unfairly. Here are some guidelines for healthy career management during transitions:

1. Assuming that managers know their people relatively well, you should be alert to clues in behavior, attitude, and speech that might indicate that a transition is approaching. Does an employee seem troubled, out of synch, mismatched, or in some kind of turmoil? Has a problem occurred—a divorce, a death, a midlife crisis—that may have triggered a major internal life change? These factors, even if not work related, may spill over into the work life. Perhaps the trauma is purely personal and what is most needed from you is some short-term realignments ("time out"). Your role is simply to acknowledge the

pain and stress and offer empathy. If there are implications for work, recognize and acknowledge them. Steer the employee into counseling or a support group. The faster personal issues are resolved, the faster the employee will be able to turn his or her attention back to work. However, avoid suggesting that your primary interest is to "fix" the problem so that your employee, like a faulty machine, can get back on track.

2. As a manager, try to give your employee the space necessary to work things out. Be supportive in terms of time off or a lessening of demands that will release energy for the nonwork problem, if you can. The long-term payoffs will be increased loyalty from your employee.

3. It can be helpful to have an exploratory conference where the main agenda is to seek understanding, give information, and provide reassurance. Remember that the conference itself is a problem for an employee who is, more likely than not, reticent, confused, and probably scared of you. After all, you represent the interests of the organization. No matter what the presentation, no matter how confidently and positively he or she answers questions, you can count on an underlying confusion. The bits and pieces of the career search have almost certainly not yet been put together in any coherent way. If you press for information, you are asking for more definitive reports than he or she probably has. Do not ask for commitments. Do not offer rewards or threats. The purpose of this interview is to indicate support and present yourself as a source of information.

You should know, at this point, what kind of company support is available. If you can offer in-company career counseling or counseling from a private contractor that the company helps pay for, it communicates powerfully that the employee is valued and that the company has a strong interest in the outcome. (In general, outside counseling is more reassuring to people worried about privacy. Any rumor of spillover will kill the effectiveness of an in-house program.)

Does your company allow such options as applying for other jobs within the division or company? Does it supply job-posting services or job-matching programs? Do lateral moves and multiple career tracks give employees options to pursue? As a manager you could profitably explain the various education and training programs available.

As part of this initial interview, set up a tentative plan for the search and indicate convenient times when you and the employee can check back in, both formally and informally.

4. Once the search process is under way, you are then in a position to have a more specific session—even a performance review—to take the new information and anticipated career changes and match them with the employee's interests. This is a potentially painful step. The employee may decide to leave your division or even your company. If, however, the option is to stay—either with you or somewhere else in the company—the organization has gained a more useful human resource.

 ELEVEN

Assessing Individual Career Orientations

Chapters Five through Nine explained five different definitions of career success, with individual examples, strategies for achieving maximum success, and suggestions for managing people with these different career success orientations. This chapter presents the self-assessment tools that can be used to evaluate and interpret an individual's internal career success map. These tools will help you to assess four factors that affect your career orientation:

1. *Motives*—those factors that provide enjoyment, stimulation, and fulfillment at work. They usually depend on the content and/or process of the work itself and are often conceived of as what you really like about work versus what you really dislike.
2. *Values*—your guiding beliefs, philosophies, attitudes, and norms as they are related to work. They usually depend on the context of the work, especially the organizational culture. Values are often defined in terms of what kinds of causes and life values the careerist is most dedicated to.
3. *Talents*—the abilities—especially the knowledge, skills, and other personal resources—that give you a competitive edge over your peers. They are usually associated with performance in the content, process, and context of the work and

are often perceived as areas where you excel in comparison with others in your reference group.

4. *Perceived constraints*—the situations that you feel prevent you from making career decisions solely on the basis of your motives, values, and talents. They are often thought of as a combination of constraining personal situations (for example, relationship constraints) that may not change in the short term (one to five years) and that thus alter your internal career perspective.

Assessing Career Orientations

It is possible in a rather precise way to determine the internal career success orientation that you carry around inside by using this formula:

$$CSM = (M + V + T) - PC$$

CSM, *the career success map,* equals *motives* plus *values* plus *talents,* minus *perceived constraints.* Let's take one of my potential admirals. He is not really motivated to get ahead. Instead, what he really wants is to have a cushy desk job in a place like Newport News or San Francisco and, as he puts it, "stop wading through the movers to get to the front door and be able to find the bathroom at night without a map." Security and a comfortable routine are important for him. His talents are considerable: after all, the navy thinks of him as a potential admiral and he will be able to work his way up rapidly through the necessary shoreside and shipboard positions until he can make the choice of taking permanent sea commands or opting for shore duty, which he will. A perceived constraint, however, is his wife's health. She has asthma. Some of the climates they have lived in have been hard on her and he is worried about being gone for six months at a time. Putting together his career success map must accommodate and weight his motives, his values, his talents, and his wife's health to get an accurate picture of the whole.

A *career success map* requires more than just feeling an

affinity for a certain work orientation (M + V + T). The internal career depends on what seems possible given your desires and also what you can realistically achieve. Furthermore, with knowledge and a range of options, we may discover the ability and the motivation to modify our career orientations. We can also change the intensity of our internal career to make whatever map we follow more manageable in light of our perceived constraints.

Freud once observed that a fully mature person would be able to do two things: work and love. Work has its own reality, demands, and satisfactions. Beyond work, however, are the personal constraints that coexist with our work lives, directly influencing the internal career. Many workers act on "hidden agendas" when personal goals conflict with organizational goals, as Virginia Schein (1977) points out. In such cases, people play career politics (usually covertly) to make some sort of match between their needs and those of the enterprise.

What are some of these personal constraints (or freedoms) which might influence the internal career orientation someone eventually chooses? They can include being in a dual-career partnership and needing to accommodate the spouse's career, having a supportive or unsupportive spouse, being geographically rooted and unwilling to move or willing to be mobile, providing high-quality intensive parenting at a given point or being comparatively free from family demands, poor health or good health, emotional problems, and having or lacking crucial friendship or support networks. All of these factors can ultimately influence your internal career success orientation and those of your employees.

Determining the career success map is, however, only part of the process. The context in which that orientation becomes operational is the external career—the company and what it wants (Chapter Three). If you accurately understand the first two elements—the internal career and the external career—you are then in a position to make wise decisions about the third element—strategies and tactics—or, as we are calling it, career politics. Only by understanding each of these three elements (what is behind much of the employee's long-term behavior, the realities of the organization or occupation, and how employees are trying to maneuver to achieve their career agendas within a certain context) can a manager effectively direct career diversity.

The tools presented in this chapter should be used critically and cautiously. Six caveats apply. First, though individuals try to assure their long-term self-interests according to their career success maps, their work experience itself helps shape those maps. For example, although many employees begin their careers by believing that success means getting ahead, work lets them experience their limitations and strengths (Sally may not be particularly adept at office politics, but she is a genius at marketing). Furthermore, they will observe close up those who have achieved hierarchical success and perceive the costs as well as the benefits. In the process, a careerist may discover that getting high is really his or her definition of career success.

Second, the specific whens, hows, and whats of actually following a certain career success map depend on several contextual variables. Organizational culture is such a variable. So are an individual's career stage and the career opportunities that come with an organization or occupation. Luck also comes into play for most of us. In addition, most people must work very hard to pay their dues early in the career to acquire enough job security to exercise their particular strategy. Actually attaining a satisfactory version of personal career success is thus a long and complex process (Derr, 1982b), but it begins with formulating a career success orientation—a process that is part decision but also part discovery.

Third, research has shown (Derr, 1980; Seligman, 1981) that, while many have a career, not everyone is career oriented. Some do not really plan or try to shape their long-term work histories. They allow events and opportunities to dictate the course of their career, and the relationship of forces in their career is controlled mostly by outside factors. Thus, a good portion of those employed may not be able to articulate a career map because they do not have one.

Fourth, these internal career orientations can change with new self-discoveries or personal events that "trigger" major conceptual-emotional shifts. Mihal and others (1984) report that when a person's "threshold" for discrepancies between the internal and external careers is surpassed, he or she will launch a search to resolve the dilemma. One result of this process may be a change in the internal career orientation. Some people, therefore, find themselves in career transitional states. Under such circumstances, they are unable to declare a clear sense of internal career direction, because they are still searching for it. Of course, such a search might end in reconfirming the old career success map or following a new one.

Fifth, the force of the direction associated with a particular career success map may vary markedly from person to person. One person may be a very strong getting-ahead individual, while someone else may have that internal career orientation but to a lesser degree. There are few "pure types." Rather, a continuum of very strong to moderately strong to mild usually exists.

Finally, self-perceptions are often less accurate than external observations. A clinically trained career counselor, for example, would observe motives, values, talents, and perceived constraints from a different (and often more experienced and theoretically grounded) point of view than the individual. Many social scientists have pointed out that even ardently espoused theories do not always match our actual behavior. Thus, it is easy for us to engage in wishful thinking or to be overly influenced by a problem or event of the moment. Sometimes we even have trouble being completely honest and open with ourselves.

When I engage in individual career assessment in the role of career counselor, I usually ask to speak to one or two intimate acquaintances of the client—a spouse, grown child, close friend, or colleague. I ask this "significant other" to give me his or her perceptions of the client's motives, values, talents, and constraints. This provides me with cross-checks on the self-assessment of the person in question. In assessing your own career, you should find someone whom you trust, who knows you well, and who is both candid and perceptive. Share with him or her your self-assessment. If possible, do this with at least two close associates. Ask them to confirm or correct your analysis, and, of course, ask them to give you reasons for and examples of their perceptions. As an additional confirmation, you could have these associates complete a questionnaire about you and then compare their scores with yours.

Your Career Orientation

Assessment. DeLong (1982, p. 60) has pointed out that the use of a survey to assess the internal career has some methodological problems. He states: "The multi-dimensional nature of the career anchor constructs makes measurement of the constructs very difficult." Schein (1978) identified his range of career anchor results primarily by using in-depth interviews. Thus, the questionnaire may not be as beneficial for assessment of the internal career as the interview. The brief questionnaire shown in Exhibit 1 will help you, however, to assess your internal career orientation in general terms. If your getting-high score

Exhibit 1. Career Success Map Questionnaire.

Basic talents, values, and motives all affect your decisions about your career. The following survey is designed to help you understand your career orientation. You cannot fail this test; there are no right or wrong answers.

Each item contains two statements. Choose the one that you feel more accurately reflects you or is more true of you. You must choose one of the statements, even though you may not like either or you may like both of them. Do not skip any pair of statements or circle both alternatives in one set. Circle the letter corresponding to the *one* sentence you select as the most reflective of you. Do not spend a lot of time weighing your answers.

1. I see work as a team sport and like to organize myself and oth-   V
   ers to win.
   I like to do my own thing in an organization.   X

(continued on next page)

Exhibit 1. Career Success Map Questionnaire, Cont'd.

---

2. Work must be balanced by time for leisure and the develop-   Y
   ment of significant relationships.
   Personal needs must be subordinated for me to get ahead.   V

3. I would like to work in an organization that rewards hard   W
   work, loyalty, and competence.
   I like setting my own goals and accomplishing them at my own   X
   pace and in my own way.

4. I am aggressive and have good analytical skills.   V
   I am able to keep a good perspective between the needs of my   Y
   work and the needs of my family.

5. I would like to work independently.   X
   I like to be part of a stable organization and to have my own   W
   place in it.

6. I enjoy working as an expert or "troubleshooter" and being   Z
   able to demonstrate my expertise in a particular area.
   I enjoy working in a situation where I am the leader and am   V
   responsible for achieving certain objectives.

7. My spouse/partner is as important to me as my career.   Y
   My spouse/partner takes a back seat to my work when I am in   Z
   the middle of a very exciting project.

8. The most important thing to me is:
       Freedom.   X
       Maintaining perspective.   Y

9. I am competent, loyal, trustworthy, and hard working.   W
   I am politically skillful, a good leader, and a good administra- V
   tor.

I can be described as:
10. Self-reliant.   X
    Flexible.   Y

11. One who gets "turned on" by exciting work.   Z
    One who likes to be his or her own boss.   X

12. In equilibrium but divided.   Y
    Adventurous and competitive.   Z

13. Self-reliant, self-sufficient.   X
    Imaginative, enthused.   Z

Exhibit 1. Career Success Map Questionnaire, Cont'd.

---

14.   Stable and tenacious.   W
      Independent and self-directed.   X

15.   One who plans and organizes extremely well.   V
      One who analyzes situations and develops creative new solu-   Z
      tions.

16.   An expert in my field.   Z
      A solid citizen.   W

17.   Able to modify my own goals to accommodate to organiza-   W
      tional goals and leaders.
      Intent on finding a way to make the organization's goals and   Y
      my own personal goals converge.

18.   A personal goal is to:
          Control my work circumstances.   X
          Not let work interfere with the needs of my family.   Y

19.   It is important to:
          Have a job where there is security and a sense of belonging.   W
          Be able to devote time to family and other activities.   Y

20.   I prefer:
          A career with potential for promotions.   V
          The opportunity to tackle challenging problems or tasks.   Z.

21.   I like being in the center of power.   V
      I value long-term employment, acceptance, and being valued   W
      by the organization.

22.   I view knowing the right people and making the right friends   V
      as important to career advancement.
      I view being able to develop my career along my own areas of   X
      interest as the critical factor.

23.   The bottom line for me is gaining a sense of balance between   Y
      work and private life.
      The bottom line for me is stability, benefits, and having a se-   W
      cure place.

24.   I would like a position with maximum self-control and auton-   X
      omy.
      I would most like to get work that is crucial and central to the   V
      organization.

(continued on next page)

Exhibit 1. Career Success Map Questionnaire, Cont'd.

25.	The bottom line for me is stability, benefits, and a secure place.	W
	The bottom line for me is advancing up the organization.	V
26.	I view financial success and increased power and prestige as important measures of career success.	V
	I view success in my career as having equal time for work, family, and self-development.	Y
27.	I would rather:	
	Excel in my field.	Z
	Be considered dependable and loyal.	W
28.	I prefer:	
	Managing people on a long-term basis.	W
	Managing people on a task-force or project basis.	Z
29.	Professional development and continued training are important for their own sake.	Z
	Professional development is important as a means to becoming an expert and gaining more flexibility and independence.	X
30.	The bottom line for me is to seek an equilibrium between personal and professional life.	Y
	The bottom line for me is excitement and stimulation.	Z

Scoring

The scoring is quite simple. Follow these instructions and then plot your CSM profile on the grid below. Once you have completed the test, go back through it and add up the number of times you circled the letter V. Then do the same with each of the other letters, writing the number in the space provided. If you have completed the test accurately up to this point, the total will be thirty ($V + W + X + Y + Z = 30$).

Ahead	*Secure*	*Free*	*Balanced*	*High*

Score: $V =$ ____ $W =$ ____ $X =$ ____ $Y =$ ____ $Z =$ ____

Once you have totaled the letters and checked to make sure the totals equal, plot the answers on the graph below. The highest peaks indicate your career orientation.

Exhibit 1. Career Success Map Questionnaire, Cont'd.

CSM Profile.

Intensity	12	.	.	.	.	.
	11	.	.	.	.	.
Strong	10	.	.	.	.	.
	9	.	.	.	.	.
	8	....	....	....	....	....
	7	.	.	.	.	.
Average	6	.	.	.	.	.
	5	.	.	.	.	.
	4	....	....	....	....	....
	3	.	.	.	.	.
Weak	2	.	.	.	.	.
	1	.	.	.	.	.
	0	.	.	.	.	.
		Ahead	Secure	Free	Balanced	High

on this questionnaire is 6 or higher, an additional instrument will help clarify this profile. As Chapter Eight demonstrates, this general career orientation includes entrepreneurs, adventurers, specialists, and altruists, making it the most complex of the career success maps to measure. The inventory in Exhibit 2 will supply more precise information and is valid to the extent that the getting-high score was particularly strong for you. See Chap-

Exhibit 2. Getting-High Inventory.

Circle *a*, *b*, *c*, or *d*, indicating the item or answer that most represents you or that you most prefer.

1. a. I want to dedicate my life to a meaningful cause or to the service of others.
   b. I want to concentrate on advancing my field and developing my expertise.
   c. I want most to have very exciting experiences or adventures—even if that means potential physical dangers or financial ruin.
   d. As a life goal, I want to create new businesses, products, or services that will endure and become significant.

(continued on next page)

Exhibit 2. Getting-High Inventory, Cont'd.

2.   a.   More important than the money are recognition of my contributions and being moved into positions where I can influence policies that advance the cause.

      b.   I want to be remunerated according to my education and skill level, commensurate with what my peers receive.

      c.   I would like a reward system that gives me very substantial pay and other benefits (time off and so on) for completing extremely difficult assignments or missions critical to the organization.

      d.   I want to be the owner and reap the rewards or failures of my own efforts.

3.   a.   A good manager is someone who agrees with important values and issues and supports my trying to do something about them.

      b.   A good manager feeds me challenging work in my area of specialization and recognizes my contributions.

      c.   I do not care so much whether a problem is in my area of expertise, but a good manager will feed me almost impossible assignments that others will not or cannot do, giving me the autonomy I need to get the job done.

      d.   There is no such thing as a good manager. I manage myself, and I need new creative opportunities to develop new products, services, or organizations.

4.   a.   The bottom line for me is realizing my goals and influencing the world around me to make a difference.

      b.   The bottom line for me is making a contribution by exercising my special talents and applying myself to my area of expertise.

      c.   The bottom line for me is succeeding at new, difficult, thrilling, adventurous tasks.

      d.   The bottom line for me is using my creativity in the pursuit of new ventures: products, services, or organizations.

5.   a.   I most fear having to abandon what I think right or best—in short, what has become a bit of a crusade for me.

      b.   I most fear having to abandon my profession and do more general work or otherwise being cut off from interesting and challenging work in my field.

      c.   I most fear becoming bored by mundane and routine work and not having access to stimulating, difficult, and adventurous tasks, even to my own "impossible dreams."

      d.   I most fear having to work for someone else and not being able to fully exercise my own creativity.

	Ideo-logical	Special-ist	Adven-turous	Entre-preneurial
Total	a _____	b _____	c _____	d _____

ter Eight for a more complete discussion of these categories. The ideological person gets excited about particular issues, client groups, or causes. The specialist careerist is turned on by increasingly challenging work in his or her area of expertise. The adventurer gets high from the pure excitement and challenge of impossible, adventurous (often dangerous) assignments. And the entrepreneur is driven by the need to create new products, businesses, or services and get them going.

Interpretation. In interpreting your career success map profile on the scoring sheet of the survey, consider: (1) To what extent is one internal career orientation clearly dominant over the others? A clear dominance—which will not be apparent in all cases—probably suggests that your career success map is well developed and has proved satisfactory to you. Do not be alarmed if no clear dominance emerges, however. (2) What is your backup internal career orientation, or what general pattern seems to develop? In general, getting high and getting free complement one another and should receive close scores. Getting ahead and getting secure have the same relationship. Getting balanced usually sides with getting free and getting high. It would be highly unusual for getting secure and getting free to be paired. Thus, in addition to finding the single strongest orientation, you should find in the chart a sense of direction. However, a very mixed pattern might lead to the third question. (3) Is your career success map drawn yet? If you have a very balanced profile where all of the scores are about equal, where the intensity is generally weak, or where an unconventional pairing occurs, your career success map may either not yet be formulated or be in the process of being redrawn. Possibly you are not a career-directed person. Many people, even those with long and successful work histories, still do not have a planned, long-term, inner-directed sense of their work futures. For some, work is not a central value or variable in life.

One reason for an unclear or weak pattern in your career success map may be that you are in the middle of a major life change, questioning a former internal career orientation and considering adopting a new one. In the search mode, it is normal for a career success map profile to look complex. A second possibility in interpreting a complex and unclear type of profile is that circumstances may be compelling you to pay attention to one orientation right now but that you do not consider it to be your "real" long-term internal career orientation. This often happens, for example, to people who have lost jobs or are switching jobs and feel a high need for security. Once the need for security is met, they will not necessarily stay getting-secure people. As another example, a getting-ahead careerist may feel temporarily burned out and be concentrating on personal needs and personal relationships, but this does not indicate a genuine getting-balanced profile. What it does mean is that such factors will score high on the survey, confusing the identification of the real long-term internal career orientation. Unfortunately, there is no built-in filter on the questionnaire to let you determine with certainty whether you are in the process of changing or just falling back temporarily to a different orientation.

Another caution on evaluation is appropriate at this point. If you are a manager considering this questionnaire's utility in assessing your employees, you should be aware that the chances are not good of getting valid data. Like many surveys used for such purposes, this one is vulnerable to the astute employee who knows what answers will be most acceptable and gives politically advantageous responses to "look good." Remember, information about real feelings, beliefs, and long-term intentions is highly political. Revealing strategy is dangerous if it does not happen to be what the boss wants to hear. If these obstacles can be overcome and the information can be used in a genuinely helpful setting, then the survey will be valuable to both manager and employee. A manager would want, of course, to remove the score sheet from the back of the questionnaire to reduce categorization bias while the employee is taking the test. The instrument could be scored and the profile plotted after the questionnaire is completed.

Perceived Personal Constraints

The second assessment task in identifying the career success map is determining the impact of your perceived personal constraints. Here we let reality speak to the ideal—the limitations, too-high costs, and disadvantages that modify moving full steam and single-focusedly toward working out your internal career orientation. The advantage of such a process, of course, is that it provides a more inclusive and hence more accurate career success map, because it includes nonwork elements that definitely affect our work lives. It is not possible, given our definition of a career, to segregate work from the other critical aspects of our lives. Sometimes we must alter our hopes and aspirations because of our personal circumstances. Whether these are real is not as critical as the fact that we perceive them as real and act on them; the entire internal career is highly subjective and personal.

Assessment. Here is a way to assess the most commonly mentioned constraints that, once perceived and accepted, can cause you to change your internal career orientation. The survey in Exhibit 3 should provide you with information about the cumulative impact of your various personal constraints and your career direction. If you are somewhat or greatly constrained,

Exhibit 3. Perceived Constraints Survey.

A. *Your Immediate Constraints.*

      Assign a value to the personal but work-related factors listed below. Think of your personal situation only in relationship to your career. Arrange your ratings of the various items on a scale of 1 to 5, where 5 represents a constraint that is very typical of your situation and that you must take into account and 1 represents a constraint that does not apply to your case.

1.   Unsupportive spouse/partner   _____
2.   Need to accommodate to your spouse's career   _____
3.   Very demanding responsibilities as a parent   _____
4.   Other encumbering relationships, such as caring for aging family members   _____
5.   Poor physical health   _____
6.   Unresolved psychological/emotional problems   _____
7.   Lack of financial resources   _____
8.   Lack of geographical mobility   _____
9.   Employer discrimination against the group with which you are visibly identified (for instance, a minority)   _____
10.   Starting your career late   _____

(continued on next page)

Exhibit 3. Perceived Constraints Survey, Cont'd.

---

11. Lack of mentors or sponsors   _____
12. Lack of influential peer group and connections   _____
13. Lack of friendship and support network   _____

        Total Points   _____

B. *Estimated Future Constraints.*

    Now complete the same form as above, with this important difference: complete it as you best imagine your circumstances *five years* from now. If, for example, you are planning to become part of a supportive friendship network or your family circumstances are likely to change (children become more independent, for example) over the next five years, your ratings on the factors below would change. Supposing it is five years from now, assign a value from 5 (very typical) to 1 (does not apply) to the personal constraints listed below.

1.   Unsupportive spouse/partner   _____
2.   Need to accommodate to your spouse's career   _____
3.   Very demanding responsibilities as a parent   _____
4.   Other encumbering relationships, such as caring for aging
     family members   _____
5.   Poor physical health   _____
6.   Unresolved psychological/emotional problems   _____
7.   Lack of financial resources   _____
8.   Lack of geographical mobility   _____
9.   Employer discrimination against the group with which you
     are very visibly identified (for instance, a minority)   _____
10. Starting your career late   _____
11. Lack of mentors or sponsors   _____
12. Lack of influential peer group and connections   _____
13. Lack of friendship and support network   _____

        Total Points   _____

    From the above list or from factors not listed above but rather unique to your situation, list the two or three major constraints that affect how you define your internal career. Explain them.

---

you may not be able to see yourself pursuing a highly absorbing career path, such as getting ahead, getting high, or getting free. The score sheet and work sheet at the end of the survey will help you interpret the impact of these constraints on your overall career success map. If you are a manager, you can use this instrument with the same cautions and awareness mentioned in connection with the questionnaire.

Interpretation. The various factors listed in Exhibit 3 represent personal constraints that would conflict with a work-intensive or more absorbing career pattern. Some combinations of variables tip the scales on the work/nonwork balance and make people rethink their internal career orientation. The total scores of both the immediate and future ratings must be considered for assessing the internal career. In general, a significantly lower future score shows that you are becoming less constrained and could plan for, without alteration and regardless of intensity, the most appealing and representative internal career orientation $(M + V + T)$. The matrix shown in Exhibit 4 will help you understand your scores from the survey.

Exhibit 4. Interpretation of Perceived Constraints Survey.

Score	Category	Immediate (A)	Future (B)
13–25	Free to choose		
26–44	Somewhat constrained		
45–65	Constrained		

Instructions: Write in the appropriate space your total scores for both times you answered the questions: Column A, "Your Immediate Constraints," and Column B, "Estimated Future Constraints." Now look at your scores. If you are not particularly constrained now or in the near future, you can feel free to follow your internal career orientation. If you are constrained, you may need to modify your internal career success map or remove some of the personal constraints so that you can better follow your internal inclinations.

Summarizing Your Career Success Map Assessment

At this point, you can identify your career success map on information from the earlier steps. First, determine your initial career orientation score: your dominant orientation and your backup orientation, as measured by the Career Success Map Questionnaire. Now, from the matrix of the Perceived Constraints Inventory, decide whether, within the next five years, you will be free to choose, somewhat constrained, or constrained.

Given the constraints, decide whether your career success map is getting ahead, getting secure, getting high, getting free, or getting balanced. Finally, explain the extent to which you feel this describes your internal career success identity. How strong or how weak is it? What is the likelihood that it will change at some point in your career? And if so, to what?

 TWELVE

Applications
for Managers:
Working Effectively
with All
Career Orientations

Because career success maps are such potent and personal instruments, learning how to assess them can be particularly valuable for a manager interested in diagnosing the internal career of his or her various subordinates, peers, and bosses to better work with them. For that same reason, their misuse can be extremely damaging.

I am assuming that managers are both intelligent and well meaning. But managers get their work done through people. To be successful and productive, they have to constantly try to analyze the best way to motivate, influence, and even control their valuable human resources. Managers are also very busy people. Both Mintzberg (1973) and Kotter (1982) help us to understand the pressures and complexities of the schedules of high-level managers, who sometimes have a propensity, even in human resource management, to search for a quick fix, a "one right answer." Understand this: no theory can be complex enough to match the complexity of a human being. Any theory describes only part of an individual's underlying thought, attitudes, and actions.

What makes the task even more difficult is the natural role managers play where their employees are concerned. It is not possible for managers to divorce themselves entirely from an evaluative role in which, on many occasions, they must represent the interests of the company rather than those of the individual. Examples are evaluating employee performance each year and recommending promotions, pay raises, and job changes. Consequently, employees are likely to disguise or withhold information from their manager in their own self-interest.

Some further complications muddy the waters of career orientation assessment. Employees who are career oriented may be experiencing a career transition (Chapter Ten). Others may not be career oriented. It is usually quite possible to differentiate those for whom work forms a central aspect of their lives from those who simply work to survive economically or take whatever opportunity presents itself without any internal career orientation. Even for getting-balanced careerists, it is quite clear that one of the important pillars of their self-concept and personal plans is their career. While they are concerned about equilibrium, they will become very dissatisfied if their work is not meaningful and directed. People in transition, however, are more difficult cases and may even appear to lack a career orientation. While some have strong and clear internal career orientations, others who are also career oriented have weaker, less developed profiles. Some persons take longer than others to clarify an internal career perspective, sometimes making such discoveries in their middle or late thirties.

Diagnosing Career Orientations

Given the complexity of people and the probability that they will be very cautious when interacting with someone in authority, how can the manager diagnose an internal career orientation? The questions below, which a manager can answer on the basis of interactions with a given employee, may be helpful in supplying an accurate overview, but they should not replace an in-depth interview with the employee and others who know him or her.

Motives. Questions that can be helpful in diagnosing this area include:

1. What kinds of events, tasks, and assignments does this employee particularly enjoy? What kinds of work "turn on" this person?
2. What kinds of assignments, tasks, and events "turn off" this person? What does he or she dislike doing?

The value of this information is obvious. Knowing what a person likes doing is the key to providing work that will, in itself, be rewarding.

Talents. Useful questions in this area include:

1. What are this employee's major professional strengths or talents?
2. In which areas, if any, does he or she excel in comparison to peers?
3. What are some of his or her key weaknesses?
4. How much do these weaknesses affect his or her professional performance?

Values. So far, these questions have followed the classic human resource pattern of management. The questions on values make the task more difficult. Life values can stem from one's family of origin, religious or cultural heritage, and formative experiences in childhood, many of which are not even known on a conscious level. A way must be found to incorporate these life/work values into any description of the internal career success map.

1. What philosophies or beliefs seem to guide this individual?
2. To what causes, people, or tasks does he or she seem most dedicated?
3. What sorts of things seem to offend him or her most?
4. Of what does he or she seem proudest?

Values can be determined by ascertaining philosophies, beliefs,

objects of dedication, and sources of pride. It is often difficult
to differentiate between personal and professional values, but
the important point for managers is to determine to what extent these values affect the careerist's work and how.

Personal Constraints. The career success map formula
shows that internal career success depends on motives + values
+ talents — perceived personal constraints. Most people, even
those with strong and clear internal career orientations, formulate their personal career plans during a definite period of time
with respect to significant aspects of their personal or nonwork
lives. Managers must also consider these factors.

1. Is this person's partnership life constraining? How?
2. Is this person's parenting life constraining? How?
3. Is this person's extended-family life constraining? How?
4. Is this person's health a constraint? How?
5. Is this person geographically mobile?
6. Is this person's educational or social background con-
    straining? How?

I call these normal life elements (which vary for each of us) *constraints* only because they act as forces that can alter the career
success map perspective. They can also be important sources of
personal happiness that an individual would not choose to alter.
They represent realities that affect—positively or negatively—an
individual's ability to make career dreams come true.

By asking these questions and trying to determine the answers, within the limits of the information, managers can arrive
at a basic perception of the internal career success orientation
of a subordinate, a peer, or a boss. The accuracy of a diagnosis
depends, of course, on the accuracy of the information, much
of which will be purposely concealed in the politically charged
world of organizations. Accuracy also depends on a manager's
skill at psychological diagnosis and the clarity, strength, and stability of the other person's career success map. Given human
complexity and change, no evaluation should be taken as absolutely final.

Another option to the manager's private analysis is to ask

subordinates to read this book and place themselves in a category. In this case, a manager should allow for distorted self-perceptions, the play of career politics, and the possibility of evolution toward another career success map. The manager and subordinate could then discuss their joint perceptions and try to arrive at a career direction that, when matched with various opportunities, would enhance productivity. Whatever else happens, effectively matching the internal and external careers of individual employees requires mutual recognition of essential information and contracting about future behavior on the part of both the individual and the organizational representative.

Effective Managerial Tasks

My experience convinces me that these diverse career orientations can be well managed and that the organizations that make the best use of their diverse human resources will, ultimately, be most effective. Managers who use this material to "weed out" the deviant cases will not only be on shaky ground ethically but will also do their organization a disservice. Given these cautions against being too much of a psychologist, what, then, is a manager's most productive role in managing career diversity?

As representatives of company interests, managers must evaluate, set standards and controls, and insist on certain levels of productivity. A vital element in managing career diversity is specifying clear guidelines and limits within which subordinates may negotiate their career agendas. It is probably never effective for a company to demand complete uniformity and conformity, but organizations must achieve common objectives to survive. It would, therefore, be as ineffective for the diverse individual needs to prevail without concern for the company good as it would for the company's needs to dictate all behavior. Managing career diversity requires some compromise on the part of both the individual and the organization. It requires that employees understand their choices and also the limits beyond which exercising those choices becomes disruptive and punishable.

On the positive side, the most valuable employees are usually those who make themselves valued because they fill a need vital to the company. It is also useful for managers to help others understand where and how they can become valued (thereby increasing their own ability to negotiate a situation more to their liking), even in their own unique and diverse way. Some of the organizational pressure points that a manager could help any type of careerist address in creative and useful ways are: how to increase productivity and accomplish the work; how to achieve objectives; how to maintain quality; how to better recruit new employees; how to prevent premature turnover; how to assure a spirit of innovation; and how to enhance the department/company image. However, managing the new careerists in their diversity requires additional perspectives.

Have a Careers Attitude. The first step begins with an attitude of valuing career diversity and making good use of it. One of the most powerful ways to intervene in the life of an organization is to alter the underlying assumptions and attitudes of those in power (Schein, 1985). Managers who value career diversity find that employees share more about their true career intentions and work willingly to effect a better match between their needs and those of the organization. Subordinates and colleagues will feel valued and willing to make the best use of their various strengths. A spirit of reciprocity and corporate pride emerges. People who might feel deviant and marginal in other enterprises respond to being valued with greater loyalty and greater willingness to subordinate some of their own agendas for the good of the company. This situation may especially be true as they consider the policies of organizations that value only one type of person—one who looks, acts, and thinks like the other general managers.

A second strategy is to encourage the organization to develop human resource/career development programs and systems that increase options for employees with diverse career orientations. These actions are part of every manager's *policy-making role* in which he or she is able to initiate and/or influence key organizational decisions. In this role, line managers are usually more influential than staff specialists, although human resource managers in some companies will be helpful allies in this task. For example, good managers have a sense of the internal careers of their people. What would the best career placement moves be? Up? Out? Sideways? Down? And when? When the economic picture is bleak, movement slows down. Employees would rather have a less-than-perfect job than no job. This makes your task as a manager both easier and harder—it makes it easier to keep people but harder to get turnover when you want it and harder to move your own career along. A number of professions, such as education and engineering, are pretty flat, without much room to maneuver. Getting-ahead people look for the kind of company that has many vertical levels and, consequently, many ways to move up.

Two current career development options are the dual-ladder plan and lateral moves. The dual-ladder system merits serious attention. It has been frustrating for many talented individuals who want to be at the cutting edge of their craft to be "rewarded" by being moved away from their tools, putting them in the position of managing other people to do the projects they really want to do themselves. Yet how can they retain their status in the company if they refuse the promotion? For example, of seventy-three large American, British, French, German, Swiss, and Swedish multinational companies that I recently surveyed, sixty defined a high-potential employee as a general manager who has the best prospects of moving up two or three levels in the managerial hierarchy by a certain point in time. However, thirteen innovative and very successful companies were beginning to include technical or functional specialists and internal entrepreneurs as part of the high-potential group and provided different but significant career paths and rewards for them. Employee morale in these companies is high, and, by all indications, the direction is a promising one. These industry leaders are Apple Computers, Esso Chemicals, Honeywell, and Hewlett-Packard (United States); L. M. Ericcson, Pharmacia, and IKEA (Sweden); Schering, Sandoz, Dornier, and Porsche (Germany and Switzerland); British Timken Company, Imperial Chemicals, and STC (United Kingdom); and Thomson (France). According to Kaufman, "The dual-ladder approach is generally formalized into parallel hierarchies; one provides a managerial career path, and the other advancement as a professional or staff member. Ostensibly, the dual ladder promises equal status and rewards to equivalent levels in both hierarchies" (Kaufman, 1974, p. 125).

As Michael-Roth points out, "The 'Y' concept of career progression is popular and provides for a parallel 'branching' of career paths along either the managerial or professional ladder often at the third or fourth level of hierarchy" (Michael-Roth, 1984, p. 11). Some lateral movement across the management and professional tracks is allowed early on but discouraged at the upper levels of either hierarchy. Movement up the professional ladder usually leads to autonomy and the advanced practice of one's specialty. Providing such a path for technical/specialist/professional employees makes good sense from a career management perspective. Many of them operate in areas critical to your company's success. Since this kind of expertise is not cheap, keeping such employees satisfied is a simple matter of getting a good return on your investment. Such expertise is also scarce; you need to retain them. Furthermore, because economic growth is often slow and managerial positions are scarce, it makes sense to find a better reward for this particular group of workers. Here are the benefits of such a system:

1. A high-potential employee who does not like or want management can see this option as more satisfying and motivating, thus leading to greater long-term productivity.
2. Some technically oriented careerists have, in the past, taken managerial positions simply because they can get their hands on more challenging assignments this way (Bailyn, 1982). The cost to the business is a set of first- and second-line supervisors who are not really interested in managing or particularly competent at it.
3. It is a way for the company to recognize and reward the contributions of its technicians/specialists/professionals by providing career opportunities and rewards specifically for them. In a sense, it is a symbolic way to recognize the organization's commitment to these values.

4. As growth slows in many industries and liberalized retirement policies reduce the number of scheduled retirement vacancies, baby-boom demographics put many in the mid-career "glut" or "bulge." The natural tendencies of any hierarchy mean that opportunities for promotion simultaneously narrow at the third to fourth levels. Thus, this dual-ladder approach becomes a way to open up opportunities to a valued part of the work force.

Some of the disadvantages to this dual-ladder system reported by companies and individuals follow:

1. In practice, there are glaring inequalities in pay, status, and fringe benefits in comparison with the managerial ladder. Usually, there are fewer rungs and a ceiling that cuts off advancement much sooner. Some professional positions are also more insecure and temporary than managerial positions.
2. Many of the professional-technical ladders have been used as "dumping grounds" to get rid of managers who could not be promoted further. Needless to say, technically oriented employees are cynical about the system when such pollution occurs.
3. Many dual-ladder systems suffer from a lack of imagination. Instead of providing such important nonmonetary rewards as more education and training benefits, better staff and clerical support, better equipment, publicity, larger and better-equipped offices and laboratories, and better access to professional activities and colleague groups, some companies have insisted on the traditional managerial rewards of money and status. Although specialists, like everyone else, value money and status up to a point, these are often not the most valued rewards.
4. Many technically oriented careerists want to be involved with top management in planning and decision-making sessions on areas relevant to their expertise. They assume that increased status means more access to top management and are disappointed when their authority and influence do not increase.

5. Many dual ladders have not adequately defined the techni-
    cal and functional jobs associated with various levels of ad-
    vancement. Instead, the levels on the professional ladder
    have been created by analogy with the managerial ladder,
    with ambiguous or confusing titles. As a result, the profes-
    sional track is less substantial than the managerial option,
    and internal confusion reigns about what the professional
    option means.

Clearly, to solve some of these problems, management
must take aggressive action to be sure that the professional-lad-
der option really is as viable as the traditional managerial one
and that the perception matches the reality. This means being
sure that it is not polluted by managerial rejects, that specialists
routinely consult on plans and decisions that touch on the technical work of the institution, that creativity is expended to produce meaningful, nonmonetary rewards, and that progress up
this ladder will be defined by its own standards in ways that reward technical competence, not simply in ways that are managerial evaluations in disguise.

Another popular strategy right now is the lateral assignment. The baby boom, a sluggish economy, and later retirement ages intensify the competition for available slots. People
whose ego and sense of success are tied to a major promotion
every three years have no option but to dub themselves failures
when the promotions do not come. Bailyn (1980) suggests instead a "slowburn" way to the top. Two or three lateral moves
between hierarchical promotions mean that executives have a
much-prized chance to get some new training, to learn a new
aspect of the job, and to pace their own growth. As a manager, you should explore this option for your employees if your
company is not already considering it. You should be aware,
however, that the results are not all in on this proposal. Some
getting-ahead people are justly suspicious that a lateral move
dead-ends them out of sight and out of mind. How can you re-
assure them, especially if it is still experimental? In areas where
expectations and schedules have been more clearly spelled out,
lateral moves seem to be energizing.

Sometimes lateral moves are moves to the center—making

someone an assistant to a vice-president with a critical assignment or shifting a high-potential candidate to a unit that has an important function in the company. Furthermore, moves need not always be formal. Some companies are using their high-potential candidates as one-of-a-kind project managers, sending them on special assignments, pulling them out for special training, getting them involved in consulting, or allowing sabbaticals and non-work-related leaves. The best organizations know themselves and what they need. As a manager you can help your careerists know what they need and how to find the best match. Still, moves are sometimes downward. Those who refuse to retire, refuse to leave, or refuse to upgrade their training but who cannot simply be eased out are often moved back down in other assignments, often with a change in pay. People whose competencies do not keep pace with the job or the company's needs are sometimes in the same position. Sometimes, the best decision is to move a person out of the company. There are humane ways of doing it by providing counseling, workshops for career redirection or retraining, or even using the services of a search firm.

Actively Mentor and Coach Subordinates. A career counseling relationship is inherently difficult for a manager because of his or her evaluative role, the hidden agendas of employees, and the political environment of the relationship. Still, many employees and even colleagues will seek out a knowledgeable and helpful executive for advice about options within the organization. In this case, the manager is an *information giver.* This does not mean that a manager must be all knowing, but he or she should at least know where to go (for example, a career information center) or whom to contact (company career counselor, the training department) to find out about options. In this role of information and advice giver, the manager will want to be well informed about the company's career development policies and programs. It is more important in this role to be company specific than to try to play the part of a more generic career counselor.

Broaden Access to the Top. From an organizational perspective, all employees at first look somewhat alike. All new employees have to earn the right to have a career at a given firm. They must demonstrate their technical competence and gain a reputation for being able to do the work, they must learn the corporate culture and demonstrate that they fit comfortably within that framework and can be effective working in it, and they must pay their dues and be willing to work hard, do their fair share of the dirty jobs and those reserved for new employees, and become good citizens of the corporation. Beyond this basic apprenticeship and early career period, however, come some crucial questions, including career diversity.

Some will have performed better than their peers and seem to fit the culture better. These will usually be labeled high potential, and they will be given more than their fair share of time, energy, and company resources for development. The key organizational issue here is whether the high-potential group should be narrowly defined (a small elite group who are homogenous, "clones" of top management) or more diversely defined. In the typical U.S. firm, these individuals will be getting-ahead careerists. Simultaneously, however, individuals who are not part of the high-potential group will continue to perform well and productively. It is important to manage them properly, because, while they may not be future leaders, they are vital to the success of the company. How they feel about their exclusion from the high-potential group is all important. If they still feel appreciated and valued for their own contributions, they will be able to come to terms with the firm in a mutually beneficial relationship. Those who fail to achieve this compromise may leave the company, costing it the years and resources used in training and experience. After five to eight years, they may choose to remain, and it is then difficult for the company to fire them. If they are mismanaged, they will probably plateau or become unproductive. Some may engage in destructive organizational politics to meet some of their "deviant" (in the company's eyes) career agendas. Deprived of the carrot—even though they may not have liked carrots—and threatened with the stick, they perform at a minimum level. Well managed and rewarded for their unique strengths, they would become equally valuable, though in a different way, as the most promising young general managers. Other career-oriented employees could have been more vital and contributive to organizational goals if they had been better managed.

A Case Study

Bill, the thirty-eight-year-old division chief of the computer graphics company described in Chapter One, used the career success map concept to rethink his management techniques for getting-ahead Garth, getting-secure Rex, getting-free Elizabeth, getting-high Casey, and getting-balanced Don and Doris. He had been correct in feeling that Garth could not be counted on to be loyal and patient. The best thing Bill can do to manage Garth is to show him the various ways to go up the hierarchical ladder and to offer him sponsorship and career opportunities in return for service and reciprocal help. Garth will clearly be a tremendous asset if Bill can find ways to match Garth's self-interests with Bill's organizational interests. What Bill needs to remember is that all attempts to quiet Garth's ambition are likely to be futile; if Bill does not assume a sponsor role, somebody else will. Thus, Garth's usefulness may be short-lived. Given a better opportunity, Garth is likely to transfer, terminate, or readjust his loyalties very quickly.

Rex, on the other hand, is available for long-term assignments and can be relied upon to be loyal, hardworking, and trustworthy. He always has the company's concern at heart. How can Bill provide him with continuous tokens of appreciation, sincere thanks, and symbols of lifelong company reciprocity? Rex is a high-maintenance employee who demands sensitivity and consideration from Bill, a very busy and often harried manager. Moreover, it is sometimes difficult for Bill to keep coming up with salary raises and more responsibilities for Rex. As the pyramid gets narrower at the top, loyalty and personal security are assumed, but political savvy and competitive edge are rewarded. So Bill's managerial balancing act is to keep Rex motivated enough to keep tapping that loyal service while at the same time not letting Rex get unrealistic expectations about promotions or letting him consume too much management time and energy.

Elizabeth is a more difficult case. Bill is willing to meet her autonomy halfway. There is a definite place for someone who is very competent and can be trusted to meet objectives on time and within cost. To be effective with Elizabeth, Bill must be very clear about the objectives, the time parameters, the limitations, and the sanctions for failing to meet these conditions. She needs to understand that she will have to gain his full trust over time by trustworthy performance. In return, he can afford to give her more and more freedom. An end goal might be for Bill to be relatively unconcerned about whether Elizabeth observes basic work rules as long as she performs. But that is the end result of a process. Bill has to be sure she merits the trust. He also needs to coordinate and control if he is to be viewed by the rest of his superiors and peers as a good manager. Elizabeth must understand his constraints, observe the essential minimal norms, and keep Bill informed.

Casey will likely stay happy and productive, no matter what the rules are, if Bill can keep feeding him interesting and challenging problems, provide him opportunities to learn and progress in his specialty (for example, through attending conferences and workshops), and, hopefully, put Casey on a special career track for technical specialists that will reward his expertise and knowledge. Casey will probably also appreciate the opportunity to present his ideas or new specialties to peers and superiors, be delighted to be consulted about decisions in areas in which he is knowledgeable, and respond, like Rex, to special (even inexpensive) recognitions of his status and knowledge.

Don and Doris, like Elizabeth, are hard employees to manage. Their personal life does, at times, interfere with their professional commitment and their performance. It is important for Bill to communicate that they cannot expect the same organizational rewards and interesting assignments as those who routinely put in sixty-hour weeks, even while he communicates their value to him and his appreciation of their competence. The managerial challenge for Bill is how he can best utilize their talents while they are available. In return for his understanding and flexibility, Don and Doris will probably be ready to work hard and well when they are on the job and, at times, to work intensively on an important assignment—partly out of reciprocal appreciation and partly to earn the right to keep negotiating interesting but not overly demanding work for themselves.

 THIRTEEN

Applications
for Multinational
Corporation Managers

The twenty-year trend toward the creation of a global economy is one of the facts of corporate life that executives must deal with. Many managers are experiencing diversity on multinational levels as they are tapped for service at overseas offices by American-based firms or are offered positions by multinational companies based elsewhere. One French executive I interviewed about his company's recruitment, training, and development policies for high-potential managers observed that his company was typical: the president was British; one vice-president was French and another Italian. The same mix permeated the company right down to the division level in the sixty countries in which it operated. Although, like most, it relied primarily on local people as employees, supervisors needed to be prepared for diverse nationalities among their workers, peers, and superiors. "One of the traits we definitely look for in recruiting is the kind of cosmopolitanism that will let a manager move into situations like this and deal sensitively with the local culture instead of trying to impose his own assumptions," this officer observed. I heard a similar remark from literally dozens of executives charged with finding and training future managers for their companies. Cosmopolitanism was a clear value, but, for most, spelling out the criteria was difficult. Did they require

language ability? Not necessarily, although linguistic facility was
certainly a plus, and most European firms assumed that their
executives would have acquired at least a second language as
part of their education. Nor did they necessarily require experience in living in another country, although that was also quite
an advantage. It was something deeper, "a sense for nuance,"
the French executive put it, "that lets an individual read, understand, and work with a different culture."

A great deal of fascinating work is in progress on corporate culture, but it deals primarily with American firms in
American settings. Deal and Kennedy (1982) started managers
across the country thinking about "the way we do things" and
attempting to move toward the deeper levels of understanding
called for by Schein (1985), who points out the problems of
dealing with "artifacts" such as dress, hierarchy, and decision-
making models as though they were the culture itself. He defines culture as "a pattern of basic assumptions—invented, discovered, or developed by a given group as it learns to cope with
its problems of external adaptation and internal integration—
that has worked well enough to be considered valid and, therefore, to be taught to new members as the correct way to perceive, think, and feel in relation to those problems" (p. 9). He
also asserts that "companies operating in the multinational context sometimes did things in dramatically similar ways, even in
widely different cultures. Companies thus seemed to have cultures of their own that were sometimes strong enough to over-
ride or at least modify local cultures" (p. ix). This statement,
made in the preface and not later developed in the book, certainly deserves his further analysis. My own experience of working with multinational firms and national firms on their home
ground would make me wary of announcing the primacy of any
given corporation's culture. Although a French person in Shell
will, as a first impression, look more like an American in Shell
than like a French person in Exxon, it has been my experience
that essential personal and national qualities of character,
values, and style are too deeply embedded to be erased by training in a corporate culture, no matter how willing and apt the
pupil.

Andre Laurent, a professor at the European Institute of Business Administration (INSEAD) at Fontainebleau and a leader in cross-cultural management research, concurs. He collected data (Laurent, 1981) from 772 upper-middle managers in nine Western European countries and the United States, through a questionnaire that probed values in various aspects of management and organization. He found clear national differences on all fifty-six dimensions identified in his questionnaires, differences that were not reduced by working in the same company. In one case—an American chemical firm with affiliates in France, West Germany, and the United Kingdom—the managers' scores resembled those of other managers from these three countries working for other companies, more closely than they resembled each other.

It seems to me that the position of strength for the multinational manager of the future is not to ignore or disregard national differences but instead to study them, appreciate them where possible, and respect them always. That includes the manager's own culture. An instructive example is the approach to training multinational executives used by INSEAD. This school was founded in 1959, in the early days of the Common Market when French economists saw a chance to compete with the United States for the global market. INSEAD was their means of training a new generation of managers. It was the first full-time graduate school of business in Europe independent of a country, a university, or a business; at that time, the only other European business schools were France's *grandes écoles,* known more for their rigorous traditions than for innovation, and the private business schools in Switzerland run by Nestlé and Alcan. General Georges Doriot, a Frenchman who was then a professor at the Harvard Business School and founder of America's first publicly owned venture-capital company (American Research and Development), was crucial in INSEAD's birth, as was Olivier Giscard d'Estaing, brother of France's former president and the school's first director general.

About 1,500 students apply per year for INSEAD's intensive ten-month course. There are many tests and screening procedures, but each candidate must speak French and English

(German will be a compulsory course if the candidate does not already speak it) and have a clear commitment to an international career. The students come from thirty countries, and no one country, not even France, can supply more than one-fourth of the student body. The faculty is also multinational, but they agree that the real teaching takes place in the study groups, whose makeup is assigned by computer for the greatest possible diversity in nationality, goals, ages, business experience, and personal background. The purpose is to maximize the possibility of conflict.

"We think that the study groups are far more important than the classrooms," says INSEAD public- and alumni-relations director Jean-Pierre Salzmann, himself a former executive with Digital Equipment Corporation [which had been funded by Doriot's American Research and Development and which now is a major funder for INSEAD]. "All of the case work is done in the groups, and each group must reach a consensus before the participants go into class. In the process, all of the cultural differences come out, with all of the stresses they will have to cope with in the real world."

The clashes come in the first weeks, when everybody insists on solving the case problem by his own method. The vehement American hammers that profit-making is the first goal of business. The Scandinavian disagrees: what about social accounting [accountability]? The Italian thinks the way to negotiate a deal is to sweeten the pot. The Japanese says yes and means no, and the Frenchman advises a nice long lunch. . . .

The angst pays off. Students learn to accommodate the Israeli who cannot confer by telephone on Saturdays; tone down for the Japanese to whom a critique is loss of face; reckon with diverse managerial styles and the customs, politics, economies, and history that produced them. Andre Laurent, a professor of organizational behavior whose corporate research is used in both hemispheres, distills the lesson: "We used to think there was a body of knowledge titled 'Universal Management,' which was on a plate in a church called Harvard. It was a myth. There is French management, Japanese management, British, American, Swedish, Italian, and every other kind of management. Modern executives will need to know them all, to know what will work best for them."

Or, as 1974 graduate Alasdair Findlay-Shirras notes, "You go to INSEAD to learn from your friends before you have to learn from your enemies." . . . He is an international investment banker [in New York], now managing director of Associated European Capital Corp., corporate financiers [Linden, 1985, pp. 96, 100, 102].

Multinational Managers: Case Studies

Presented here are reports from three managers who were forced to consider the impact of a national culture on their personal and institutional operating styles.

One of France's largest automobile companies is a quasi-government-owned public company. In 1984, this company lost 73 billion francs and received sizable government subsidies. Because of its special relationship with the government, many decisions are made in this company for political reasons. The Communist labor union, Confédération Générale du Travail, has a great deal of control, and the relationship between its 93,000 employees and management, under intense pressure to turn it around, can best be described as adversarial. Thus, it has plenty of problems at home.

This automobile conglomerate owns a controlling share of an American auto company. One of the French executives I interviewed, an up-and-coming high-potential candidate, told of being sent to the United States to receive some international training and to occupy a key slot in the American management system. His French superiors encouraged him to try to develop some ideas about how to install close controls on cost, production, and personnel supervision in the American firm. These instructions were harmonious with the centralized, hierarchical, by-the-book French style, but he came up against the American style of decentralizing authority, which outlines a person's area of expertise and then allows considerable freedom to act within its boundaries. This "federal" system of discretion over decision making seemed loose and sloppy to the executive who was accustomed to working within a very tight system of rules.

He lamented to me the "incredibly difficult" time he had in the United States trying to understand how Americans thought so that he could suggest ways to transpose the French system. His approach was to work closely with his French bosses back home to get new information about what to do with the resistance that he was encountering rather than trying to figure out the best solution on the spot. He described his effort to develop a plan as a "complete disaster." Most of the American workers refused to go along with it from the beginning, creating "outright anarchy," from his point of view. If he had met overt agreement and covert sabotage—which might have happened in a French setting—what he considered to be the workers' contract would have been met to the satisfaction of everyone, and he could have shrugged in eloquent helplessness but not felt responsible or, within certain limits, been held accountable. The open refusal of the workers to go along with the new system would have signaled the need for re-evaluation, renegotiation, and recommitment to an American manager. This manager was simply baffled. What is more, there were few government laws or court decrees to force a settlement between management and workers.

In the second example, a Swedish friend went to Holland to help manage one of his company's engineering and manufacturing subsidiaries. He worked for a large multinational firm with offices in over seventy countries around the world. His assignment in Holland, he reported, had required very little cultural adjustment, probably because the national styles are somewhat similar. But when he was transferred to the French operation, he reported a high frustration level. The labor unions were a major difference. In Sweden, the powerful unions, by law, occupy positions on the policy-making boards in each plant. The representatives are highly participative, argue openly, and compete for resources. However, once a decision is made, the union has ownership in that decision and is fully supportive. In contrast, French unions have no formal representation on decision-making forums and, in fact, refused invitations to participate. Instead, they maintained an openly adversarial position, sabotaging decisions that they disagreed with, exercising their strike power and calling slowdowns almost at random, and interpreting jointly negotiated agreements differently at one time from another. Only the intervention of a powerful third party, such as the courts or the government, could enforce these agreements, my friend complained, bewildered by what he perceived as sheer irresponsibility. Even though Swedes are famous for encumbering protective legislation and right-to-work laws, he also found French paternalism almost suffocating. It was impossible, for instance, to fire anyone who had been with the company for more than six months without going through a complicated process that sometimes took two years.

In an executive training session that he attended with some of his French colleagues, he took part in a problem simulation in which the participants were required to select a problem that could actually be solved within the given time period. It was obvious that one of the problems was impossibly complex for the time allotted—in fact, probably incapable of a solution in any amount of time. To his amazement, his French colleagues promptly launched into a heated debate about this very problem and whether it was structurally capable of being solved. The debate consumed the entire time period, and none of the other problems—the simpler and, consequently, less intellectually interesting problems—were even considered. This, he said, was typical, and he sighed, "For a rest, give me the Swedes." However, he was enchanted by the ready French susceptibility to the temptations of philosophy, even though practical considerations were the frequent victims, and found the richness of French intellectual life and the very suppleness and deviousness of French style to be highly stimulating.

He saw this same fascination with the theoretical as

undermining the French ability to market. "They're clever engineers. They are superb technicians," he said and rattled off a list of technical advancements that included the new "smart" credit card and the TGV, one of the fastest trains in the world. "But they get snarled in the philosophical implications of an idea and never find the right way to get a product out." As a result, Swedes occupied most of the powerful marketing positions in his firm.

He humorously told of getting a ticket for speeding, in itself almost unheard of, since flagrant traffic violations—even extremely hazardous ones—are almost universally tolerated in France as long as one's papers are in order. In Sweden, a driver's license contains a national code; by entering this code in a computer terminal, a police officer has complete access to all kinds of information: not only past violations but tax levels, former residences, and educational information. Very worried about the possible repercussions from his traffic ticket, my friend expressed his concerns to his French counterpart, who laughed, said, "Come with me," walked him over to the commissariat, and presented a couple of bottles of wine to the right officers. The ticket and its record simply disappeared. He also understood quickly how his own social-democrat style was counterproductive in France and learned to assume the public manner of assurance, direction, and aloofness that matched French assumptions of "the boss." Although omniscience was not a comfortable role for him, it made dealing with his workers much easier.

Another acquaintance, Peter, was head of management development for the European division of a large U.S. multinational, one with 95,000 employees worldwide and a financial volume of $6 billion annually. A fast-moving, innovative company, it employs 18,000 people in fourteen European countries. A young careerist with a supportive wife who is willing to follow him around Europe with their children, Peter had come to Europe for this first overseas assignment. This firm, like most U.S. multinationals, decentralizes and gives decision-making discretion to its local managers while retaining quality control, standard performance review procedures, and other standard devices that make a somewhat uncomfortable fit between the local culture and American standards.

The manager of this multinational in Europe, also an American, sensed a great deal of pressure to produce profits and demonstrate his ability to meet short-term goals. Peter naturally had to help the manager meet this goal but also had to help him identify procedures and systems that would work well in a European context, thereby ultimately enhancing profits. For Peter, these two goals were often in tension with each other. Like all multinationals, the U.S. parent company preferred to hire nationals. Expatriates would be used only in a few key staff positions at headquarters to supervise the overall flow. Within the larger corporate guidelines, Peter keenly felt the need to allow for national cultures.

Many businesses are competing on the global market in a diverse and fast-paced world. Peter's firm is not unusual in slotting several key positions specifically for international human resource development—for example, in marketing, research and development, and production. Otherwise, they ask, how can such a company prepare its people to acquire this multinational perspective so that they can be used effectively in a variety of management jobs? The U.S. parent company is not simply interfacing with Europe and imposing its perspective; it must genuinely deal with a variety of regions, each with its own culture.

Peter sees a tension in his personal career as well. It is important to cycle back to the United States for key assignments, since that is the top section of the ladder. At the same time, he needs to keep looking for international assignments that will give him the valued expertise that will keep him highly marketable, participate in the task teams that work on specific international problems, and find individuals who are willing to move around from country to country to move into the company's high-potential fast track. Peter is such a person himself.

In an attempt to improve human resource management practices in Europe in a culturally relevant way, he set up a special board consisting of people who could represent a human resource perspective from the organizations in several of his firm's national countries to help him implement management programs. Their job is to advise him on specific human resource management programs, such as the feasibility of an executive training center, personnel policies, pay systems, and so on. These teams periodically meet with him in Brussels and seem to be working very well; but one of his problems is how to create an interdependent team and work collaboratively, American-style, in sharing information, making group decisions, and having ownership of the results. Some of these locals do not trust groups and do not like working in groups. At the same time, the larger organization imposes constraints: budgets, time and authority limits, and parts of other programs that cannot be touched. There is also a feeling that the final decision is made by higher authority and that the real task of a committee is to generate some creative options.

Peter faced the challenge of imposing the team decision-making model on European nationals. French and Italians were instantly suspicious of those kinds of task forces. They wanted a decision that they could either agree with or disagree with to come down from the top. Participative decision making seemed coercive to them. The British members of his group were extremely cooperative in discussing the programs, but the value for them was the ability of this group to enhance social relations. This tendency was especially irritating to the Americans, who were creative brainstormers but pushed to accomplish certain spelled-out goals by a certain deadline. Scandinavians were model group members, but they expected chunks of power in making and implementing the final decision that seemed unrealistic to the Americans. They resisted when they saw the boss reserving the final decision for himself. The German idea of a group was to bring together the technical experts who informed the rest how to solve the problem. If the experts happened to disagree, the group frequently stalemated. For an American manager, this diverse range was extremely frustrating; but Peter had the perseverance to stick with it. After two years, the European nationals have picked up enough of the "company way" to fit into the team mode, if only to safeguard their own careers. Peter does not know, however, whether any consensus is emerging that task teams really are an effective way of operating.

When he goes out to work with the managers of the various organizations in each country, he finds that he has to deal with their own personality differences as well as their own national mode. They look most American in Brussels, but back in Italy or Norway or Germany, they have to switch back to their own national style to keep communicating with their employees and their clients.

Peter also runs a management development center that periodically brings valued employees into Brussels for training seminars and coaching. He reports, as do many professors at INSEAD, the excitement and difficulty of teaching in such a potpourri of differences. How can he teach the "company way" in such diversity? How can he get agreement on what the "company way" is? Should he emphasize more conformity or more local discretion? What kind of advice should he give people about their careers, since doing the kinds of things that would make an American manager look good frequently backfire in national locales? A fourth task for Peter is being a member of the central policy board for his company in Europe. It is made up of the main staff managers in Brussels plus the main country managers. Here he has to compete for budget and turf against marketing, data-processing, accounting, and production chiefs, playing a political executive game with other executives and dealing with the diversity of styles of all those individuals and their agendas. A final challenge is dealing with the Brussels staff. All of them speak English (he also speaks French), but his peers and subordinates are culturally diverse. The simple task of getting papers typed or rooms scheduled for meetings brings him up against different styles of doing things.

Peter, a fairly typical getting-ahead person, comes out of a technical specialty rather than a general-manager perspective. Because of his particular point of view, he may not have the flexibility of the more conventional general manager. Should he adapt to European ways rather than training others to adopt American ways? But, if he does, what will be the impact on his American career? Moreover, this is an American company, and others must learn to work effectively within it.

Each of these case studies represents some of the dilemmas and problems associated with working with very diverse styles and internal career orientations in a multinational context. Each of these managers, whether general or functional, needs tools to conceptualize both individual and cultural differences in working with subordinates, peers, and superiors.

Manifestations of National Culture

Whether from reading, travel, or a college anthropology class, we have all received at least an overview of national characteristics, complete with warnings about the dangers of stereotyping. The heightened awareness in the United States of racial and sexual stereotypes that has come with the civil rights and women's movements has created a salutary reluctance to act on the basis of stereotypes. The fact remains, however, that in any new situation, we import expectations about how others are going to act. Quite frequently, an American executive expects his or her counterparts in other countries to have very similar values, priorities, and styles. When they do not act in expected ways, the executive, through no lack of intelligence or imagination, falls back on whatever bits of information he or she has about Italians, Brazilians, Japanese, or Swedes. It is an altogether healthy process for a person to move from using himself or herself as the touchstone to using mental images as the touchstone. Reality thus challenges and modifies those first assumptions, then the second assumptions. The danger is that the process will stop before it is complete—before the mental image can be replaced by many experiences with many different Italians, Japanese, or Swedes. Often, executives do not have the opportunity to spend months at a time in a country, absorbing those crucial differences. Painful encounters may, in fact, actively discourage an executive from seeking such crucial opportunities.

For the multinational manager, the process is even more challenging. He or she seldom has a leisurely learning period. Instead, learning about a national culture and managing nationals occur simultaneously. The question is not whether mistakes will be made but how to minimize the inevitable mistakes and to learn from them as rapidly as possible. Even in broad terms, it is helpful to know that when several hundred European and U.S. managers were asked to define characteristics of a good manager, 41 percent of the British respondents cited the ability to communicate; only 12 percent of the French managers and 14 percent of the Germans identified this as an important characteristic. Germans—50 percent of the sample—said it was most important for managers to have competence, knowledge, a creative mind, and intelligence, compared with 34 percent of the British managers. Perhaps most revealingly, when asked to identify the most important thing that a manager should be doing, a full 52 percent of the French managers said "to control," contrasted with 2 percent of the British managers. Germans identified this function 32 percent of the time (Laurent, 1985).

Little information has been compiled to help an executive directly, but I have here some anecdotal eye-openers to help you think about differences beyond those of language, diet, dress, and hours. During the eight months I most recently spent in Europe, teaching and doing research at INSEAD, I interviewed executives in seventy-two companies that were based in Europe or were strong overseas branches of U.S. companies. All of these companies were multinational and heavy competitors in the international market. For all of them, dealing with many other languages, nations, and cultures was a fact of their daily business life. Although my research was not focused on analyzing the problems facing the multinational manager, the reports of the managers I interviewed almost invariably included segments of their own education in becoming cosmopolitan.

These reports all cite men as respondents and examples, a pattern that reflects a reality of European multinational life. Women were simply not represented at high levels in most of the giant companies included in my studies. I certainly encountered women in European companies and as students, but in significantly smaller numbers. In fact, I was reminded of the United States of fifteen years ago in at least two ways: (1) Women were assumed to be less interested in and less competent at management than men. (2) In addition to the pervasive sexism of such attitudes, cultural controls were often in place that subtly discouraged social change, on either an individual or an institutional level. Perhaps even more tellingly, work is often not the chief source of identity and self-esteem for European women *or* men as it is for Americans. In some ways—from the inside of some European cultures, not from an American perspective—women working is simply not much of an issue, at least not yet. Moreover, many Scandinavian and German women have careers in medicine, law, and education, while men cluster in business. For them also, feminism seems to be something of a nonissue. And the horrendous problems with unemployment and underemployment in Europe prevent governments from encouraging additional workers to enter the labor market. The multinational business scene is, then, for the most part still a male domain. American women executives operating in an international context must be prepared for that difference.

A colleague at INSEAD told me about a French executive getting a new boss, an American. In the first interview, the American asked the Frenchman the rather standard question "What are your goals?" The Frenchman was dumbfounded, unable even to frame a reasonable response. When curious colleagues, waiting for him after this interview, asked him for his impressions of the new boss, the Frenchman warned, "We're in real trouble. He's weak and incompetent." Had the Frenchman himself been in the American's chair, he would have never asked such a question of a subordinate. A French executive is supposed to know all the answers, set all the goals, and formulate all the policies. A subordinate's task is to make those goals his own and to execute them admirably.

It goes without saying that no French executive really can know all the answers, and no French subordinate really expects him to. But in the world of strategy, no adept French executive would allow himself to create the appearance of vacillation, lack of information, or hesitance. The image is all important. By not understanding this deep-rooted cultural characteristic, the American had sent an ambiguous message to his subordinate. Ironically, the subordinate's obvious bewilderment and inability to respond meant, to the American, "We're in real trouble. Here's the second in command who's been here for several years, and he doesn't even know what the division's goals are."

As might be expected, this insistence on the image of authority and deferring to strict hierarchy imposes immense strains on executives in a French context. When I was exploring different companies' ways of finding, training, and managing their high-potential employees, I made arrangements to interview the division head of a large French automobile company. He was extremely cordial about granting the interview but seemed curiously evasive. Finally, after a two-hour conversation in a location that had already taken two hours to reach, I understood. He had been in his position for only two weeks and did not have the information to give me a specific response about some career development policies. He asked, as a great favor, whether I would allow him to delegate answering some of the questions to some more knowledgeable subordinates. From an American perspective, the executive should, with no hesitation, have taken the identical action within five minutes after receiving my initial request.

In one aspect of Laurent's (1981) study, he asked for responses to this statement: "It is important for a manager to have at hand precise answers to most of the questions that subordinates may have about their work." Only 10 percent of the Swedes agreed, 18 percent of the Americans, 18 percent of the Dutch, 27 percent of the British, 38 percent of the Swiss, 46 percent of the Germans, 53 percent of the French, and 66 percent of the Italians. Latin Europe, therefore, places a very high value on the manager's information level. Yet the French system is well known—almost notorious—for a kind of cultural autonomy that produces some of the more eccentric driving habits in Europe, a small merchant's assumed right to open and close his or her shop at will without regard to the customer's convenience, and over 500 kinds of cheese. How can this deference to authority be coupled with such deep-seated and all-pervasive manifestations of individuality? To the outside observer, the ferociously individualistic American is a mere conformist by comparison. It is helpful for me to remember that, as a rough rule of thumb, a French company will often obey the letter of the law but not the spirit, while an American company will obey the spirit of the law but not the letter. At the risk of pronouncing another national stereotype, I have observed that the rule book in France is sacred and that these rules are never flagrantly violated. However, no set of rules can be tight enough to cover every contingency, and there is a kind of French genius at finding the loopholes. In contrast, an American company would define outcomes and norms on a project but then delegate considerable authority and decision-making powers to the person in charge to follow through, defining the results but not the process.

In France, I met an American executive from the central headquarters staff who was visiting the French-based subsidiary. "How on earth do you get anything done in this country?" he demanded. He had arrived to work on an important but limited problem and had come with a tight mental schedule: arrive, spend an hour defining the problem, an hour probing solutions, and an hour getting consensus and detailing the chosen solution, and get back on the plane. Almost stereotypically, they had spent the morning in a three-hour meeting defining the problem and rationale in a thoroughly Gallic fashion, leaving them without time to work on the solution until after a lengthy (again typically Gallic) lunch, in which business could not be discussed until cheese and dessert. After a full day of this, he was at his wits' end.

I was sympathetic. That same week, as part of my research on management practices in European multinational firms, I had come for an appointment that had begun at 11:30. The entire half hour passed in formal introductions and exchanges of pleasantries. At the stroke of twelve, my interviewee announced that we must go to lunch and that, of course, it would not be possible to discuss business matters until the cheese. This was hardly my preferred schedule, but it was hardly a surprise, either. We spent three hours in a leisurely and far-ranging discussion that covered our childhoods, our educational experiences, our impressions of each other's countries, our wives and children, our political views, and our favorite leisure-time activities. At the end of three hours, when the cheese arrived, we were on a first-name basis, and the executive shifted easily into the agenda with which I had originally arrived, giving me answers that were models of candor and insight, complete with examples. It would have been totally impossible to have reached the same result without going through the process, but this process is acutely frustrating for Americans who have been trained to focus on getting short-term results efficiently and quickly. If it is any consolation, Scandinavians and Germans express the same frustrations working in a French setting.

A Swedish manager in Saab, newly appointed to be in the French company, tried to learn the business by doing a bit of everyone's job in the best social-democracy tradition, including bringing coffee for his secretary and cleaning up his own dishes after a break. He genuinely did not see himself in a differentiated position of authority, but his French subordinates were extremely confused by him and labeled him as a weak supervisor. In the Swedish tradition, social equality is extremely important. Few people want to be boss, because there are so few rewards for it; the job often comes with little authority—in fact, having more authority than anyone else is viewed as negative. Part of his success as a manager depended on his ability to adopt the French style of management, even though it was not personally compatible with his own.

A German colleague told about the experience he and his partner had when they were hired to do management training for Finnish executives. Finns are known stereotypically as very serious, poker-faced, and impersonal. These Germans were frustrated, bewildered, and shaken by what they perceived as a total lack of responsiveness. They pulled out every joke they knew, tried to chat informally at breaks and before and after sessions, urged participation in discussions about the case studies, and invited the Finns to proffer their own examples, but to no avail. After two days with little eye contact, few smiles, and minimum answers to discussion questions, the Germans were ready to write it off as a bad experience in which they were simply the wrong people for this group and then go home. This was a devastating experience, since they were excellent teachers who had conducted successful and popular seminars all over the world.

On the second night, they went to the sauna at the hotel, where nearly all of the conference participants were lounging around passing quart bottles of vodka from hand to hand. It was a transformation. Within an hour, the thoroughly relaxed Finns were roaring with laughter, saying, "Remember that joke you told at 11:10 on the first day? That was fantastic. The funniest joke I've ever heard." Or, "That case study about the Italian vice-president? I know exactly why he reacted that way. When I was in Italy three years ago. . . ." The German trainers could not believe that they were with the same group. Conviviality reigned supreme. They got spontaneous feedback on every aspect—practically every paragraph—of their presentations. They were exultant and sailed into the third and final day of the training seminar in high spirits, despite slight hangovers. There they met the same rows of blank-faced, motionless, unsmiling executives. After the initial shock, they quickly concluded that everything was going in, even though no feedback was coming out in this setting, and finished their seminar.

The British think that interpersonal communications, face-to-face contact, and easy sociability are very high priorities for an executive, according to Laurent (1981). The club and the bar are far more important than desk work, since contacts *are* an executive's work. This characteristic can also be frustrating for Americans who allow for business small talk—but not extensive interactions—and tend to segregate socializing into weekends and evenings in settings strikingly different from work. Also, Americans may tend, much more than the British, to relate to individuals more in their roles: "Harvey is a sales manager." In a British context, Harvey would be known not only as a sales manager but also as a member of the opera guild who has a brother who is in local government and who also has a place in Surrey where he raises prize dahlias. Another British executive might know and relate to all of these roles, not only because the probability is extremely high that he moves in the same weekend and evening circles but also because information about the dahlias, the brother, and the opera is part of the social currency exchanged as part of interactions that an American would think of as reserved for strictly "business."

I found my British students at INSEAD extremely helpful and candid. Many of them were being sponsored by companies that were also responsive to requests for information about some of their practices. However, when a group of my students, as part of a practicum, tried to conduct telephone interviews with British executives in several major multinational firms, they got nowhere. No one would talk to them. No one would provide information. No one would even take them seriously. A couple of executives openly told them, "Sorry, we don't do business this way. If you'd like to come over to London, then we'll see what can be done."

I thought at first that these executives were simply busy and reluctant to talk to students; but when I approached them by phone, I received an identical response. They were reluctant not to talk to students, not to supply data on their companies, not to deal with INSEAD because they did not like it or any other institution, but simply to do business by phone. It seemed strange to me that the telephone was not seen as a valid instrument for certain kinds of communication, but my British students confirmed that this was so. When I understood this cultural difference, I made arrangements to go to London and interview the same executives. I found them most hospitable in person, insightful and candid about their firms, and extremely generous with their information. Although they did not require the same kind of social getting-to-know-you rituals over food that French executives did, the timing and pacing of the interaction had to be observed. It was according to this internal sense of the rhythm of the relationship that it became appropriate to introduce "business."

In one case, I must say, I found that sense of rhythm extremely irritating. I had arranged to interview on the same afternoon two executives of different companies whose offices were only a few streets apart and had explained this scheduling fact to the first executive. He was gracious and hospitable in the best tradition; but it also became apparent, as the interview progressed, that there were certain areas of interest to me in which he did not want to disclose his company's practices. Rather than saying so (which I would have expected from an American and, as an American, accepted), he deftly turned the conversation to other topics and launched into a string of delightful but largely irrelevant anecdotes, displaying a dazzling ability at filibustering through the last thirty minutes of the interview that left me, hardly a novice at interviewing, without a chance to get a word in edgewise, probe for more information, or ask related questions. Yet not an uncooperative or uncivilized word had been spoken throughout the interchange.

Some elements of this style may be uncomfortable to American executives. If they are used to keeping their private life as a "retreat" from business concerns, this easy social intermingling may threaten their sense of privacy. Since British executives have traditionally been recruited as classical generalists from elite schools, Americans may also be unprepared for the wide variety of topics and classical subjects on which one is supposed to have highly informed and well-articulated opinions. Some may feel distinctly at a loss in a conversation that ranges over contemporary art, dog shows, Greek beaches (with suitable quotations from Homer), the children's schools, and the latest biography of Gandhi before coming, in the same cordial and interested tone, to sales figures or production standards. It can also be disconcerting to U.S. executives to feel the subtle manipulation of formal and informal elements going on around them when they would place a high value on "spelling it all out" and quickly resolving the problem at hand.

A further problem is that different cultures have different ways of handling disagreement. For example, I dealt with an executive in a French company that was a subsidiary of a large U.S.-owned multinational. He had contacted INSEAD about doing some executive training for his employees, since the parent company had required them to "train X number of individuals at X level by X date to X specifications." This kind of goal was not, to this executive's way of thinking, helpful to their situation; but, rather than going back to the top office to explain what kind of training would be helpful and getting a different ruling, he proposed to INSEAD a "paper" compliance while simultaneously supplying a different program. INSEAD was unwilling to accommodate this not-uncommon request, and he ended up finding a French firm that cooperated with what amounted to sabotage of the formal program. Laurent (1981) asked his respondents to react to the statement "Most organizations would be better off if conflict could be eliminated forever." While only 4 percent of the Swedes, 13 percent of the British, and 18 percent of the Germans agreed with this statement, 24 percent of the French and 41 percent of the Italians agreed.

Another instructive example, reported by a colleague I encountered, concerns a group of Italian students at a European business school who were caught cheating by British and German students. The cheating was not subtle. It involved openly passing notes back and forth in the examination room. The British and Germans provided names, dates, places, and eyewitness testimony to the dean, who confronted the offending students. They were surprised at being confronted, and one Italian said, puzzled, "But you didn't want us to fail, did you?" It was a manifestation of according full respect to the formal system and, almost by reflex, subverting it with an informal system. Laurent (1981) found that 75 percent of the Italians agreed with: "In order to have efficient work relationships, it is often necessary to bypass the hierarchical line."

You will notice that this discussion of authority and interaction has not yet mentioned the German fascination with hierarchy. As a rough rule of thumb, Germans would also rate obedience to authority and hierarchical deference as an extremely high value; but, unlike the French and Italians, they are also very interested in constructing a formal system that actually works. The French and Italians would tend to construct two: a formal one that works on paper and an informal one that works around the formal one. Several U.S. executives, although expressing dismay with the German emphasis on authority, noticed it only when, for some reason, they wanted to resist the system or change it in some way. If their goals were not at cross-purposes with the hierarchical flow of direction, the Americans did not perceive it as "rigid" or "unreasonable."

My research included sixteen large German and Swiss multinational firms. One of the initial surprises for me after dealing with French and British organizations was that I could simply pick up the phone, without having had the way paved by a prior contact who "knew the right person," and ask for a high-level official, such as the director of personnel. In nine out of sixteen cases, the call simply went right from the switchboard to the official's office, and the next voice I heard was that of the director himself or his secretary when he was out. In the other cases, I talked first to an executive assistant. In short, I found that if I could define exactly whom I needed, no intermediaries were necessary.

Part of Laurent's (1981) study posited a matrix situation where a given employee would have both a functional head and a line head. In response to the statement "An organizational structure in which certain subordinates have two direct bosses should be avoided at all costs," 79 percent of the Germans, 83 percent of the French, and 81 percent of the Italians agreed, as opposed to only 54 percent of the Americans and 64 percent of the Swedes. With the statement "The more complex a department's activities, the more important it is that each individual's functions be well-defined," 66 percent of the Swedes, 69 percent of the Americans, and an extremely high 93 percent of the Germans agreed.

Another characteristic of both German and Swiss companies—one that contrasts markedly to the broadly classical "style" of British executives—was an emphasis on technical expertise that communicated an impressive value accorded to actual knowledge and skills. In Germany, universities do not recognize business administration as a valid field of study, but advanced degrees command respect. Specialists can advance surprisingly high, in contrast to American firms, before they need to shift to a broader general-management perspective. The American preoccupation with seeing the "big picture" would become part of a manager's repertoire only quite late.

National Patterns and External Career Opportunities

Although a great deal of study needs to be done on how national culture affects the internal career, I can offer a few generalizations for careerists in European settings, based on my

research about how European multinational firms identify, recruit, manage, and develop their high-potential people. Such a
process reveals a firm's values. Whom do they want? Whom are
they willing to spend time, energy, and money on? More important to career diversity, how broad or narrow is the image of
"high potential"? Who can be included as a valuable employee
on these terms?

During the spring of 1985, I interviewed human resource
managers in seventy-three multinational companies based in
Germany, Switzerland, France, Great Britain, Sweden, and the
United States. These organizations were chosen by three criteria: a reputation for progressive human resources practices,
their willingness to collaborate in INSEAD research, and their
positions in various industrial groups. For example, I studied at
least one automotive firm in each country to get a sense of what
industry-representative practices might be and also to see
whether significant differences existed between similar companies with different national origins. This study was supple-
mented with one completed during the summer of 1985 that
queried 150 executives from seventeen countries about their
internal career orientations and the perceived attitudes of their
companies toward diverse career orientations. Since these individuals were in INSEAD's executive-development programs—
most of them at their companies' expense—they would by definition be considered high-potential candidates.

In general, European companies value high-potential general managers as much as do American organizations. Of the
150 executives, 71.8 percent agreed with the statement "Our
company values high-potential general managers and provides
special developmental opportunities and rewards for them."
When the same question was asked about "technical/profes-
sional specialists," 67.8 percent agreed. When a third question
was posed, about "internal entrepreneurs and creative people,"
53.9 percent agreed. Another statement read, "One is judged to
have been successful in this organization if he or she attains a
high-level position of authority," to which 74.8 percent of the
respondents agreed.

Furthermore, most companies had specific and highly
elaborate systems for recruiting, identifying, and training peo-

ple perceived as high potential. Usually, speed of promotion is both the test and the confirmation of high-potential status. Some companies are quite specific about which positions a high-potential candidate must be ready to occupy at three- or four-year intervals. Most also agree that a high-potential person must be able to head up a major division or fulfill an important function by about age forty. About 75 percent of the large multinational firms required international experience and multicultural sensitivity as critical criteria for becoming a high-potential candidate.

Although the selection, recruitment, and training processes are marked by distinctive national differences, a highly generalized—and hence oversimplified—checklist of cultural characteristics may be helpful in explaining some of the most conspicuous differences. The German companies assigned a much higher status to the technical/functional aspects of the career ladder, as mentioned, and the respect accorded to a proven expert is conspicuous. Advanced degrees are very important, but, in keeping with the respect for expertise, both Swiss and German companies rely more consistently on industrial psychologists and testing centers to help identify and select high-potential candidates.

British companies reflect two competing philosophies. The tradition of British management is to recruit graduates from an elite public school or university (perhaps from a known military unit). They seek a candidate who is a "gentleman," who can converse knowledgeably and agreeably on the classics, philosophy, history, and current events, and who can approach business problems from a broadly humanist perspective. However, intensified competition for the world market is forcing British companies to question whether it would be more profitable to recruit those with technical business educations.

French companies actively recruit graduates of the science and engineering *grandes écoles* and then allow them a great deal of autonomy in marshaling resources, forming alliances, and defining projects within a company. This strikingly clear value on autonomy butts up against the rigid internal hierarchy and fully formulated set of procedural rules each company has, thus testing a recruit's ability to learn the informal structure quickly and develop political skills. An interesting contemporary development is elaborate career pathing with the use of sophisticated computer systems so that possible promotions and backup candidates can be predicted three and even four moves ahead. American companies value people with master's degrees in business administration more than do other nationalities, usually use some kind of fast-track option, tend to encourage "intrapreneurs" (in-house innovators), and stress short-term results. Fewer Swedish companies (54 percent) had specific programs for high-potential candidates, and 70 percent reported extreme resistance when they tried to place employees at preparatory international posts outside the country. Many executives, it was reported, have wives with careers of their own—usually in the professions or education—who refused to accept a husband's transfer.

With the statement "Above all, our company values steady, hardworking, competent, and loyal lifelong employees rather than individuals of high-potential," 40.8 percent of all respondents agreed, whereas 51.4 percent disagreed; 7.7 percent neither agreed nor disagreed. In a comparison of French, British, Swedish, and German companies, those who worked for British companies were least in agreement, whereas those who worked in the German firms were most in agreement.

Getting-high people who love their craft generally have high esteem in German and Swiss companies. The respect for competence and technical creativity rewards those who establish technical and functional specialties. British and French companies tend to view such persons as "mere technicians," particularly if they do not move quickly through the career phase of establishing their expertise, then broaden their perspective to a wider, more generalist view. In fact, an engineering background, while highly valued in France, is an actual liability in Great Britain. Entrepreneurs are similarly regarded as disruptive in French, German, and British firms. Entrepreneurs must almost unanimously seek an area for action in small businesses in these countries. An indication of this sentiment lies in responses to the statement "Our company values high-

potential internal entrepreneurs and creative people and provides special developmental opportunities for them." In agreement were 53.9 percent of the respondents, while 40.4 percent
disagreed; 5.7 percent neither agreed nor disagreed. Those who
worked for Swedish companies agreed most with this statement,
and those who worked in German firms agreed least, when
French, British, Swedish, and German firms were compared.

Getting free would be very difficult in the British tradition because of strong normative controls. It would be easier in
France, because national culture allows a high degree of individuality. Even though French organizations are highly bureaucratic, their actual operations still permit autonomy. German
bureaucracies are designed to work in real life as well as on paper, and it would be difficult to find private "space" within
them. Swedish companies allow and even encourage a great deal
of negotiation, but the very emphasis on consensus might make
it difficult for a "noncooperative" person to operate. It is even
more difficult to go into business for oneself in Sweden. This
career success map is traditionally difficult for a large organization to tolerate, but a study of small businesses rather than
multinationals might disclose different results.

Getting balanced is already an established style in a country such as Sweden, where the laws are quite protective, where
norms are relatively nonprescriptive, and where social democracy allows a great deal of time and attention to one's personal
interests rather than assuming that the corporation "owns" its
workers. A similar situation exists in Germany, except that the
apprenticeship phase seems to last until about age thirty-five.
This requires workers to delay gratification until they have
reached a certain "safe" level at which they can voluntarily
plateau and attend to some personal interests, such as starting a
family, accommodating a working spouse, or developing hobbies. Three of my four German students had well-developed career plans that included gaining impressive credentials (which
they had acquired before coming to INSEAD), working very
hard for the first five to eight years, achieving a certain level or
position in their company in a chosen geographical location,

and then leveling off. French culture, with its frequent holidays, ritualized relaxation over long dinners, and weekend retreats, allows for balance without extraordinary efforts, even though it is certainly possible to be completely absorbed in work as well. The British companies would be less hospitable to this career success map. Since loyal conformity is so highly prized in Britain, insisting openly on time and space for one's own interests might be seen as negative.

Getting-secure people also have a place in most companies as the solid, dependable workers who will keep things going at a consistently high level. As in the United States, where careerists with this success map are tolerated and appreciated but not awarded anything like the glamorous status of the getting-ahead executive, many conservative multinational companies seek out these people and rely on them. Unlike the U.S. situation, once the initial hurdles of getting a job and performing at acceptable levels for a certain period of time are passed, it is very difficult—or even illegal—for a company in Europe to fire someone. If I were looking to be appreciated and rewarded as a getting-secure careerist, a solidly profitable German bureaucracy would be an ideal setting. Reciprocity is very clear. Loyalty and dependability are highly valued and rewarded. It might be harder in France, simply because education in a *grande école* and subsequent manifestation of political skills are more crucial to assuring one's value in the complicated informal structure than mere hard work and company loyalty. At the same time, no one can deny that merit-based French bureaucracy exists and is highly protective of its own, especially in the public sector.

Despite these differences, the seventy-three multinationals of the study were similar in requiring their general managers to be bright, efficient, politically skilled, geographically mobile, and willing to work extremely hard. In exchange, the usual rewards of money, promotions, power, status, and attractive fringe benefits make getting ahead a highly marketable career success orientation. However, individual career diversity is one of the facts of multinational life as well.

Although the research and observations cited in this chapter focus on Europe, with particular attention to France where I was able to observe companies in operation over a more sustained period of time, it is highly probable that observers would be able to supply the same kinds of information about South American and Asian firms. The diversity of national styles adds a layer of complexity to any corporation's assumptions about what will motivate workers, which is further complicated by the individual worker's own desires. It is possible that all three styles may coincide, producing remarkable singleness of purpose and, we may suppose, equally remarkable productivity. But it seems clear to me that a calm assumption that interests will coincide is premature. Any company doing business overseas needs skilled managers who can absorb new information quickly from a variety of sources, spoken and unspoken, and who can serve as cultural interpreters between the home office and the field office.

FOURTEEN

Applications for Human Resource Professionals

Human resource management is a comparatively new branch of management. Its general task, broadly defined, is to improve the human side of the organization. Included within it are four sometimes-overlapping specialties: organization development, training, personnel, and career development. The material in this book is directly relevant to human resource professionals in several ways. The best people are not limited to just personnel problems or just training but are able to think broadly, draw on a rich background of theories, skills, and behaviors, and intervene appropriately for their particular companies' dynamics. Understanding career diversity can be extremely helpful for human resource specialists in performing these tasks. When an employee's behavior seems puzzling, sometimes it is because he or she is working out a personal career success map. Understanding diversity helps human resource experts be more effective at career counseling and at heading off some of the negative consequences of career politics.

A less obvious task of a human resource specialist is to understand the problems and opportunities of general managers. As most of the recent human resource materials for general managers, such as *In Search of Excellence* (Peters and Waterman, 1982) and *Theory Z* (Ouchi, 1981), demonstrate, it is the manager's task to direct all aspects of the company—including its human resources. A human resource specialist will be most helpful to a manager when he or she can supply insightful, helpful data about managing a company's people most effectively. The contents of this book represent another viable way for managers to consider people problems and human resource opportunities.

Organization Development Specialists

Organization development (OD) specialists work within a company to improve its ongoing performance programs through initiating companywide changes in policies and procedures. They emphasize large-scale human resource interventions. They focus on people's reactions and potential reactions to various companywide or unitwide initiatives. Collaboration is their preferred methodology, which means that employees often can participate in the change process and come to feel a sense of ownership for decisions. Assuring more effective communication, running assessment centers, appraising replacement needs, and managing high-potential candidates are career-related parts of the OD job. OD specialists also collect data about needed changes, then feed the information back to management and work for broad-based change.

In general, most organization development specialists are themselves humanistic in their orientation and champion the cause of individuals within the context of the organization. A high goal for them is to make a good match between individual employees and the enterprise. However, it is important to recognize that organization development has historically been based on participative motivational theories. Consequently, OD often models an ideal type of employee and a "one best way" to manage. As this book documents, the pluralism and diversity of the global work force demands a basic shift in understanding how to motivate workers. For organization development specialists to keep their companies at the cutting edge, they must acknowledge this diversity. Four of the five career success orientations discussed in this book are very different from the traditional getting-ahead assumptions that are made by most managers and often supported by organization development staffs. One challenge for OD specialists is to match the internal career diversity of individuals with diversity in offerings and programs in the external career.

Another challenge for organization development people is to reappraise their traditional reliance on team-building interventions: project teams, management teams, committees, and so on. The thread within organization development that has stressed small-group methods above all, including the often uncritical adoption of Japanese management styles such as quality circles, must be modified and used only where appropriate as diversity continues to proliferate. Any of the career management programs listed in Table 1 that are not currently part of a given company's repertoire might be profitable to consider.

An ongoing challenge is how to integrate the people-management system with management as a whole—how to take a "big-picture" interventionist approach instead of isolating people problems in one department. If managers cannot see human resources as part and parcel of their whole complex task, then they will always be compartmentalizing in one or two areas. If OD specialists do not accept human resource development as part of general management and, therefore, accept their role as staff assistants to various general managers, the importance of the company's people may be sidelined as materials and finances get top management attention. If people cannot find meaningful ways to match their desires with a variety of jobs and work conditions as they take their places in the whole scenario of the business, the inevitable result will be covert and dysfunctional career politics. A certain amount of politics is normal and natural, but at some point, it can turn into sabotage and subterfuge. Sensitive organization development specialists can turn negative political energy into positive productivity.

A fourth challenge for organization development specialists is to add a careers orientation to their individual and systems perspectives. It is helpful, in dealing with an individual employee, to understand some of the constraints of the external career, as described in Chapter Three. In the early stages of a career, the main tasks are recruiting and socializing young employees so that they understand "how things are done around here" and can tell quickly whether they will fit in comfortably. They need to learn the company culture and develop a sense of timing about moves. Anxious and eager to please, they may be unsure whether they are in the right career, let alone the right company. If there is not a good fit, the usual choice is to leave.

At slightly later stages, the company needs to be able to test employee competence, loyalty, and commitment. For those who are still with the company, the organizational challenge is to select high-potential candidates from that group and, correspondingly, to decide how to manage those who are not high potential but who are solid citizens and who belong in the company. What should a company do about midlife or personal crises among valued employees? Then, during the later stages, how do they best use people in preretirement stages and effect useful service up to retirement? Understanding these stages helps organization development specialists plan programs that can match a variety of long-term company needs with a shifting map of individual requirements and preferences.

It is useful in orchestrating a large-scale program (a system) to also consider the career point of view. If the problem is how to recruit, train, and develop women employees, for example, it is useful to recognize that many of the best candidates on the entry level will not be typical entry age—a fairly common problem of incongruity between career stage and careerist age. Many women, after serious attention to child rearing, are usually equally serious about developing their achievement sides and are very valuable employees if they can receive special mentoring and sponsoring, qualify for fast-track programs, and otherwise be easily acculturated.

I consulted with a large public utility in the Southwest that had a training department but not an organization development department. The training department conducted an outside evaluation to determine employees' attitudes toward the company and was dismayed to discover that employees liked the climate, the culture, and the company but simply did not see it as providing any kind of clear career futures. Instead, they described it as chaotic, with advancement dependent on capriciously available sponsors and hard-to-read informal connections. A second survey, with high-potential candidates within the same company, turned up precisely the same data. A numerically impressive array of personnel programs, training programs, flextime, and a variety of individually selected benefits still did not add up to any overall concept that would communicate career opportunities clearly to its employees. This situation has now been defined as the company's key human resource issue, and it is studying how to create an organization development plan with a career perspective. When a controlling concept comes together—if it does—it will require companywide change. Organizational change technology will be required to define it, sell it, and implement it over three to five years.

Training Specialists

Part of a $40 billion business, these staff experts see themselves using their teaching talents to train people in the company about how to improve their performance and absorb change-making concepts and programs, usually through courses, workshops, and seminars that are taught within the organization. Trainers also provide computer-aided instruction and other education-intensive programs.

Training is almost a subcategory of organization development, since it is a form of planned intervention to improve the ongoing operations of the organization. Many organization development specialists also conduct training sessions, and many "trainers" see themselves as organization development specialists. However, training is a genuine subspecialty. It has its own professional associations, journals, and jargon. What is more, it is much more concrete than organization development. Training specializes in pedagogy, application, and applied technology, while organization development is often more theoretical, complex, and systems based. Trainers come far down the abstraction ladder to discuss the best use of overhead slides, class size, and computer software. They distinguish among training experiences that transfer knowledge, those that build skills, and those that change behavior. They differentiate among levels of trainees: management training for executive development is different from skills sharpening for technicians and other specialists. They are also concerned about measuring the effectiveness of training interventions. A recent topic of interest is how to make better use of computer and video technology for individualized instruction. Many of these people have a technical orientation. They are interested in perfecting the techniques and skills involved in their specialty.

Training has a controversial side. As one trainer reported to me, "My company was all for it as long as they just thought it was going to get production up. But when my boss saw that some important topics about identity and work were going to be discussed—and discussed in quite a lot of depth—he got really nervous. He saw a lot of women getting more aggressive about negotiating their careers, and he didn't want that. He saw a lot of the young fathers and mothers making more demands for flextime and on-site day care, and he didn't want that. And he was frankly baffled by discussions on how to integrate a good marriage with a career. His final proposal to me was to see if we couldn't have a couple of seminars on time management and goal setting."

An effective strategy for trainers might be to collaborate with organization development people. For example, a major multinational computer and aerospace company with 90,000 employees brought me in to consult with its research division, a segment of the company that included about 300 employees. For them, a pluralistic work force is having immediate, specific, and concrete consequences. In a boom period, they have the largest backlog in history, and any kind of turnover would be painful. But right now, they are losing over one-third of their employees a year. Even knowing that some of that turnover is to other sections of the company is no consolation; and traditional programs to keep them happy and productive are not working. Somewhere between 10 and 15 percent of their work force are members of minorities, especially Asian, so English is not their first language. A quarter of their employees are women. Many of their senior people are not available to mentor because they are also leaving.

Their getting-high people, many of them recruited from places such as MIT, arrived with their briefcases full of pet projects and were dismayed to find a marketing component as part of their job. A lot of them do not like it and are not good at it. Their getting-free people chafe under a system that currently calls for a great deal of teamwork and interdependent groups. The getting-secure people are willing to work hard and plug along, but the company is moving so fast and hard and puts such a priority on getting-ahead marketing that they end up feeling as though they do not quite fit. Getting-balanced people like the flexibility of the hours and the looseness of the culture, but a clear requirement is staying until the job is finished, even if that means moving in for the weekend with your sleeping bag.

The company instituted a dual-track career ladder a few years ago in hopes of making a more appealing situation for its technical people, but it is not a popular option. It is not seen as having the same status, opportunities to progress, or pay scale as the managerial track. Since managers are the only ones who do not have to account for their time on a particular contract or project, some engineers go into management, not because they like it or are good at it but because they want the free time to work on their own projects. Furthermore, since technical people at a certain level have to charge for their time at a very high rate, budget-conscious project managers would rather have "the kids," as long as they can do the work, than senior people.

The top management team decided that the key to current and future business success was to stay at the cutting edge of research and development. That clearly meant redefining some of its procedures so that it could keep more of its talented people. Organization development people faced the quandary of a loose organization, highly competent people, and the need for change. An organization development specialist at the company read this book in manuscript and brought it to her manager's attention. He agreed with her that their main management problem was accommodating the diversity of their bright, hardworking, but very marketable employees. I conducted two days of training on career diversity and how to manage it for the company's managers and two days for some of the employees the company most wanted to keep—engineers, scientists, technicians, accountants, and marketing people. In these workshops, they learned how to assess their internal careers, appraise the opportunities in the external career, and then plan their strategies for achieving their internal career agendas. Follow-up workshops planned by the research and development people went very well. At their end, OD personnel reported, individual careerists felt they could appraise their own diversity in a managerial context that communicated "We like your diversity. We need your diversity. This is how we'll reward it." It started a groundswell of managerial interest in career diversity. A series of committees were set up by the two organization development people I had trained, which included some top management people. They focused on such key issues as why the technical ladder was not working as effectively as it might and how the research and development center might manage its diverse careerists more effectively. Top management decided to refocus, all the way down to the recruitment level, on getting-secure people who would be willing to do the profitable but relatively unglamorous meat-and-potatoes projects. Restricting committee work and cutting back on interdependence were good ways to make getting-free people feel better. They also decided to allow more entrepreneurs to market actively if they so wished and to allow more technical assignments for the getting-high people. Relieving managers of some of the marketing responsibility also communicated the value of diversity down the line.

These recommendations are currently being studied throughout the company to see whether they will work in other settings. Obviously, the R&D center is only at the beginning of its reappraisal; but because its organization development people were able to see a concept that spoke to its problems, they were in a position to sell it to top managers. By selecting representatives for the workshop from all constituencies and by selecting people who were change agents and opinion leaders, they assured their own credibility if the concepts made sense on that level, which they did. They also kept in touch with top management so that the constructs made sense and did not exceed management's willingness to change.

Because such information is so political, I was careful in the training workshop to allow ample time for individual work and consultation. Small groups work best with strangers, not colleagues who know better than to share very personal strategic information. Giving these employees permission not to share certain types of information was an important part of establishing trust and credibility.

Personnel Specialists

Personnel specialists are also concerned about people-management programs, but their context is usually ongoing programs designed to channel the human resources of a company into the most productive effort. For example, personnel specialists work with pay and benefit programs, performance review programs (often linked to the pay system), personnel policies and manuals, adjudication mechanisms, personnel files and records, and government regulations that shape many internal personnel policies (for example, equal opportunity regulations). They also are often in charge of recruitment; run the orientation programs for new employees; work out career-path options; develop policies and programs for internal transfers, flexible scheduling, benefits, leaves of absence, sabbaticals, life-long employment, part-time employment, and help for spouses; implement succession planning; conduct performance reviews; and administer job postings. It is easy to see that a large part of any career development program is in the hands of personnel specialists.

Quite often, the personnel specialists I work with describe themselves as having a company-first orientation. They feel loyalty to the company and see themselves as helping the other employees but also protecting the company's interests from employee abuse. Unlike the organization development experts, they often view their primary clients as top management, rather than the individuals who make up the organization.

It is precisely in this strength that a limiting weakness lies. To the extent that personnel people are perceived as "guardians of the files," they often lack the credibility and power base to initiate change. The contemporary shift toward diversity means that other groups within the organization will be pulling the personnel specialists along, rather than receiving leadership from them, unless they are able to incorporate a careers perspective and career diversity in some of their attitudes and policies. If they can, they are in a position to represent the needs of individuals, communicate that the company values diversity, and see that its reward system corroborates that attitude.

Career Development Specialists

This emerging group of human resource experts grows out of a combination of organization development and personnel specialties but is different from either. Career development means the set of activities and resources a company provides to help employees achieve their career objectives (career enhancement), coupled with the organization's own attempts to recruit, develop, and move its employees according to its own short-term and long-term human resource needs (career management). The distinction between career enhancement and career management is an important one. In many organizations, attention to the employee is limited to only what the company needs. If your company takes a purely contractual view of relationships ("money in, work out"), sees any employee as largely replaceable by any number of other employees, and views all nonwork activities as strictly the employee's business unless they infringe on work time, you are dealing with career management rather than career enhancement. (See Chapter Three.)

A study by Walker and Gutteridge (1979) pointed out that, while managers in their sample of 225 companies believed in career development, they often took an organization-centered, career management approach. Most companies supply information on job opportunities and employee benefits, but the attitude accompanying this information ranges from actively encouraging employees to explore options to doing nothing, assuming that ambitious employees will somehow try to find out about the various opportunities open to them. Most companies, of course, operate out of expediency rather than career development commitments. They reorganize to sell a new product, move an entire division from New Jersey to Florida, or add a publications section when they discover the need for user manuals. They react to solve a business problem rather than plan ahead to meet development needs. Although these expedients are often necessary, a manager should try to smooth them out through planning. They should not substitute for planned career development, even when they turn out well. They often have a significant impact—sometimes a negative one—on an individual's career. Probably in every company, the line between "careful decision making" and "crisis management" will vary, but the advantages are on the side of the planners.

Career development specialists need to be knowledgeable in career dynamics, career development theory, and the varieties of career development practices. This expertise may range from a doctorate for some sophisticated consultants to a master's degree or equivalent experience for internal staff. Part of what they should be able to do is understand the interrelation among career development and training, personnel policies, compensation and benefits, human resource information and planning systems, performance appraisals, organization development, strategic planning, and social-trend data.

In most companies, the career development specialist will initiate and coordinate policies and programs that support individual career planning and organizational career management. He or she will usually be expected to provide career counseling and assessment, to run workshops on various aspects of career training, to propose and implement various career paths and structures, and to deal with such typical problems as premature turnover, the midcareer plateau, and preretirement stagnation. Other critical career-related pressure points that the career development practitioner must be able to address are organizing well-matched recruiting, identifying high-potential candidates and providing ways of developing them, managing diverse internal career orientations, and helping to plan for succession. Many times, the career development specialist will consult and work with managers about problem employees, provide them with strategies for coaching, and counsel their subordinates in career-related matters.

Typical organizational programs related to career development include establishing information-gathering systems for profiling employees, running career information centers, coordinating multiple career paths and rewards (including benefits) for diverse careerists in the system, and designing relevant performance reviews, or at least coordinating career planning as part of the performance review. Table 1 provides an overview of some typical programs currently in use by some firms, examples of companies implementing such programs, and the different types of career-oriented individuals that would find the various programs especially appealing.

One large multinational bank has given its career development specialist, Steven J., a comparatively free hand in setting up the program to meet the company's current and future needs. A job-posting service has been available at his company for a long time, as have a workshop on retirement planning, a skills inventory to profile various levels of managers, a management review and promotion committee, and an attitude survey, which periodically measures the climate within the organization. Transferred from organizational development to career development, Steven is working to balance immediate and long-range needs by launching seven or eight projects to integrate existing programs and to initiate new ones. He needs to "pull a menu into a meal," he says, and his goal is to ease the transition into a clear career philosophy for his bank and also be sure that a workable, though piecemeal, system is not discarded out of hand in favor of a new one that has not yet been tested. "One of my biggest jobs," he says, "is to get people here to agree on the nature of career development. How much should be weighted toward the individual and how much toward the bank? What does it mean? How is it different from other ongoing human resource programs?"

Steven's initial effort is an intensive study of the information and data system needed. "We need to decide how to provide data, project job vacancies, ascertain the age groupings of employees and their forecasted retirements, anticipate new-staff needs, develop accurate forecasts about the internal and external labor market, and put together individual profiles." The next two or three years will be spent building up the job-posting

Table 1. Contemporary Career Development Programs.

Program	Description	Implementing Companies	Appropriate Career Types
Assessment centers	Simulated activities and analogous work situations that give participants feedback on their performance and potential for managerial success in a particular organization, often used to help companies discover managerial potential	AT&T, Alcan, Union Carbide	Getting-ahead
Career counseling and coaching by managers	An emphasis on encouraging and training managers to act as career guides and developers of their subordinates	Hughes Aircraft, Bell of Pennsylvania, 3M, ARCO, Ford, IBM	Getting-ahead Getting-secure
Career counseling by others	Counseling by career development specialists within the company or career counselors on contract from an external agency	Crocker Bank, U.S. General Accounting Office, Lawrence Livermore Laboratories, Sun Company	Getting-high Getting-free Getting-balanced
Career information centers	Sharing of information about career opportunities within a company through brochures and workbooks, videotape presentations, electronic display information about future projections, a general reference library, career counselors, and career workshops	Crocker Bank, 3M, U.S. General Accounting Office, NCR, Polaroid, Aetna, Portland Electric	All
Career information systems	Pooling of data about existing and projected job vacancies, employee demographic data (for example, age, race, sex, anticipated number of retirees in various years), forecasts of internal and external labor-market trends, and employee profiling for study and planning	Union Oil, NCR, Citibank, American Express, Ford, IBM	Getting-ahead Getting-high Getting-free

(continued on next page)

Table 1. Contemporary Career Development Programs, Cont'd.

Program	Description	Implementing Companies	Appropriate Career Types
Career pathing	Structuring of clusters or streams of job assignments and movement options, each eventually leading to increased pay and status, often advocating technical career tracks along with managerial ones to reward nonmanagerial but high-potential employees	Sears, Corning Glass, Aetna Life	Getting-high Getting-free
Computer-aided instruction and information systems	Accessing computer information relevant to individual's career planning: various career paths, career-related benefits (for example, educational benefits, counseling), in-house courses and programs, and company philosophy about career development.	IBM, Sears Roebuck	Getting-ahead Getting-secure
Educational and professional development benefits	Provision of a menu of benefits that supports an individual's efforts to learn, develop, grow, and enhance his or her own career-related objectives	World Bank, Utah Power and Light Company, Digital Equipment Corporation, IRS, IBM, Westinghouse, AT&T	Getting-high Getting-free Getting-ahead
Fallback-position transfers	Lateral moves or transfers to another function with the possibility of returning to the former position or a similar one if the move is unsuccessful	Connecticut General, Procter & Gamble, Continental Can, Connecticut General, Lehman Brothers	Getting-secure
Flexible scheduling and benefits	Allowing options such as flextime, leaves of absence, part-time employment, and sabbaticals	Exxon, Shell, World Bank, IRS	Getting-balanced Getting-free

Family-related benefits	Help for spouse during transfer, child-care benefits, maternity and paternity leave	Procter & Gamble, IBM, Merck & Company, Exxon	Getting-balanced
High-potential identification programs	Systematic efforts to identify promising young employees (usually potential managers) by the use of assessment centers, surveys, managerial committees, testing, fast-track programs, and managerial recommendations	RCA, NCR, Agrico Chemical, Metrobank, IBM, Exxon, Citibank	Getting-ahead Getting-high
Individual development plans	Comprehensive career plan initiated by employees for review and approval by management	Bell of Pennsylvania, Merrill-Lynch, TRW, First Chicago, IBM	Getting-ahead Getting-secure Getting-high
Integrated career planning	Integration of personal career planning and assessment with performance review	Hughes Aircraft, NASA, Exxon, Marriott Corporation	Getting-ahead Getting-secure
Job matching	Matching of vacant internal positions with the individual development plans of employees, with first preference given to employees who match, posting the job for other employees only if it is not filled through matching	First Chicago, IBM	All
Job posting	Announcement of vacant positions (with accompanying job descriptions) to employees inside the firm before external recruiting and application criteria are spelled out	World Bank, Citibank, Polaroid, Sun Company, First Chicago	All
Lifelong employment	A "psychological" contract of lifelong employment with steady progression and benefits over time if certain minimum standards are met	Eastman Kodak, IBM, Eli Lilly, Hewlett-Packard, Honda U.S.A, many government agencies	Getting-secure

(continued on next page)

Table 1. Contemporary Career Development Programs, Cont'd.

Program	Description	Implementing Companies	Appropriate Career Types
Mentor programs	Official assignment of mentors or sponsors to promising young employees to help them develop their careers	Security Pacific Bank, IBM	Getting-ahead Getting-balanced
Succession planning	Identification and training of a small number of people as backup candidates for certain key jobs	Exxon, IBM, Union Oil, Citicorp	Getting-ahead
Workshops and training events	Career information workshops, orientation sessions, life/career planning, self-assessment, career development for women and minorities, aid in making career transitions, outplacement, and preretirement workshops	3M, ICI, Crocker Bank, U.S. General Accounting Office, NASA, Merrill-Lynch, Honeywell, Aetna, Syntax, Sun Company, Lawrence Livermore Laboratories, ARCO, Polaroid, IBM	Getting-high Getting-free Getting-balanced

system so that there is a clear and visible connection—not a rigged one—between what it says and what is really available, enabling people to choose among options for movement within the bank. Ultimately, Steven will oversee a new career information center, with brochures, career workbooks, video presentations by top management about their views on career advancement, a general library of career planning materials, computer terminals that give people up-to-date information about planning and trends, more workshops, and better counseling.

A second long-range goal is a better system for identifying high-potential managers, doing succession planning, and addressing the problems of professionals within the bank who are not interested in the managerial career track. "We've got a traditional grading and pay system that gives points to certain jobs. It rates managerial positions the highest," Steven explains. "I'm working closely with people in the compensation area to change the weightings so that this pay system doesn't give unintended negative messages about long-term career rewards to our specialists and professional people." He is also training managers to be better coaches and counselors and is linking the career planning process to the annual performance appraisal and review. The goal here, he says, is to have a serious career planning session every fourth year with a supervisor, producing a career plan that can be filed and put on line. A series of workshops on career development for women, minorities, couples, careerists in transition, and those approaching retirement is also on the boards.

Steven's situation is somewhat unusual in that he has the support of top management for this extensive program. Shirley, the career development specialist with a high-tech organization in Massachusetts that has just slowed down after explosive early growth, observes, "I was hired because all the gee-whiz kids hired in the first three years are starting to look around and say, 'What next? If I stay here, where do I go?' I'm supposed to fix that, but the real attitude at the top is, 'People come and go, but there will always be enough interesting projects here to attract the best.'" She discovered early that flowcharts and bar graphs are the best way to convince her audience. "The eyes glaze over when they hear something like 'social trend.' Too touchy-feelie for them." The problem of getting good people and retraining the good ones they have without letting their skills become obsolete or seeing them turn into deadwood makes the idea of lateral moves and a technical track an appealing one to her, but she still must persuade the people at the top.

Both of these career development specialists are encountering residual attachment on the part of top management to a system of job grading that determines the compensation system. The problem is that job grading assumes a getting-ahead orientation from employees and assumes that a company wants and rewards only getting-ahead employees. This assumption ignores the real diversity of the new careerists, especially when it comes to getting-high people. Many professional jobs are different from managerial ones. They are frequently hard to define, rely on peer assessment to evaluate performance, and emphasize nonfinancial rewards. The most competent individual contributors frequently work alone and do not supervise staff. The grading criteria simply do not account for such situations and therefore cause discrimination in titles and salaries. Simply detaching title from salary would be a step in the right direction. Flexible benefits, pay systems, and status symbols tied to a variety of criteria besides hierarchy would be another. Giving managers responsibility for career development would also be helpful.

Conclusion

I help train career development specialists as part of a master's degree program in human resource management (HRM) at a residential degree program for experienced and mature learners. In five-day training sessions for experienced HRM people, we supply subspecialties. Mine is training career development specialists. We have three teaching goals: (1) We teach the students to consider their own career goals and planning as a prerequisite to being effective with others. After all, the primary intervention tool is the HRM professional himself or herself. Our students do personal career assessment using the instruments described in Chapter Eleven and the microlabs briefly described in Chapter Two. (2) In teams, we focus on career counseling methods by having the students work in dyads on career development issues. Here they use the interview questions suggested in Chapter Twelve along with a range of in-depth instruments described in Chapter Fifteen. (3) The final phase approaches the management/organization side by helping the students to appreciate the organizational perspective, better understand the managerial problems related to careers, and become skillful at managing people using the careers framework. Career stages, management of diverse careerists, career politics, high-potential selection, premature turnover, management of the midcareer plateau, and preretirement issues are discussed here. At the end of the week-long seminar come two or three large case studies, some generated from the group members' own organizations, in which they are asked to apply their knowledge of self, another person, and a whole organization.

The results have been quite successful, indicating that, even with limited training, human resource people can absorb these concepts easily and transfer them into action without a great deal of difficulty. One human resource specialist in a large government agency used the concepts of these career types as the basis for designing career development programs to meet his agency's needs. Another, in a large public utility, developed workshops for those who wished to do self-assessment and career planning. An independent consultant developed workshops for women using this framework, discussing appropriate settings for women to match their internal careers. An employee of an insurance company is using this material to broaden her company's definition of high-potential candidates and develop ways to utilize and reward them.

Human resource specialists are at a crucial juncture in an organization. Companies cannot demand complete uniformity and interchangeability from their employees, but individuals must recognize that organizations have to achieve their own objectives to survive. Managing career diversity requires both the individual and the organization to make compromises between internal and external careers. Employees need to understand their choices and also the limits beyond which exercising those choices is not acceptable. Human resource specialists can, in some respects, represent both sides in negotiating fair, workable compromises.

 FIFTEEN

Applications
for Career Counselors

Career counselors help individuals better understand themselves
so that they can make more appropriate career choices and implement those choices more effectively. From a career diversity
perspective, the career counseling task has four components: (1)
Is the individual career oriented? (2) If so, to what extent? (3)
What is his or her internal career success map? (4) Given that internal career, what strategies are appropriate for maximizing it?
This fourth question moves the counselor into areas of discussing how to find the "right" organization or occupation, what
proper timing for different moves might be, and appropriate
tactics given the restrictions existing in particular companies
and professions. The ultimate goal is to effect a good career
match.

 This definition differs in several ways from conventional
career counseling. First, the career diversity–oriented counselor
is not helping the client find a particular job. Placement centers,
employment agencies, professional associations, colleagues, and
want ads provide that specific reference service. Second, he or
she is not doing occupational matching. Many career counselors
use such well-known and useful psychological tests as the
Strong Vocational Interest Blank, the Kuder Vocational Reference Record, the Edwards Personal Preference Schedule, the
Allport-Varnon-Lindsay Test, or Holland's Vocational Preference Inventory and Self-Directed Search. Although these diagnostic tools are all helpful in providing feedback to clients

about their profiles and, hence, how they might correspond to various occupational choices, they sometimes fail to identify talents, motives, and values in a useful way (Schein, 1978). DeLong and Schein's Career Anchor Orientation questionnaire (DeLong, 1982) focuses on filling this gap, as do the assessment instruments presented in Chapter Eleven. Psychological tests frequently have no way of identifying perceived personal constraints on careerists, thus failing to help careerists move from aspects of the internal to the external career in their analysis. This chapter is designed to help counselors collect data in a variety of ways and then assist their clients in arriving at career agendas, putting them in context, and implementing them through appropriate strategies and tactics. Being able to identify a career type is good, but equally important are the issues of dynamic personal growth, change, and compromise (politics).

Third, career counseling is not simply a life-planning exercise, with its attention to self-development, life-stage problems, relationship problems, or internal well-being. In this view, career counseling is little different from any other kind of counseling. Naturally, the long span of a career coincides with the span of a life, but I see career counseling as focusing on work-related concerns (the career) and acknowledging and accounting for other personal life concerns where they have an impact on work.

Counseling Prerequisites

My experience indicates that career counseling is generally most effective when the client has had enough life or work experience to be able to determine a career success map. This kind of knowledge usually takes between five and eight years of on-the-job experience. Since career counseling requires a significant commitment of time and energy, another prerequisite is that some need—whether the internal need to know more about oneself or the external need of solving a career problem—motivates the counseling.

I usually begin any kind of counseling by "contracting"— that is, by ascertaining the client's expectations and desires, by explaining what the counseling can and cannot accomplish, and by setting some time limitations. The client needs to be willing to complete assessment instruments, participate in at least one in-depth interview, arrange interviews with at least one significant other person, and meet at least twice to discuss the diagnosis, career plans, and working strategies.

Although you might assume a client's willingness to meet these conditions, spelling them out has sometimes saved a great deal of time and effort when it has become apparent that a client is not really serious about working on it. One San Francisco acquaintance, deeply involved in a large family business, was contemplating a career shift. His cousin, who had been a student of mine and had done some career counseling with me, urged John to contact me and made complicated arrangements to bring us together when we were both in a different city on other business. I complied out of willingness to accommodate my former student. John was willing to talk with me and filled out the questionnaire, but it was obvious that he did not feel a need for much help. "The company's got a terrific personnel department," he said. "I can spend the next two weeks filling out questionnaires and taking tests if I want to. But I already know what I want to do." In fact, he had confessed some serious doubts to his cousin about the "terrifying prospect" of attempting a small-business venture and "falling flat on my face" and had postponed a career move for another eighteen months. When he finally decided to make his move into an independent entrepreneurial situation, he did very well and discovered that it was exactly what he wanted and needed. Effective career counseling almost certainly would have helped him ascertain the strength of his getting-high need and helped him plan strategies to get there faster; but, as it was, I simply could not help him very much.

In contrast, Nelson, the getting-high physician described in Chapter Eight who found himself bored once his esoteric arthritis research turned into a fairly routine treatment of arthritis patients, could probably have echoed John's statements about knowing himself and having other resources. He came to me when he had spent almost a year thinking about the sources of his dissatisfaction and analyzing different strategies. He was actively searching and had already focused closely on the problem. He was serious about doing the work involved in counseling, and his wife cooperated as well in the interviews and diagnosis. I am not sure that my diagnosis and discussion provided any brand-new options for him, but they quickly clarified the strength of his career success orientation and helped him sift out his priorities. He made his transition to a research specialty quickly and relatively easily.

Data Collection and Diagnosis

The Preliminary Interview. I use a three-phase model of data collection and diagnosis. In the preliminary interview, we spell out expectations with each other and do our basic contracting, and I give the client the Career Success Map Questionnaire and Perceived Constraints Survey (Chapter Eleven) to be completed and returned later. These two instruments help me ascertain the client's perceived internal career orientation and constraining limitations. If a client knows himself or herself well, then the instruments usually confirm hunches and impressions he or she already has. Invariably, however, these instruments indicate areas for probing more deeply during the career interview. I also ask for a current curriculum vitae or resumé that includes his or her employment history, educational background, and particular honors, experiences, and other hobbies or special interests of which the client is particularly proud or otherwise wants an employer to know of. The third instrument included in this assessment phase is the future resumé, which asks these questions:

1. By 1996 I would like to be doing the following kind of work: (Describe below an ideal job for you. Be creative and let yourself go—now is not the time to be constrained by present-day realities. In answering these questions, you may note key phrases and words that capture central ideas.)

2. Associated with this job, the kind of role, benefits, organi-

zational setting, colleagues, and working conditions I would most enjoy (if not elaborated above) are:

3. The kind of life-style that would most appeal to me is: (Describe here your house, your car, your use of leisure time, where you live and what you do in that environment, commitments to community and other volunteer agencies, and self-development and other personal growth activities. Emphasize the most important life-style components.)

4. My ideal relationships life in 1996 (for example, with friends, spouse or lover, children, extended family) would be:

5. My ideal personal life in 1996 would be: (Include hobbies, other use of leisure or time alone, personal service commitments to voluntary and community organizations, health and exercise programs, counseling or therapy, spiritual development, and so on.)

6. Now outline below a more likely or realistic scenario for yourself in 1996. What do you suppose will be the nature of your work, life-style, and relationship life at that time?

7. How frustrating has this exercise been for you? Why? How far into the future do you typically plan? Please comment.

From the client's current resumé, I plot possible motives, values, and talent trends that seem to be unique. If clear trends emerge, they indicate a profitable line of questioning during the interview. If no clear trends emerge, the data may help me confirm certain positions during the final diagnosis. For example, what types of courses has Gloria typically pursued? Do her honors and special experiences say anything about her values? What does she seem to like about work? What is her task orientation as indicated by her resumé patterns? How much has she moved? Changed jobs? Are there hints that she is willing to compromise work for personal concerns or vice versa? What kinds of things does she want employers to know about her? What are unique achievements or personal situations? The future resumé is, of course, unfettered revelations of dreams, hopes, motives, and values. The question about a realistic scenario identifies perceptions of constraints. Both provide a place to begin talking about possible changes.

The Career Orientation Interview. The career interview follows the initial phase of data collection. Schein's (1978, pp. 257–262) interview schedule poses questions that assess both the internal and external career. My interview borrows some elements from the Schein internal career questions but does not include his external career questions. I place great importance on this interview. In a climate of trust and an open exploration of work and life, it is possible for a skilled counselor to ascertain the career success map of most career-oriented people. The resumé and questionnaire confirm or deny this diagnosis.

I usually begin with the following questions, probing more deeply or exploring more thoroughly when the information seems either puzzling or promising. This portion of the interview usually takes between forty-five minutes and an hour.

1. Identify some moments, tasks, or events during your work life that you particularly enjoyed. What about those occasions did you find so stimulating? Give specific examples.
2. Cite some times or tasks you did not enjoy. What did you dislike about them?
3. What are the two or three philosophies that guide your life, either implicitly or explicitly?
4. To what causes, people, or work do you feel most dedicated? Why?
5. What sorts of things offend you most?
6. Of what in your life are you proudest?
7. What do you consider to be your principal strengths, talents, or abilities at work?
8. Give some examples of times you performed very well because you capitalized on these talents.
9. Are there any of these areas critical to your career success where you really excel in comparison to peers?
10. What are some things you do not do very well?
11. Give some examples of times you performed poorly because you lacked certain talents.

Questions 1 and 2 help identify motives; questions 3, 4, 5, and 6 help identify values; and questions 7, 8, 9, 10, and 11 help identify talents. Thus, the pattern of response to all of these questions helps chart a profile of motives, values, and talents.

In addition to these questions, I also like to ask questions that establish values and background factors more clearly, a portion of the interview that usually takes another forty-five minutes to an hour. These questions were worked out in collaboration with Susan Nero when we cotaught in the human resource development program discussed in Chapter Fourteen.

1. What work and life values did you learn from your family of origin? Explain your family's values and view of the world.
2. Discuss your childhood. What was the setting (house, geography, pets, neighborhood)? Who were the people closest to you who influenced you the most (immediate family, extended family, friends, neighbors, youth leaders)? What was your ethnic, religious, or geographical heritage?
3. Did the larger history of your region or the country (economic depression, war, and so on) greatly influence you or your family when you were growing up? How?
4. Who were your early heroes or heroines? Your role models? What impact did they have?
5. How has being a member of your particular generation affected you? How strongly do you identify with other members of your age group?
6. Name any special affiliations with groups or communities (religious, ethnic, political, social, and so on) that have particular importance to you. Describe why they are important.
7. If you see yourself as a member of a minority (or minorities), how does that view of yourself affect your life?
8. What are the most significant demands and responsibilities placed on you by your current intimate relationships? What are the key pleasures and satisfactions they give you?

9. Who have been your cultural heroes and heroines? Your significant role models? Why did you choose them?

10. What fantasies and desires would you like to be able to fulfill in your life? What things would you like to do that you have not yet begun to (or dared to) act upon?

11. Write your own obituary as you would like others to remember you.

The Significant Others Interview. The third phase of data collection and diagnosis is the interview with significant others. It is very useful to cross-validate your client's perceptions by conducting at least one and sometimes three or four shorter interviews with people who have known the client in a work setting over a long period of time and intimately enough to have opinions about his or her work history. Informants, say the anthropologists, are most valuable when they know the information, can articulate it clearly, and are willing to be honest about it. I usually ask my clients to arrange interviews with a spouse, long-time colleagues, friends, or family members who have remained close. In these interviews, I ask the following questions:

Professional Factors

1. What do you think are [the client's] principal strengths, talents, or genius at work?

2. What are some things he or she does less well?

3. What would you say has been his or her main business or life philosophy?

4. To what has he or she been most dedicated during his or her career?

5. What moments, events, tasks has he or she seemed most to enjoy or relish? Give specific examples of high-pleasure activities.

Personal Factors

6. What, in your opinion, are some times or situations that he or she has not liked very much, even if he or she per-

formed well and did not complain? Why? Give specific examples.

7. How did he or she balance the demands of work with the requirements of family life?
8. What activities outside of work and family (for example, hobbies, church service, community service) have seemed particularly important to him or her?
9. What moments in his or her career and life have seemed to you to be particularly rewarding? (Be specific.) Why?
10. What moments have been most trying or difficult? Why?
11. If you were asked to give a speech at a banquet honoring this person for his or her career achievements, what main points would you make?

One of my recent clients, Ike, a state social services counselor, had just shifted to the administrative side and was experiencing some qualms about that particular move and about his career in general. Did he like the technical challenges of counseling? Did he want to shift back? Go into private practice? Some aspects of administration appealed to him. Did he want to really plunge in there? He came to me for help in sorting out his confusion within a few weeks of making the shift. In many ways, it was an ideal counseling situation. He was used to contracting and was motivated to dig into the issues. He did not have an up-to-date resumé, so, as part of the data collection process, he produced a masterpiece of thoroughness, including annotations on some of the portions that he considered relevant. He was eager to have me interview his wife, Lila, his brother Claude, who had also been his partner for a short time in an insurance venture, and two colleagues who had worked with him as counselors for four or five years. In his own interview, he was thorough and thoughtful. Lila was thoroughly involved in the process with him, not only giving me a fine interview about him but also coming to the second session, where we talked about diagnosis. Both of them were objective and analytical about the data, providing information about what did and did not seem to fit, identifying aspects that "really clicked" and taking ownership for them, and working hard on implementing strategies for change. The conclusion from several hours of intensive work was that Ike had a getting-ahead orientation that fitted him beautifully for administration. In fact, the question was not whether he would make a good manager in this state agency but whether it would provide enough challenges to keep him excited and fulfilled.

A contrasting example was Gavin, the altruistic attorney described in Chapter Eight who had dreamed of drowning in money. He had come to me for career counseling after reading a report of my research in a popular publication and was quite interested in "trying this system." I discovered that he had a well-worked set of self-perceptions from years of taking every popular and professional personality profile and personality inventory that he had encountered. He found my questionnaire interesting and mildly insightful, but he flatly refused to involve his wife in a significant other interview and refused with equal firmness to put me in touch with other members of his family or colleagues who might be interviewed about him. I could understand how threatening it might be to Lisa to learn that Gavin was collecting career data. She would immediately feel panicky at the idea that he would do something other than earn the comfortable income for which she had so long postponed other pleasures and even necessities. But I gathered that having other people understand his career orientation was also threatening to Gavin. Although he engaged the data well, agreed that he had a clear career success orientation, and discussed it insightfully, just getting the information seemed to be his goal. The information did not in itself seem to lead to any desired action.

Data Feedback

After the data have been collected from these instruments and interviews, the next counseling task is to make a diagnosis and feed information back to the client. The purpose of this interview is to share information, give the client an opportunity to consider and validate the facts and conclusions, get the client to identify where he or she wants ownership for the conclusions, and begin the process of addressing the problems. It is important at this stage that the initiative for action shift to the client and away from the counselor.

I have found it useful to sort information into a most- to least-important order and go over the findings one point at a time, leaving plenty of time to discuss each finding separately. When we have finished the list, we talk about how the findings are interrelated. The critical issues in the discussion of the career success map are the major motivations, values, talents, and personal constraints that make up that map; the extent to which this orientation seems strong or weak; the extent to which the client is career oriented; and whether he or she is currently in a period of discovery, transition, change, or conflict. In my opinion, the most important question I ask is a repeated one: "Does this seem to fit with how you feel?" I ask this question or a variation of it after discussion of every point in the data, share my reasons for arriving at my conclusion, and try to model acceptance of the client's own reactions. I have the data, true; but my possession of them is merely temporary. I want to transfer them to the client as quickly as possible so that we can move from fact finding to problem solving.

Career Counseling Sessions

After the data-feedback meeting, I usually schedule one or two meetings for more traditional counseling. Here I adopt a less active role, trying to help the client solve his or her own problems rather than giving advice. Typically, it is not difficult to hand the responsibility back to the clients. Nearly always, they are energized by some of the findings, excited by the insights they are receiving, and anxious to explore ideas and test options. I try to be a good listener, ask probing questions, and be a resource for additional information: a good book on a certain topic, a good career information center, or specific career opportunities. At this point, it is usually helpful to steer clients to consider the implications of the internal career for the external career. Some kinds of careerists fit best into certain organizational cultures. Timing issues are crucial. A careerist needs to understand his or her organizational context in mapping out strategic options. Chapter Three is a useful reference for analyzing the external career, while Chapters Five through Nine explore some of the strategies appropriate for each type of careerist.

Occasionally, someone who has had a successful experience right up to this phase will develop sudden resistance. Barclay, the rabidly independent New Hampshire filmmaker we met earlier, was an example of this puzzling phenomenon. He was sufficiently distressed and depressed by his inability to "get my career off the ground" that he was highly motivated during the data-collection and interview phases. Susi was deeply involved in the process with him, and both of them seized on the getting-free concept as something that really made sense in explaining Barclay's fundamental motivations. But when it came to the career counseling phase, things just did not click. The information did not seem to lead to a strategic plan or tactic development. Barclay had insisted that Susi be present at the career counseling sessions, but he seemed to become more withdrawn and confused the more suggestions Susi made. From my perspective, and despite my intervention, she seemed to be taking charge of this information for Barclay. I finally realized that career counseling was probably premature until they had dealt with some of the issues in their marriage and personal lives. The information was simply not empowering to him until he had a different construct with which to handle it.

Another challenge during the career counseling session is the deeply motivated client who dreads the conclusions he or she can see are being reached. Emily, the getting-secure careerist who looked so much like a getting-ahead venture capitalist, fit this problem profile. We had had the initial intake interview in the San Francisco Bay Area when I was there on a business trip, but virtually all of the rest of the process had been conducted in the next two weeks by telephone. She had been meticulous, even obsessive, about filling out the questionnaires, providing a complete resumé, putting me in touch with significant others to interview, and giving me supplementary information, including results of psychological profiles and tests that she had taken earlier. During the feedback and career counseling sessions, however, it was most apparent to me that she resisted the getting-secure identification—not because she felt it was inaccurate in her case or misapplied in any way but because it had such negative implications for her. Her entire background and upbringing had trained her to be a corporate whiz kid, and she felt almost ashamed of having a getting-secure orientation. One of my challenges was to phrase the information in a way that she could accept and discuss before I could deal directly with her response to identity issues.

A career counselor who understands career diversity has a much better opportunity to provide the kind of flexible counseling and useful strategic planning needed by today's careerists. In some ways, his or her job still boils down to the traditional task of finding the right job for the right person, but the career diversity approach exposes and undercuts the traditional assumption that there is a way to make an individual into the right person for a given job. Instead, it begins from a much broader base of analyzing and appreciating the roots of diversity in individual careerists and then goes on to identify and feed back the information that people need to make informed choices about their own careers.

References

Allen, F. "Executives' Wives Describe Sources of Their Contentment, Frustration." *Wall Street Journal,* Dec. 15, 1981a.

Allen, F. "Executives' Wives View Marriages as Combining Rewards, Sacrifices." *Wall Street Journal,* Dec. 16, 1981b.

Allen, F. "Executives' Wives Describe Effects of Husbands' Careers on Children." *Wall Street Journal,* Dec. 17, 1981c.

Allen, F. "Wives of Executives Offer Advice to Women Marrying Rising Stars." *Wall Street Journal,* Dec. 18, 1981d.

Argyris, C. *Integrating the Individual and the Organization.* New York: Wiley, 1964.

Asimov, I. "Creativity Will Dominate Our Time After the Concepts of Work and Fun Have Been Blurred by Technology." *Personnel Administrator,* 1983, *28,* 42–47.

Bailyn, L. "Accommodation of Work to Family." In R. Rapport and R. N. Rapport (eds.), *Working Couples.* London: Routledge & Kegan Paul, 1978.

Bailyn, L. "Taking Off for the Top—How Much Acceleration for Career Success." *Management Review,* 1979, *68,* 18–29.

Bailyn, L. "The Slow Burn Way to the Top: Some Thoughts on the Early Years of Organizational Careers." In C. B. Derr (ed.), *Work, Family and the Career: New Frontiers in Theory and Research.* New York: Praeger, 1980.

277

Bailyn, L. "Trained as Engineers: Issues for the Management of Technical Personnel at Mid-Career." In R. Katz (ed.), *Career Issues In Human Resource Management.* Englewood Cliffs, N.J.: Prentice-Hall, 1982.

Bailyn, L., and Schein, E. H. *Living with Technology: Issues at Mid-Career.* Cambridge, Mass.: MIT Press, 1980.

Berg, B. "Early Signs of Infertility." *Ms,* 1984, *12,* 68–72, 164.

Bralove, M. "Problems of Two-Career Families Start Forcing Business to Adapt." *Wall Street Journal,* July 15, 1981a.

Bralove, M. "Husband's Hazard." *Wall Street Journal,* Nov. 9, 1981b.

Bralove, M. "Ma Bell's Orphans." *Wall Street Journal,* Jan. 26, 1982.

Byrne, J. J. "Occupational Mobility of Workers." *Monthly Labor Review,* 1975, *98,* 53–59.

Cavanagh, G. F., Moberg, D. J., and Velasquez, M. "The Ethics of Organizational Politics." *Academy of Management Review,* 1981, *6,* 363–374.

Clark, A. R. "Nancy Brandt." Unpublished manuscript, Institute for Case Research and Development, Graduate Programs in Management, Simmons College, Boston, Mass., 1977.

Clopton, W. "Personality and Career Change." *Industrial Gerontology,* 1973, *17,* 9–17.

Dahl, R. A. "The Concept of Power." *Behavioral Scientist,* 1957, *2,* 201–205.

Dalton, G. W., Thompson, P. H., and Price, R. L. "The Four Stages of Professional Careers: A New Look at Performance by Professionals." *Organizational Dynamics,* Summer 1977, pp. 19–42.

Deal, T. E., and Kennedy, A. A. *Corporate Cultures: The Rites and Rituals of Corporate Life.* New York: Addison-Wesley, 1982.

DeLong, T. J. "The Career Orientation of MBA Alumni: A Multidimensional Model." In R. Katz (ed.), *Career Issues in Human Resource Management.* Englewood Cliffs, N.J.: Prentice-Hall, 1982.

Derr, C. B. "More On Career Anchor Concepts." In C. B. Derr (ed.), *Work, Family and the Career: New Frontiers In Theory and Research.* New York: Praeger, 1980.

Derr, C. B. "Career Politics." Working paper no. 003-82. Institute for Human Resource Management, University of Utah, 1982a.

Derr, C. B. "Career Switching and Organizational Politics: The Case of Naval Officers." In R. Katz (ed.), *Career Issues in Human Resource Management.* Englewood Cliffs, N.J.: Prentice-Hall, 1982b.

Derr, C. B. "Living on Adrenalin: The Adventurer-Entrepreneur." *Human Resource Management,* Summer-Fall 1982c, *32,* 6–12.

Derr, C. B. "Ken Garff: Small Business Entrepreneur." Working Paper no. 005-84. Institute for Human Resource Management, University of Utah, 1984.

Derr, C. B., and Chilton, S. K. "The Career Directionality of High School Principals." *High School Journal,* 1983, *67,* 11–19.

Driver, M. J. "Career Concepts and Career Management in Organizations." In C. L. Cooper (ed.), *Behavioral Problems In Organizations.* Englewood Cliffs, N.J.: Prentice-Hall, 1979.

Driver, M. J. "Career Concepts and Organizational Change." In C. B. Derr (ed.), *Work, Family and the Career: New Frontiers In Theory and Research.* New York: Praeger, 1980.

Driver, M. J. "Career Concepts: A New Approach to Research." In R. Katz (ed.), *Career Issues in Human Resource Management.* Englewood Cliffs, N.J.: Prentice-Hall, 1982.

Emerson, R. M. "Power-Dependence Relations." *American Sociological Review,* 1962, *27,* 282–298.

Etzioni, A. (ed.). *The Semi-Professions and Their Organizations.* New York: Free Press, 1969.

French, J. R. P., Jr., and Raven, B. "The Bases of Social Power." In D. Cartright and A. Zander (eds.), *Group Dynamics.* New York: Harper & Row, 1968.

Gilligan, C. *In a Different Voice: Psychological Theory and Women's Development.* Cambridge, Mass.: Harvard University Press, 1982.

Gottschalk, E. C., Jr. "Promotions Grow Few as 'Baby Boom' Group Eyes Managers' Jobs." *Wall Street Journal,* Oct. 22, 1981.

Gottschalk, E. C., Jr. "More Women Start Up Their Own Businesses, with Major Successes." *Wall Street Journal*, May 17, 1983.

Gouldner, A. W. "Cosmopolitans and Locals: Toward an Analysis of Latent Social Roles." *Administrative Science Quarterly*, 1957-58, *2*, 281-306.

Guyon, J. "Life on the Job." *Wall Street Journal*, Apr. 29, 1981.

Hall, D. T. *Careers in Organizations*. New York: Scott, Foresman, 1976.

Hill, R. "Once a Frenchman Always a Frenchman." *International Management*, June 1980, pp. 45-46.

Holland, J. L. *Making Vocational Choices: A Theory of Careers*. Englewood Cliffs, N.J.: Prentice-Hall, 1973.

Ingrassia, L. "Situations Wanted." *Wall Street Journal*, Nov. 13, 1984.

Kaufman, H. G. *Obsolescence and Professional Career Development*. New York: AMACON, 1974.

Kets de Vries, M. F. R. "The Entrepreneurial Personality: A Person at the Crossroads." *Journal of Management Studies*, 1977, *14*, 34-57.

Klaus, G. "Corporate Pyramids Will Tumble When Horizontal Organizations Become the New Global Standard." *Personnel Administrator*, 1983, *28*, 56-59.

Korda, M. *Power: How to Get It, How to Use It*. New York: Random House, 1975.

Kotter, J. P. "Power, Dependence and Effective Management." *Harvard Business Review*, 1977, *55*, 125-136.

Kotter, J. P. *The General Managers*. New York: Free Press, 1982.

"Labor Letter Column." *Wall Street Journal*, June 26, 1984.

Lane, H. M., and Morley, E. "Neiman-Marcus." In J. P. Kotter, L. A. Schlesinger, and V. Sathe (eds.), *Organization: Text, Cases, and Readings on the Management of Organizational Design and Change*. Homewood, Ill.: Irwin, 1979.

Langway, L., and others. "A New Kind of Life with Father." *Newsweek*, Nov. 30, 1981, pp. 93-97.

Laurent, A. "Perceived Determinants of Career Success: A New Approach to Organizational Analysis." In K. Trebesch (ed.),

Organizational Development in Europe. Bern, Switzerland: Houpt, 1980.

Laurent, A. "Matrix Organizations and Latin Cultures." *International Studies of Management and Organization,* 1981, *10* (4), 101-114.

Laurent, A., and Ingerilli, G. "Managerial Views of Organization Structure in France and the USA." *International Studies of Management and Organization,* 1983, *13* (1-2), 97-118.

Laurent, A. "The Cross-Cultural Puzzle of International Human Resource Management." Unpublished manuscript, European Institute of Business Administration, Fontainebleau, France, Aug. 1985.

Levinson, D. J. *The Seasons of a Man's Life.* New York: Ballantine Books, 1978.

Levinson, H. "The Abrasive Personality." *Harvard Business Review,* 1978, *56,* 84-94.

Linden, P. "Schooling Europe's Business Elite." *Town and Country,* Apr. 1985, pp. 96, 100, 102, 104, 106.

McGinley, L. "Cautious Approach: Despite the Expansion, Many Companies Trim Their Labor-Force Size." *Wall Street Journal,* Oct. 26, 1984.

Maccoby, M. *The Gamesman.* New York: Bantam Books, 1976.

Michael-Roth, L. "A Critical Examination of the Dual Ladder Approach to Career Advancement." Unpublished paper, Center for Research in Career Development, Graduate School of Business, Columbia University, 1984.

Mihal, W. L., and others. "A Process Model of Individual Career Decision Making." *Academy of Management Review,* 1984, *9,* 95-103.

Mintzberg, H. *The Nature of Managerial Work.* Englewood Cliffs, N.J.: Prentice-Hall, 1973.

Moberg, D. J. "Organizational Politics: Perspectives from Attribution Theory." Working paper, Graduate School of Business Administration, University of Santa Clara, 1977.

Moyer, J. "Stag Poker Aggravates Women at CBS." *Wall Street Journal,* Nov. 9, 1981.

Naisbitt, J. *Megatrends.* New York: Warner Books, 1982.

Nero, S. "How Female MBAs Align Their Needs for Career

Progress and Family Life." Unpublished doctoral dissertation, University of California at Los Angeles, 1984.

Nickles, E. *The Coming Matriarchy: How Women Will Gain the Balance of Power.* New York: Seaview Books, 1981.

Ouchi, W. G. *Theory Z.* New York: Addison-Wesley, 1981.

Peters, T. J., and Waterman, R. H., Jr. *In Search of Excellence.* New York: Warner Books, 1982.

Schein, E. H. "How Career Anchors Hold Executives to Their Career Paths." *Personnel,* 1975, *52* (3), 11–24.

Schein, E. H. *Career Dynamics.* Redding, Mass.: Addison-Wesley, 1978.

Schein, E. H. "Individuals and Careers." Technical Report 19, Office of Naval Research, 1982.

Schein, E. H. *Organizational Culture and Leadership: A Dynamic View.* San Francisco: Jossey-Bass, 1985.

Schein, V. E. "Individual Power and Political Behaviors in Organizations." *Academy of Management Review,* 1977, *2,* 64–72.

Scism, T. E. "Employee Mobility in the Federal Service." *Public Administration Review,* 1974, *34,* 247–254.

Seligman, D. "Luck and Careers." *Fortune,* Nov. 16, 1981, pp. 60–72.

Tarnowieski, D. *The Changing Success Ethic.* New York: AMACON, 1973.

Tocqueville, A. de. *Democracy in America.* New York: Knopf, 1945. (Originally published 1851.)

Toffler, A. *The Third Wave.* New York: Bantam Books, 1981.

Walker, J. W., and Gutteridge, T. G. *Career Planning Practices.* New York: AMACON, 1979.

Walsh, M. W. "Career Women Rely on Day-Care, Nannies to Meet Child Care Needs." *Wall Street Journal,* Sept. 25, 1984.

Yankelovich, D. "New Rules in American Life: Searching for Self-Fulfillment in a World Turned Upside Down." *Psychology Today,* 1981, *15,* 35–91.

Yankelovich, D., and Immerwahr, J. "The Emergence of Expressivism Will Revolutionize the Contract Between Workers and Employers." *Personnel Administrator,* 1983, *28,* 34–41.

Index